D0875021

DAY BY DAY IN
DODGERS
HISTORY

A publication of
Leisure Press.
597 Fifth Avenue; New York, N.Y. 10017

Library of Congress Catalog Card Number: 82-83940

ISBN: 0-88011-108-9

Text photographs courtesy of the
Los Angeles Dodgers Public Relations Department

Library of Congress Cataloging in Publication Data

Gewecke, Clifford George.
  Day by day in Dodgers history.

  Includes indexes.
  1. Brooklyn Dodgers (Baseball team)—History.
  2. Los Angeles Dodgers (Baseball team)—History.
  I. Title.
  GV875.B7G48 1984 796.357'64'097494 84-7825
  ISBN 0-88011-108-9

DAY BY DAY IN
DODGERS
HISTORY

BY CLIFF GEWECKE

LEISURE PRESS

NEW YORK

ACKNOWLEDGMENTS

This book is dedicated to my late father, Cliff Gewecke Sr., who rarely missed a game on radio (or TV) and whose longstanding faith and knowledge as a Dodger fan put my commitment to the project to shame.

I could not have accomplished my research work without the good graces of Bill Schroeder, and staff, at the First Interstate Bank Athletic Foundation, the world's greatest combination sports museum and library. Also, a variety of books borrowed from public libraries in the southern California vicinity were helpful—as were additional personal and encyclopedic sources.

Gratitude also goes to my mother, friends who encouraged, the "Babe," and the people at the Golden State Dance Association of Downey where most of the final writing and typing were achieved.

CONTENTS

1

THIS DATE IN BROOKLYN AND LOS ANGELES DODGERS HISTORY

JANUARY

January 1

1927— Dodgers greet outfielder Zach Wheat with a "Happy New Year"—his release after playing for 18 straight seasons, still the longest tenure in the club's history.

January 2

1912— Dodgers president and majority stockholder Charles H. Ebbets announces he has purchased a new location in Brooklyn and that a concrete and steel stadium will be built to accomodate 30,000 spectators. It will later bear his name.

January 4

1898— Charles H. Byrne, one of three original owners of the Brooklyn Baseball Club and the president 1890-1897, dies. The secretary, Charles Ebbets, is then named president.

January 5

1982— Vin Scully, Dodgers' announcer for 30 years, joins his predecessor Red Barber in the baseball Hall of Fame. A former neighbor and baseball announcer, Ronald Reagan, phones congratulations.

January 9

1918— Dodgers trade outfielder Jake (Casey) Stengel and second baseman George Cutshaw to Pittsburgh for infielder Chuck Ward and pitchers Burleigh Grimes and Al Mamaux.

1961— Former Dodgers' manager Leo Durocher is signed to be a coach under Walter Alston.

January 10

1909— Harry Lumley is named Dodgers' manager.

1927— Ten days after releasing Zach Wheat, Dodgers trade pitcher Burleigh Grimes to Philadelphia.

1984— In his 10th year on the ballot, pitcher Don Drysdale is elected to the Hall of Fame at Cooperstown.

January 11

1977— Dodgers trade outfielder Bill Buckner and shortstop Ivan DeJesus to the Cubs for outfielder Rick Monday and pitcher Mike Garman.

January 17

1958— Dodgers complete arrangements to play their home games in the Los Angeles Coliseum for 1958 and 1959.

January 19

1938— Larry McPhail, formerly with the Cincinnati Reds, accepts the job as general manager and executive vice president of the Dodgers with "full authority" and a three-year contract.

1972— Receiving a record 344 votes, Sandy Koufax at 36 becomes the youngest ever elected to the baseball Hall of Fame.

1983— Dodgers trade third baseman Ron Cey to the Cubs for Vance Lovelace and Dan Cataline.

January 21

1969— Catcher Roy Campanella is elected to baseball's Hall of Fame.

January 23

1962— Eight days before his 43rd birthday, the Dodgers' Jackie Robinson is elected to the Hall of Fame.

January 24

1934— Responding to a newsman's question, Giants manager Bill Terry wisecracks, "Is Brooklyn still in the league?" It becomes a Dodgers rallying cry.

Burleigh Grimes, obtained from Pittsburgh in a trade, pitched for the Dodgers from 1918 to 1927 and went on to become one of the all-time Dodger greats.

January 28

1958— The Dodgers' three-time National League MVP Roy Campanella sustains injuries in an automobile accident near his home in New York that will paralyze him for life.

January 29

1967— A year after his death, former Dodgers president and general manager Branch Rickey is elected to the baseball Hall of Fame.

FEBRUARY

February 1

1919— Former National League MVP Jake Daubert is traded to Cincinnati for outfielder Tommy Griffith after suing the Dodgers for a month's pay when the 1918 season ended early because of the government's "work or fight order" embracing men of draft age.

1959— Dodgers' all-time great Zach Wheat is elected to the baseball Hall of Fame.

February 2

1942— Infielder Cookie Lavagetto joins the Navy as a flood of Dodgers players begin to go into the service for World War 2.

1964— The "last spitball pitcher," ex-Dodger Burleigh Grimes, is elected to the Hall of Fame at age 70.

February 5

1928— At the annual Baseball Writers' banquet, mayor Jimmy Walker of New York City is twitted about his reported ambition to purchase an interest in the Brooklyn team.

February 8

1907— The Tim Jordan Association of Harlem gives a grand ball at Sulzer's in New York City honoring Brooklyn first baseman and home rum slugger Tim Jordan.

1982— Second baseman Davey Lopes at age 35 is traded to Oakland, thus breaking up the Dodger infield of Lopes, first baseman Steve Garvey, shortstop Bill Russell, and third baseman Ron Cey that played as a unit a major league record 8½ years—3½ years longer than any previously.

February 13

1971— One day before Valentine's Day, Dodgers infielder Bobby Valentine marries Roxana Castle Lisson in Stamford, Ct. They'll spend part of their honeymoon at the team's spring training camp in Vero Beach, Fla.

February 16

1961— Hall of Famer and Dodger pitching great Dazzy Vance dies in Homosassa Springs, Fla. at age 69.

February 18

1946— Dodgers .313-slugger Luis Olmo signs to play with the outlaw Mexican League for three years at $10,000 annually and is later joined by a second Dodger, catcher Mickey Owen.

February 19

1983— All in the same stroke, Dodger pitcher Fernando Valenzuela becomes (a) the highest-paid Dodger ever, (b) the highest-paid third-year player in baseball history, and (c) the first man ever to be awarded $1 million—per season—in arbitration.

February 21

1957— The Dodgers and Cubs swap minor league franchises, with the Dodgers getting Los Angeles territorial rights and 22,000-seat Wrigley Field and the Cubs Ft. Worth in the Texas League and financial considerations of $2,500,000.

February 23

1960— A cast iron wrecking ball, painted to look like a baseball, begins the job of tearing down Ebbets Field to make way for a housing project. Otto Miller, who caught the first game in 1913, is among those who attend going-away ceremonies.

February 24

1934— Coach and former Dodger player Casey Stengel succeeds Max Carey as manager, signing a two-year contract calling for $12,000 per season.

February 27

1907— The National League adopts a uniform ticket scheme proposed by Charles Ebbets, president of the Dodgers.

MARCH

March 1

1935— Rookie outfielder Stanley (Frenchy) Bordagaray arrives for spring training at Daytona Beach, Fla. wearing a beret with Van Dyke beard and handlebar moustache causing manager Casey Stengel to comment "it looked like a little French waiter joined the club."

March 4

1907— A judgement for $52,000 is awarded the Baltimore club which claimed that when Baltimore left the National League Brooklyn agreed to pay $40,000 for the franchise but failed. The balance of $52,000 is interest.

1912— Charles Ebbets turns over the first silver spadeful of frosty soil as ground is broken in the Pigtown section of Brooklyn for the new baseball stadium. It's scheduled to be called Washington Park, but a writer suggests, "Call it Ebbets Field, Charlie. You put yourself in hock to build it and it's your monument."

1983— The season-long "Steve Howe saga" begins as the Dodgers' reliever tells reporters at Vero Beach of his cocaine dependency and that he even snorted the stuff during games. Though said to be "cured" after off-season treatment in Arizona, Howe later during the summer suffers relapses that result in fines from the team and an eventual suspension from playing.

March 5

1907— The Dodgers, led by manager Patsy Donovan, leave New York by boat for Jacksonville, Fla. and spring training.

March 6

1938— Dodgers send outfielder Eddie Morgan and $50,000 of the Brooklyn Trust Company's money to Philadelphia for slugging first baseman Dolph Camilli.

March 7

1938— Longtime part-owner Steve (Judge) McKeever dies at 83 of pneumonia, his stock in the club going to his daughter Dearie (Mrs. James) Mulvey.

March 8

1966— Casey Stengel is elected to the baseball Hall of Fame, the first under the new allowance for retired executives. The five-year waiting period is waived.

March 10

1925— Having been named the National League's Most Valuable Player in 1924, Dodger pitcher Dazzy Vance signs a three-year contract with pay hikes.

March 11

1972— All-time great Dodger Zach Wheat dies at age 83 in Sedalia, Mo.

March 15

1945— Only 15 players are in uniform as the Dodgers open spring training in Bear Mountain, N.Y.

1970— At 32 Peter O'Malley of the Dodgers becomes the youngest club president in the major leagues, his father Walter moving up to the newly created post of Chairman of the Board.

March 16

1976— Andy Messersmith of the Dodgers along with the Expos' Dave McNally are declared free agents, a decision that will create financial shock waves through-out baseball.

Pete Reiser went 10-for-10 in four games during his first spring training with the Dodgers in 1939 but was shipped back to the minor leagues for further "seasoning."

March 21

1905— The Dodgers cut disgruntled manager and stockholder Ed Hanlon's salary from $12,000 to $6,000, but after a compromise is arranged he signs for $8,000 for 1905.

March 22

1939— Pete Reiser starts his first spring training game for the Dodgers, belting a home run his first at-bat against the Cardinals and following with a walk and two singles. He goes 10-for-10 in four games but is shipped back to the minor leagues.

March 24

1982— Fernando Valenzuela arrives at Vero Beach for spring training, ending his three-week holdout but refuses to sign the contract the Dodgers had automatically renewed March 1 under the "second year rule."

March 29

1983— Having sold about 27,000 tickets, the Dodgers become the first team in major league history to cut off season sales before the start of a season. The cutoff is so that group sales won't be impeded and that fans will be able to buy tickets for individual games.

March 30

1966— Pitchers Sandy Koufax and Don Drysdale end their unprecedented 32-day double holdout and sign one-year contracts, Koufax for $120,000 and Drysdale for $105,000.

APRIL

April 1

1963— After 16 years with the Dodgers, 36-year-old Duke Snider is sold to the New York Mets for $40,000.

April 2

1962— The California Angels win the 'city. championship' in their first-ever game with the Dodgers, 6-5, as Albie Pearson hits a three-run homer off Johnny Podres in the eighth inning and Joe Koppe singles home the winning run off Pete Richert in the ninth.

April 3

1966— Dodgers catcher John Roseboro, at bat, faces Giants pitcher Juan Marichal for the first time since their bloody battle of 1965 and strokes a three-run inside-the-park homer in the second inning of a spring training game at Phoenix. Dodgers win 8-4 before 7,793.

1969— The "Freeway Series" with the Angels is resumed. The Dodgers, 0-5 following the first three years, win their first game, 4-2 at Anaheim Stadium.

April 5

1913— Genevieve Ebbets, daughter of the club president, throws out the first ball before 25,000 as the new $750,000 Ebbets Field opens in Brooklyn. Nap Rucker pitches the 3-2 win over the New York Yankees and Casey Stengel of the Dodgers hits the first (inside the park) homer in the fifth inning.

1983— Ken Landreaux has six RBI's and Pedro Guerrero five as the Los Angeles Dodgers begin 1983 in Houston with a 16-7 conquest—highest season-opener run total since the move West.

April 6

1973— The "Babes of Summer"—youth-movement Dodgers—debut but the Dodgers and Don Sutton lose 4-2 at San Diego as skipper Walt Alston starts his 20th season.

1982— As their World Championship flag flies high, the Dodgers nip the Giants 4-3 in the season opener when Dusty Baker singles home Bill Russell in the ninth inning. Terry Forster gets the win in relief.

April 7

1910— Charles Ebbets and the Brooklyn team are received by baseball fan and President, William Howard Taft, at the White House.

1925— At Ashville, N.C. during spring training the Yankees beat the Dodgers 16-9 but have other concerns as their star slugger, Babe Ruth, is rushed to the hospital with the "world's most famous stomach ache."

1977— Tommy Lasorda's debut as manager to open the season is a winning one as Don Sutton beats the Giants 5-1 at Dodger Stadium.

1978— Don Sutton starts his seventh (and final) straight Dodger season opener— a club record—as he beats the Braves 13-4 in Atlanta.

April 8

1974— The Atlanta Stadium scoreboard shrieks "715! 715! 715!" as Henry Aaron in the fourth inning off the Dodgers' Al Downing hits his historic home run to surpass Babe Ruth. The Braves win 7-4 before 53,775 and a national TV audience.

April 9

1913— Only 12,000 attend as the Dodgers and Nap Rucker lose 1-0 to Philadelphia on a cold, windy day that inaugurates National League play at new Ebbets Field. Outfielder Benny Meyer drops a pop fly in the first inning allowing the lone run.

1947— For "conduct detrimental to baseball," Dodgers manager Leo Durocher is suspended for the season by baseball commissioner A.B. (Happy) Chandler. The ruling is based on a series of incidents whereby Durocher had been linked, in Chandler's view, to gambling interests and was also the source of too much public controversy.

1970— By a score of 3-0, Wayne Simpson of Cincinnati becomes the only rookie ever to shut out the Los Angeles Dodgers in his first start.

1971— At the home opener of the 10th anniversary of Dodger Stadium, the Dodgers and Bill Singer lose 6-3 before 31,413.

1976— Dusty Baker, traded by Atlanta, hits a homer in his first Dodger at-bat but the Giants win 4-2 in San Francisco.

1981— With Jerry Reuss hurt, the Dodgers turn to rookie Fernando Valenzuela, who responds with a 2-0, five-hit opening-day win over the Braves. It's the first of eight straight wins and five shutouts that start his season.

April 10

1962— With 52,564 in attendance, Kay (Mrs. Walter) O'Malley tosses out the first ball but Cincinnati wins 6-3 in the first game ever at the new $18 million Dodger Stadium. Wally Post's three-run homer in the seventh breaks a 3-3 tie and beats starter Johnny Podres.

1962— Dodgers sell their first Los Angeles World Series hero, right handed pitcher Larry Sherry, to Detroit.

April 11

1912— The final season-opener at Washington Park turns into a travesty as 30,000 spectators overflow the field and remain seated in the outfield and along the foul lines. The Giants hit 13 ground-rule doubles into the crowd and are leading 18-3 in the sixth when the game is called by darkness.

1959— For their second straight season in Los Angeles, the Dodgers open on the road and lose—6-1 in 42-degree weather in Chicago, a city they'll return to in October to become world champs.

1961— Don Drysdale starts his fourth consecutive Dodger season's opener as he trims the Phils 6-2 at the Coliseum.

1962— Behind Sandy Koufax, the Dodgers win their first game at new Dodger Stadium 6-2 as Jim Gilliam hits a homer. It launches a four-game winning streak.

1973— From Grey to Cey! Rookie Ron Cey replaces Ken McMullen, out with a muscle spasm in his back, in a 4-1 home opener loss to Cincinnati and soon becomes the Dodgers' permanent third baseman. It ends a search begun in 1958 with Dick Gray and that included 40-plus candidates during 16 years.

Dusty Baker, obtained in a trade with Atlanta, hit a home run in his first at bat as a Dodger.

From Gray to Cey! On April 11, 1973, rookie Ron Cey replaced Ken McMullen, out with a muscle spasm in his back, and soon became the Dodgers' permanent third baseman. It ended a search which began in 1958 with Dick Gray and included 40-plus candidates during 16 years. Cey is shown above making a sensational catch off a bunt by the Yankees' Bob Murcer in the 8th inning of the 3rd game of the 1981 World Series.

April 12

1884— In their first-ever game as a major league franchise, the "Brooklyns" lose 5-1 at Washington Park to the visiting Cleveland National League team. Adonis Terry allows 11 hits and the Dodgers get seven.

1960— Dodgers set a major league attendance record for a night game, 67,550, and win their first season opener since moving West as they nip the Cubs 3-2 in 11 innings at the Coliseum.

1962— Dodgers rookie southpaw Pete Richert debuts in relief of Stan Williams and sets records by striking out the first six batters to face him including four in the third inning when a called third strike gets by catcher John Roseboro. Dodgers rally and top the Reds 11-7.

1965— The Dodgers open the season for the first time in New York since leaving there as they beat the Mets 6-1 before 37,999 with Don Drysdale on the mound.

1966— Ron Fairly drives in all three tallies in a 3-2 Claude Osteen-pitched Dodgers' season-opening victory over Houston at Dodger Stadium.

April 13

1922— After a career largely spent in the minor leagues, Dazzy Vance debuts as a Dodger pitcher at age 31 but loses 4-3 to the Giants and Shufflin' Phil Douglas who also beat him in 1915 when Vance pitched one game for Pittsburgh.

1926— Jesse Petty of the Dodgers shuts out the Giants 3-0 on one hit, a Texas League double by Frankie Frisch, in the season's opener at the Polo Grounds.

1954— Walt Alston's debut as Dodgers manager is spoiled by ex-GI Willie Mays' homer in the sixth inning, 4-3, as 32,397 watch at the Polo Grounds in New York. Andre Baruch with Vin Scully assisting is the new chief play-by-play announcer, replacing Red Barber who resigned after the 1953 season.

1968— Don Drysdale at age 31 gets win number 191 to surpass Dazzy Vance as the all-time Dodgers' leader. It's a 1-0 four-hitter over the Mets with Ron Fairly homering in the second inning.

April 14

1964— Sandy Koufax twirls his ninth complete game without allowing a walk as he stops St. Louis 4-0 in his only start as an opening day pitcher before 50,451 at Dodger Stadium. Maury Wills gets three hits and Frank Howard hits a 400-foot homer.

April 15

1909— The Dodgers' Kaiser Wilhelm and Leon Ames of the Giants have a double no-hitter going until the eighth inning when Wilhelm allows his first of three. Whitey Alperman gets the Dodgers' first hit, a double, in the 10th and Brooklyn then scores three runs in the 13th to win 3-0 on seven hits.

1915— Rube Marquard celebrates his return to the Giants after having jumped to Brooklyn of the Federal League by no-hitting the Dodgers 2-0 in the season's second game.

1947— Jackie Robinson, starting at first base, becomes the first black to play in the major leagues in the 20th century as the Dodgers beat Boston and Johnny Sain 5-3 at Ebbets. Robby is hitless in three at-bats but scores the winning run in the seventh inning when Pete Reiser doubles off the screen.

1958— Don Drysdale is batted out in the fourth inning as the Giants whitewash the Dodgers 8-0 at Seals Stadium, San Francisco, in the first major league game played on the West Coast before 23,448.

1972— The season finally gets underway after a 13-day players strike and the Dodgers win at Cincinnati 3-1 behind Don Sutton.

April 16

1887— Dodgers outscore the crosstown New York Metropolitans 14-10 at Washington Park as their fourth American Association season begins.

1958— The Los Angeles Dodgers score their first-ever victory, 13-1 in San Francisco behind Johnny Podres, as Duke Snider hits two homers and Dick Gray another one.

1961— Umpire Jocko Conlan and Dodgers coach Leo Durocher engage in a shin-kicking duel at the Coliseum following a disputed popup foul hit by Norm Larker. Durocher goes to the showers and Stan Williams beats the Pirates 13-6 on a 13-hitter.

1973— Dodgers beat Houston 2-1 on Lee Lacy's hit, but they lose hot-hitting Von Joshua who breaks a bone in his wrist when struck by a Ken Forsch fastball.

1980— With Steve Yeager and Joe Ferguson injured, Derrel Thomas catches a 10-4 Dodgers' win at San Diego. Thus, he has played every position except pitcher in the major leagues.

1983— On "Steve Garvey Weekend" the ex-Dodger makes his first appearances at Dodger Stadium since joining the San Diego Padres and on this Saturday night plays in his 1,118th consecutive game, breaking Cub Billy Williams' National League record. A crowd of 50,800 gives "Garv" a standing ovation and he gets two hits. But the Dodgers win their sixth straight, 8-5, as Steve Sax (four hits) and Garvey's successor at first base, Greg Brock (two doubles and a single), sparkle.

April 17

1904— Dodgers wallop Boston 9-1 in their first-ever Sunday game at Washington Park. No admission is charged, in accordance with New York state law, but all persons who pass through the turnstiles are required to buy a grandstand-or-field-box-colored scorecard.

1942— Newly-marrieds Pee Wee Reese and Pete Reiser are both serenaded with "Here Comes The Bride" by a fan playing a trumpet in their first at-bats during a 7-1 Ebbets Field home opener win over the Phils.

1965— Don Drysdale becomes the second Dodger to fan four batters in one inning—the second—but he also gives up two homers and loses 3-2 to the Phils for the eighth straight time.

April 18

1884— The Dodgers and Giants battle for the first time as major league teams in a pre-league contest at Washington Park won 8-0 by the Giants who get nine hits off Adonis Terry.

1901— Jimmy Sheckard raps out three triples, a Dodgers' record, in a 12-7 season-opener win over Philadelphia before 6,000 at Washington Park.

1925— On the morning of the season opener, Dodgers owner Charles Ebbets dies of heart disease, leaving an estate of $1,275,811. A moment of silence in tribute is observed before the start of the afternoon's game, won 7-1 by the Giants, and the players wear mourning (arm) bands.

1939— The Dodgers' first-ever regular-season game on radio—Red Barber at the mike—is a losing effort as the Giants get 13 hits in a 7-3 triumph.

1947— Jackie Robinson smacks his first major league homer at the Polo Grounds in a 10-4 loss to the Giants. It comes the day after his first hit, a beat-out bunt against the Braves in the fifth inning.

1958— Preceded by a downtown parade in the morning, the Dodgers edge the Giants 6-5 before a record 78,672 at the Coliseum in their first-ever Los Angeles home contest. Clem Labine preserves the win for starter Carl Erskine as the Giants' Jim Davenport is out for failing to touch third base despite scoring the "tying" run in the ninth.

1967— The smallest-ever home-opener crowd in Los Angeles, 17,947, sees Claude Osteen and the Dodgers beat Cincinnati 7-2.

1975— The largest April crowd in Dodger Stadium history, 54,050, is on hand as Bill Buckner injures his ankle sliding into third base during a 3-1 loss to the Giants. He never fully recovers all season.

April 19

1890— After leading 9-0, the Dodgers blow their first-ever National League game, 15-9 at Boston despite Oyster Burns' three hits. The Dodgers score their first NL win the next day, 7-6 in Boston.

1947— Burt Shotton takes his place on the bench in street clothes as the Dodger manager succeeding suspended Leo Durocher, but homers by Johnny Mize and Bill Rigney give the Giants a 4-3 win at the Polo Grounds. Coach Clyde Sukeforth guided the Dodgers the first three games.

1957— In the first "home" game of seven that will be played at Jersey City's Roosevelt Stadium, the Dodgers nip the Phils 5-4 in 10 innings. Duke Snider and Roy Campanella drive in the tying and winning run.

1960— Johnny Podres, with help from Ed Roebuck, shuts out the Giants 4-0 in the first game between the rivals at San Francisco's Candlestick Park. Dodgers score three runs in the ninth inning.

April 21

1925— All league games are called off for the day as Dodgers owner Charles Ebbets is laid to rest in Brooklyn's Greenwood Cemetery, 700 feet away from the "father of baseball," Henry Chadwick. His funeral cortege passes both Ebbets Field and Washington Park.

1959— Don Demeter becomes the first Los Angeles Dodger to hit three homers in a game, including the winner in the 11th frame, for a 9-7 victory over the Giants. Demeter totals six RBI's and knocks the first inside-the-park homer at the Coliseum.

1967— Dodgers suffer their first rainout since moving to Los Angeles after 737 games, St. Louis scheduled. There have been ten others since.

April 22

1947— The Phils give newcomer Jackie Robinson his first big racial "test" as they invade Ebbets Field shouting invectives from their dugout. But Dodgers' Hal Gregg hurls a one-hitter and Jackie keeps his cool as he singles to open the eighth inning, advances, and scores the winning run, 1-0, on Gene Hermanski's hit.

1955— Off to a record 10-0 start-of-the-season, the Dodgers lose finally to the Giants 5-4 at Ebbets after Johnny Podres had led 3-0 going into the eighth inning. Manager Walt Alston is ejected when he disputes Don Zimmer's being called out on a Jackie Robinson squeeze bunt that would have tied the game.

1958— Dodgers beat Chicago 4-2 in the first night game ever in Los Angeles at the Coliseum.

April 23

1891— A game-ending, bases-loaded triple play in Philadelphia wipes out the Dodgers, 3-1, when Darby O'Brien lines out to third baseman Bill Shindle who steps on third base to nail George Pinckney and throws to second before Dave Foutz can get back safely.

1954— Jackie Robinson steals second, third, and home in a 6-5 win at Pittsburgh. He also doubles home Jim Gilliam in the 13th inning with the games' winning tally.

1958— Gil Hodges hits his 300th homer and Pee Wee Reese plays in his 2,000th game, but the Dodgers lose 7-6 to the Cubs on Bobby Thomson's double in the ninth inning. Before the game, Duke Snider injures his arm trying to throw the ball out of the Coliseum and is fined a day's pay.

April 25

1913— Casey Stengel's two-run homer to deep center field off Doc Crandall breaks a 3-3 deadlock as the Dodgers whip the Giants 5-3 in the first game between the two at Ebbets Field.

1976— The Dodgers nip Chicago 5-4 in 10 innings in a game made memorable when the Cubs' Rick Monday rescues the U.S. flag from two radicals trying to set it afire in the Dodger Stadium outfield.

April 26

1959— Dodgers trim the Cards 17-11 with 20 hits, five by Charlie Neal, four by Carl Furillo, to move into first place in the National League for the first time since moving to Los Angeles.

April 27

1918— Despite their 0-9 record—a start-of-the-season modern league mark—the Dodgers upend the 9-0 Giants by a 5-3 score as Larry Cheney fans seven and triples home the winning run.

1929— Dodgers relief pitcher Clise Dudley becomes the first player to hit a homer on the first major league pitch thrown to him, but the Phils win 8-3 and Brooklyn drops into last place.

1944— Knuckleballer Jim Tobin of the Braves is the first ever to twirl a no-hitter and hit a home run in the same game, 2-0 over the Dodgers before only 1,984 in Boston.

1982— Dodgers drop pitcher Dave Goltz who still has four years left on his six-year contract at $425,00 per season.

April 28

1900— Outfielder Fielder Jones hits the first grand slam home run in modern Dodgers history in the first inning off Kid Nichols in a 10-1 win over Boston at Washington Park.

April 29

1890— A Washington Park crowd of 1,222 sees the Dodgers whip Boston 5-2 behind the pitching of Mickey Hughes in the first National League game at Brooklyn.

1906— Harry Lumley hits the first pitch to him over the fence at Washington Park as the Dodgers beat the Phils 1-0.

1913— Christy Mathewson of the Giants beats the Dodgers and Nap Rucker 6-0 in 13 innings en route to setting a league record of 47 consecutive innings without a walk.

1925— Ed McKeever, the Dodgers' president for less than two weeks, dies after having caught cold at Charles Ebbets' funeral that developed into influenza. Wilbert Robinson is elected president, meanwhile continuing to manage the team.

1965— Don Drysdale gets his 28th career win over the Giants as he outduels Juan Marichal 2-1 before 30,219 at Dodger Stadium—smallest crowd for the rivalry ever at the stadium.

April 30

1898— May Ebbets, the daughter of President Charles Ebbets raises the flag and a crowd of 14,000 waves small American flags as the new—and second—Washington Park opens with the Dodgers losing 6-4 to Philadelphia. Mike Griffin scores the first run and Jimmy Sheckard hits an over-the-fence homer.

1905— Attracted by a John McGraw (Giants manager) tirade against the umpires three days before, a sellout crowd of nearly 30,000 jams its way into Washington Park but the Dodgers lose 5-3 as the Giants' Iron Man McGinnity stops them.

1919— Burleigh Grimes of the Dodgers and the Phils' Joe Oeschger both pitch all 20 innings of a 9-9 tie called by darkness.

1940— Dodgers win their ninth in a row since the start of the season, tying the 1918 Giants, as Tex Carlton no-hits the Reds 3-0 at Crosley Field in his first start as a Dodger. Cincinnati ends the streak 9-2 the next day.

1944— Dodger pitchers issue a major-league-record 17 walks—Mel Ott receiving five of them—as Phil Weintraub has 11 RBI's in a 26-8 Giants win, largest margin between the two rivals. Hal Gregg wins the day's nightcap, 5-4, his first Dodger win.

1977— Ron Cey climaxes a great April during which he drove in a major-league-record 29 runs as he hits a seventh-inning homer in a 6-4 win over the Expos. The Dodgers post a 17-3 record for the month under new pilot Tommy Lasorda.

MAY

May 1

1884— In Washington, D.C., the Dodgers play their first-ever American Association (major league) game and lose 12-0. However, the following day Brooklyn wins, 7-5.

1906— Philadelphia's John Lush pitches the first modern (since 1900) National League no-hitter, 1-0 over the Dodgers. He fans 11.

1920— Both starting pitchers, Leon Cadore of the Dodgers and Joe Oeschger of the Braves, go all 26 innings in the majors' longest-ever game called by darkness in Boston with the score 1-1. The Dodgers then lose in Philadelphia in 13 innings the next day and in 19 innings to Boston on May 3.

1922— The Dodgers' Harry Schriver becomes the first National Leaguer to hurl a shutout in his major league debut, 2-0 over the Phils.

1965— Dodgers two-time batting champion Tommy Davis breaks his ankle sliding into second base during a 4-2 victory over the Giants at Dodger Stadium.

1981— At Montreal the Dodgers go 13 innings (and lose 9-8) in 4 hours, 18 minutes—same time exactly as it took to complete a club-record (timewise) nine-inning playoff game against the Giants in 1962. Both are longer than the 26-inning game in 1920, which took 3:50.

May 2

1975— In a trade which since has been called "The Great Arm Robbery," the Dodgers get pitcher Burt Hooton of the Cubs for pitchers Geoff Zahn and Eddie Solomon.

1982— An injured Steve Garvey is on the bench as the Expos win 13-1 at Dodger Stadium. But his consecutive-games playing streak is extended to 968 when he pinch-hits in the fifth inning, striking out on four Steve Rogers pitches.

May 3

1890— Before 3,774 at Washington Park, Brooklyn wins the first-ever National League Dodger-Giants game, 7-3, behind the pitching of Parisian Bob Caruthers. The Dodgers (Grooms) steal four bases.

1946— Dodger Rookie Stan Rojek is reported to have accepted $10,000 to join the Mexican League, but he refuses them.

1947— The Dodgers trade pitchers Kirby Higbe, Cal McLish, and Hank Behrman, plus shortstop Gene Mauch and catcher Dixie Howell, to Pittsburgh for $200,000 and outfielder Al Gionfriddo. Behrman is later returned.

1979— After nine relief appearances, Rick Sutcliffe starts in place of the ill Burt Hooton and beats the Phils 5-2 at Dodger Stadium. It launches him toward a 17-10 record and "Rookie of the Year."

1981— With two outs in the eighth inning, Fernando Valenzuela's longest-of-the-season scoreless innings streak is snapped at 36. But he still beats the Expos at Montreal 6-1 to run his record to 6-0.

May 4

1919— A full house at Ebbets Field watches the Dodgers beat the Braves 6-2 in the first Sunday game following approval of the Sunday Baseball Bill by the New York state legislature.

1966— Willie Mays cracks homer No. 512 off the Dodgers' Claude Osteen at Candlestick to break Mel Ott's National League record as the Giants win 6-1.

May 5

1884— Jim Conway pitches a seven-hitter as the "Brooklyns" beat Washington 11-3 at Washington Park in their first American Association home game. A large crowd of ladies attends.

1940— The Dodgers use 22 players and the Cards 17 for a league record 39 during a 9-6 Brooklyn win at St. Louis.

1955— Don Newcombe is suspended when he refuses to pitch batting practice. But Newk apologizes and the next day pitches two innings of relief in a 6-4, 12-inning Dodgers' win at Philadelphia.

1965— Dick Tracewski hits a homer outside the park and Ron Fairly smacks one inside the park as the Dodgers top the Reds 4-2 at Dodger Stadium.

1967— Dodgers sign Sandy Amoros, a free agent, to enable him to qualify for the major league players' pension. He's released May 16.

1976— Dodgers crack a Los Angeles club record of seven homers as they outscore the Cubs 14-12 in Chicago. Henry Cruz hits two and Bill Russell, Ed Goodson, Ron Cey, Bill Buckner and Steve Yeager one each.

May 6

1916— George Cutshaw's freak home run—the "grounder that clumb over the wall" at Ebbets Field—beats the Phils 3-2 in the 11th inning. The drive landed on a hard spot near the wall at the foul line, assumed a peculiar "english," and climbed over the fence—pausing momentarily at the top before dropping over.

1941— The Dodgers trade for the pennant as they get second baseman Billy Herman in exchange for outfielder Claude Gilbert, shortstop Johnny Hudson, and cash.

1945— The Dodgers take two at Philadelphia, 7-5,10-7, as Luis Olmo gets eight hits, including a homer and two doubles in the second game.

1947— Suspended manager Leo Durocher and his movie actress wife Laraine Day watch for the first time as the Dodgers nip the Cards 7-6 at Ebbets on Pee Wee Reese's homer. Later, it's revealed some St. Louis players were planning a strike against Dodger negro Jackie Robinson being in uniform, but it was averted.

1963— Manager Walt Alston's challenge to "step outside" stifles Dodger player complaints about their cramped bus following a 7-4 loss in Pittsburgh. But the next day they ride a roomy, air-conditioned bus to the ballpark and trim St. Louis 11-5 behind Sandy Koufax's seven-hitter.

1978— Lee Lacy sets a big league record by hitting a pinch-hit homer in consecutive at-bats (the first was May 2). But the Dodgers lose in Pittsburgh, 3-2. He hits a third consecutive May 17.

May 7

1940— The Dodgers help set records on and off the playing field as they lose 18-2 in St. Louis and then become the first "full team" in the majors to fly, going to Chicago on two planes then two days later returning to Brooklyn via air. In the day's game, the Cards tie an NL record with seven homers and set a major league mark for total bass, 49. Of their 20 hits, 13 are for extra bases.

1959— The largest crowd ever to watch a baseball game in person, 93,103 at the Coliseum, attends Campy Night in honor of the crippled former Dodger catcher Roy Campanella. The Yankees beat the Dodgers 6-2 in the accompanying exhibition game.

1960— The brothers Sherry team up for the first time, catcher Norm smacking an 11th inning homer to win 3-2 over the Phils for relief hurler Larry who'd entered the game in the eighth inning at Dodger Stadium.

1970— Wes Parker's triple in the 10th inning wins 7-4 over the Mets, but it also makes him the only Los Angeles Dodger to hit for the cycle—a single, double, triple, and homer in the same game.

May 8

1896— Following a 9-5 Giants win over the Dodgers at Eastern Park the *Sporting Life* comments about New York—with two ball teams in one league—being "the hottest baseball locality on earth."

1942— Dodgers tip the Giants 7-6 on Dolph Camilli's homer in an Army-Navy Relief Game at Ebbets that makes $60,661 for the cause.

1959— In the continuing battle of Chavez Ravine, deputies forceably evict the Manuel Arechiga family then bulldoze the house the city had condemned and demanded they vacate. Later, it's revealed the "homeless" family owned at least seven houses they were renting out.

May 9

1910— Zach Wheat and Bill Davidson get five hits each, but two wild throws by catcher Tex Erwin in the ninth inning gives the Pirates a 7-6 win over the Dodgers.

1974— Don Sutton one-hits San Diego, 6-0, when Johnny Grubb singles off Bill Russell's glove in the second inning. Sutton follows with a second straight shutout, 1-0 over Houston May 14.

1983— Former Dodger Ron Cey returns "home" for the first time in a Chicago Cubs uniform and gets three hits, a warm Dodger Stadium ovation, and a yellow rose from a lady fan. But Ken Landreaux's homer in the sixth and run-scoring single in the ninth wins it 4-3 for L.A.

May 10

1883— It's the first day on the job for 23-year-old Charles Ebbets as a clerk for $75 a month.

1926— Dodger pitcher Jesse Petty suffers his first loss of the season, 9-0 to Chicago, after five straight wins.

1953— Roy Campanella drives in all five runs on a double and homer to back Billy Loes' pitching as the Dodgers win 5-0 to sweep the Phils in three games and move into first place.

1955— Gene Baker, who singles in the fourth frame then is out trying to steal, is the only baserunner as Don Newcombe faces only 27 batters and beats the Cubs 3-0.

1966— Dodgers sell pitcher Johnny Podres to Detroit.

May 11

1907— Dodgers come close to a double header shutout, beating the Cubs 1-0 behind Nap Rucker in the first game and holding them scoreless for eight frames of the second. But Chicago then wins, 2-0, with a pair of tallies in the ninth.

1963— Sandy Koufax tosses his second no-hitter, 8-0 over the Giants, a performance that is perfect until he walks Ed Bailey with one out in the eighth inning. He fans four.

1974— Jimmy Wynn hits three homers—one with the bases loaded—in a 9-6 Dodgers win at San Diego.

1979— Dodger pitcher Doug Rau, 0-4 with an 8.22 ERA, comes close to a no-hitter, Chris Spier's single in the eighth inning ruining it in a 7-0 Los Angeles win.

May 12

1883— That new professional baseball team—the "Brooklyns" or "Church City nine"— of the minor Interstate League whips Trenton 13-6 before 6,000 spectators in the first game at new Washington Park.

1922— Reds' relief pitcher Cliff Markle gets the Dodgers' Hy Myers to ground out on one pitch, ending a rally, and Cincinnati then scores two in the bottom of the ninth inning to give Markle a 7-6 one-pitch victory.

1927— Pitcher Dazzy Vance gets four hits himself and holds the Reds to four hits— all two-baggers— as the Dodgers win 6-2.

1956— Jackie Robinson at third base and Carl Furillo in the outfield make big catches as Carl Erskine stops the Giants 3-0 with his second career no-hitter at Ebbets.

1980— Rudy Law steals four bases en route to his Dodgers rookie record of 40 (since broken) as Don Sutton trips the Cubs 2-1 at Dodger Stadium.

May 13

1901— Dodgers players create a rumpus at the Polo Grounds and then forfeit, 9-0, to the Giants when the umpire rules against them. On the play in question, two Dodgers "score" on a two-out bases-loaded single by Bill Dahlen with the runner at first being thrown out at third on the peg from left field. The ump rules only one run scored, while the Dodgers claim two—which would give them an 8-7 lead instead of a 7-7 deadlock in the ninth.

1956— Dodgers purchase pitcher Sal Maglie—a former Giant—from Cleveland.

1958— Righthanded hitter Charlie Neal is the first to homer over the remote right field fence at the Coliseum, but Dodgers lose 16-9 to the Giants in a game with 37 total hits—26 by the Giants.

1966— Phil Regan, in relief of Claude Osteen, suffers his lone loss of the season 4-3 in Pittsburgh when Pirate Roberto Clemente triples and scores on a sacrifice fly.

May 14

1933— Hack Wilson belts the first pinch-hit grand slam in Dodgers history off Ad Liska of Philadelphia in a drenching rain at Ebbets as Brooklyn rallies to win 8-6 in the ninth frame.

1978— Dave Kingman of the Cubs hits three home runs and drives in eight runs in a 15-inning, 10-7 Chicago victory at Dodger Stadium decided by a Kingman three-run blast. Afterwards, Dodgers pilot Tommy Lasorda has some choice comments about "Kingman's performance."

1981— Fernando Valenzuela beats Montreal on a three-hitter, 3-2, giving him an 8-0 record and tying him with Boo Ferris of the Red Sox (1948) for the fastest start ever by a rookie. He loses to Philadelphia, however, in his next outing.

May 15

1919— Cincinnati breaks a tense 0-0 pitchers' duel by scoring 10 runs in the 13th inning at Ebbets Field off Al Mamaux, who goes the distance in the 10-0 defeat.

1965— Al Ferrara blasts a three-run pinch-hit homer with two out in the eighth inning, the lone Dodgers safety in a 3-1 win over Dick Ellsworth and the Cubs at Dodger Stadium.

Clarence Arthur "Dazzy" Vance—Hall of Fame performer for the Dodgers—pitched fourteen years for Brooklyn and was named the National League's Most Valuable Player in 1924.

1967— After 71 game appearances over a year's time, Dodgers pitcher Phil Regan is beaten, 5-3 by Houston, as Bob Aspromonte hits a two-run, 10th-inning triple.

May 16

1980— Jerry Reuss gets his first start as a Dodger in place of the ill Dave Goltz and twirls five scoreless innings. The Dodgers score six in the seventh inning and beat the Pirates 8-6.

May 17

1953— Carl Erskine's bid for another no-hitter is spoiled only by Gus Bell's safe bunt in the sixth inning as the Dodgers trim Cincinnati 10-0 in the second game of a twin bill.

1982— The "Peepul's Cherce" of Brooklyn, Dixie Walker, dies at 71 of cancer in Los Angeles.

May 18

1925— Pitcher Dazzy Vance gets a medal and $1,000 as the league's MVP for 1924 during pre-game ceremonies as the Dodgers celebrate National League "Golden Jubilee Day" with a 9-5 win over Pittsburgh.

1929— Wild day in Philly! Dodgers' Johnny Frederick gets five hits and scores five runs, giving him a majors' record of eight runs for two consecutive games, in a 20-16 opener victory while the Phils win the second, 8-6. The teams score 50 runs and get 63 hits for the day and the Dodgers perform a rare triple play— Harvey Hendrick snagging a liner and doubling the runner at first and throwing to Davey Bancroft at second.

1945— Luis Olmo has a seven-RBI day with a grand slam homer, a triple, and a double as the Dodgers beat Chicago, 15-12.

1953— The Dodgers tie a major league record for 18 stranded runners at Cincinnati as Bud Podbielen stops them 2-1 despite walking 13 and allowing six hits.

May 19

1897— Dodgers lose 13-12 at Louisville in 13 innings, the second longest game of the National League season.

May 20

1896— In the drizzling rain, Dodgers build up a 22-0 lead over Pittsburgh and in the final two innings pitcher Bert Abbey eases up so that the Pirates avoid a shutout in the 25-6 contest.

1927— Umpire Pete McLaughlin is showered with hundreds of bottles at Ebbets Field as the Cubs trim the Dodgers, 7-5.

1948— A nickname is born! Stan Musial of the Cardinals raps out four hits in a 13-4 victory over the Dodgers to complete an 11-for-15 series. As he comes to bat the Ebbets Field crowd begins to murmer, "Here comes that man again!" Thus, Stan The Man.

1972— Al Downing stops Houston 3-0 on two hits as the Dodgers play the fastest game in Los Angeles history, one hour, 30 minutes, and move into first place at Dodger Stadium. Bobby Valentine homers in the first inning.

1979— At Cincinnati, Don Sutton wins his 210th career game, 6-4, to surpass previous Dodgers leader Don Drysdale.

1981— Pedro Guerrero gets four hits, three of them off Steve Carlton, but Rick Monday's homer that leads off the 10th nips the Phils 3-2.

May 21

1952— As 19 runners reach base consecutively—and Pee Wee Reese reaches first safely three times—the Dodgers score a major league record 15 runs in the first inning and top Cincinnati 19-1 at Ebbets.

1962— Tommy Davis bats in three runs and Sandy Koufax fans 10 as the Dodgers beat the Giants 8-1 in their first-ever game at new Dodger Stadium.

May 22

1899— Jack Dunn throws an 8-hitter, winning 5-2 at Louisville, as the Dodgers move into first place en route to their second National League pennant. Dodgers win 22 straight at home this season.

1949— Don Newcombe tosses a five-hit, 3-0 victory in Cincinnati to become the third Dodger to claim a shutout in his first major league start.

1963— Don Drysdale beats the New York Mets 7-3 on two hits, home runs to Duke Snider and Tim Harkness.

May 23

1889— Fire strikes the wooden Washington Park grandstand, causing $18,000 in damage, but the Dodgers are back and playing there by Decoration Day.

1895— Because its supply of baseballs is exhausted, Louisville forfeits a home National League game to the Dodgers.

1946— Dixie Walker and the Cubs' Len Merullo fight during batting practice, a carryover from the previous day's brawl during which Claude Passeau ripped off Dodgers manager Leo Durocher's jersey. The Dodgers win 2-1 for the second day, this time in 11 (instead of 13) innings.

1953— Benched for five days because of a batting slump that actually extends back to his 0-for-21 1952 World Series, Gil Hodges returns and is 0-for-3 in a 2-0 Dodger win over Philadelphia. However, he soon gets back his batting eye.

1960— Sandy Koufax twirls a 1-0 one-hitter in Pittsburgh.

1981— Ron Cey hits his 200th career homer as the Dodgers win 9-6 at Cincinnati with four runs in the 10th frame.

May 24

1953— The Dodgers score 12 runs before a batter is out in the eighth inning at Philadelphia and win, 16-2.

1973— Willie Davis gets six of the Dodgers' 19 hits in a 19-inning, 7-3 loss to the Mets that takes a then-club record of five hours, 42 minutes to complete.

1982— Jay Johnstone lines a double for his first pinch-hit in 21 at-bats and when he returns to the dugout manager Tommy Lasorda tells him he's been released. Dodgers lose 9-3 to Pittsburgh.

1983— Dodger pitchers are on a roll as Alejandro Pena's four-hitter, 3-0 in Philadelphia, follows shutouts the two previous days—5-0 by Bob Welch over the Mets Sunday and 2-0 by Fernando Valenzuela over the Phillies Monday.

May 25

1922— A line drive off the bat of Tommy Griffith strikes Phils' pitcher Bill Hubbell in the head, sending him to the hospital, as the Dodgers win twice, 8-7, 9-6. Jimmy Johnston hits for the cycle in the opener.

1941— Pete Reiser knocks the only grand slam of his career, off Ike Pearson of the Phils who'd beaned him only a month earlier, and it wins 8-4 for the Dodgers at Ebbets Field.

1979— Dodgers set a club record for homers in one game at Dodger Stadium— seven—in a 17-6 win over Cincinnati as Dusty Baker, Rick Sutcliffe, Steve Garvey, Gary Thomasson, Joe Ferguson, Derrel Thomas, and Davey Lopes each stroke one.

May 26

1955— After hitting a two-run triple during a four-run Dodger ninth inning that nets a 6-2 win at Pittsburgh, Don Newcombe becomes the last major league pitcher to steal home.

1970— The Dodgers rake five San Francisco pitchers for 20 hits in a 19-3 win at Candlestick, their highest run total in the two teams' rivalry.

1971— Maury Wills singles in the sixth inning, his 2,000th major league hit, but the Giants score twice in the ninth inning to win 6-4 at Dodger Stadium.

May 27

1888— The Dodgers' Adonis Terry blanks Louisville 4-0 at old Washington Park as he pitches his second no-hitter and the third in the young club's history.

1957— National League club owners grant their permission for the Dodgers and Giants to draft the Pacific Coast League's Los Angeles and San Francisco territories.

May 28

1934— Ebbets Field's "largest-ever crowd," 41,209, sees the Giants win twice, 5-2, 8-6, to extend their season's record to 6-0 over the Dodgers and lend credence to New York manager Bill Terry's earlier jibe, "Is Brooklyn still in the League?"

1952— On his final at-bat before entering the Army, the Giants' Willie Mays is cheered by Ebbets Field fans who rise to their feet. Mays goes hitless, but New York ends Dodger Billy Loes' five-game winning streak, 6-2.

1954— Dodgers pitcher Ben Wade ties a major league record by giving up four homers in one inning—the eighth—as the Giants score six runs then for a 17-6 win at the Polo Grounds.

1956— Pirates first baseman Dale Long hits a homer in his eighth consecutive game—a major league record—as Bob Friend beats the Dodgers and Carl Erskine 3-2. But the next day the Dodgers stop Long's streak.

May 29

1897— Dodgers pull off an unusual triple play. Mike Griffin traps a short fly to center field, then runs in and tags the confused runner between second and third bases and throws to second base to get the forceout of the runner coming from first. The batter is tagged out as he tries to get to second on the hit. But the Dodgers lose 9-7 to Pittsburgh.

1905— Elmer Stricklett of the Dodgers baffles the Giants with a pitch they've never seen before, the spitball, as he fans five in a 4-3 victory. But the Giants win the day's morning game, 7-2 at the Polo Grounds.

1922— Clarence Mitchell, batting for starter Leon Cadore in the ninth inning, is the first Dodger pitcher to swat a pinch-hit homer but it's to no avail as Boston wins 5-4 at Ebbets.

May 30

1893— Dodgers' Brickyard Kennedy is the first major leaguer to pitch and win two complete games in one day under the new pitching distance—increased from 50 feet to 60 feet, 6 inches—as he beats Louisville 3-0 and 6-2 in a morning-afternoon holiday attraction at Washington Park. Former Dodger George Pinckney gets the only two hits off him in the opener and Kennedy tosses a five-hitter in the aftermath.

1940— King Carl Hubbell of the Giants makes 81 pitches and faces only 27 batters as he one-hits the Dodgers 7-0 at Ebbets. Johnny Hudson gets the Dodger safety in the second inning, but is erased stealing. Giants also win the nightcap, 12-5.

1949— The continuing Jackie Robinson-Leo Durocher feud gets its start in a 7-4 Giants' nightcap win when Leo gives the "swollen head" gesture after Robby has stolen second while time is out for a pitching change and is called back by the umpire. Robinson's 13th-inning homer wins the opener for the Dodgers, 2-1, at the Polo Grounds.

1976— Ron Cey goes 6-for-9, including three doubles, as the Dodgers win 6-5 then lose 7-2 in a doubleheader at Cincinnati's Riverfront Stadium.

Paul Jonas, Sports Director of WOR Radio, presents Duke Snider with a framed gold replica of an issue of *Sports Magazine* which featured Snider. Pittsburgh's Ralph Kiner looks on.

May 31

1919— Dodgers pitcher Rube Marquard doubles home two runs in the ninth inning to win his own game, 3-2, and stop a string of five straight by the Giants over Brooklyn.

1921— Dodgers ship infielder Jack Sheehan, only player ever to get as many hits (two) during the regular season as he does in the World Series, to Buffalo.

1943— Billy Herman gets the only hit, a twisting fly inside the right field foul line, off the Cardinals' Mort Cooper in a 7-0 Dodgers' defeat.

1954— Duke Snider "climbs the wall" in the 12th inning at Ebbets Field to rob the Phils' Willie Jones of a sure hit as the Dodgers with Clem Labine win, 5-4.

1968— Big D's narrow escape! Working on his fifth consecutive shutout—and the record scoreless innings streak—Don Drysdale loads the bases in the ninth inning and hits the batter Dick Dietz. But umpire Harry Wendlestadt rules Dietz made no attempt to get out of the way and nullifies the run as the Dodgers win 3-0 over the Giants.

1972— Manny Mota triples home Willie Davis in the 10th inning for the Dodgers' 10th straight win at Candlestick Park, 5-4, a record in the Los Angeles-San Francisco competition.

1975— Andy Messersmith pitches two games in one day, getting the save for Don Sutton in a 3-1 contest at Chicago continued from the day before, then starting and losing the nightcap, 2-1, on two homers.

JUNE

June 1

1888— Battle of the unbeaten boxmen! Mickey Hughes has a 5-0 record and Lee Viau of Cincinnati 8-0 when they pitch. The Dodgers' Hughes wins, 3-1.

1940— Substituting for regular shortstop Leo Durocher, rookie Pee Wee Reese is beaned in Chicago by Jake Mooty as the Cubs win 4-3 in 12 innings.

1955— Duke Snider becomes the only Dodger to twice hit three homers in one game and he has six RBI's in an 11-8 win over the Braves at Ebbets.

1974— Hooked up to an NBC "Game of the Week" TV microphone, Dodgers third base coach Tommy Lasorda calls the shot as Ron Cey hits a second-inning homer plus drives in seven runs in a 10-0 victory at Chicago.

June 2

1894— The Dodgers' Ed Stein no-hits the Cubs 1-0 in a game called after six innings.

1925— Art Nehf walks in the winning run as the Dodgers beat the Giants 6-5 on Uncle Robbie's 62nd birthday after five early-season losses to them.

1962— Phils rookie Dennis Bennett gets his first major league win, 7-0, and it halts the Los Angeles Dodgers' longest winning streak (equalled in 1965) at 13 games.

June 3

1958— By a count of 345,435 to 321,142, the Los Angeles Dodgers win the referendum election enabling them to acquire acreage in Chavez Ravine for their new stadium.

1971— Tom Seaver of the Mets extends his record to 10-1 against the Dodgers and stops Willie Davis' hitting streak at 25—six games short of his 1969 club record—in a 3-1 New York victory at Dodger Stadium.

June 4

1922— A shower of pop bottles protesting an umpire's call at Ebbets Field fails to help in the ninth inning as the Giants then score four runs to win 5-4. Casey Stengel's sacrifice fly brings home the winner.

1947— Dodgers outfielder Pete Reiser crashes into the shortened fence at Ebbets and is knocked unconscious but still holds on to a long, fifth-inning drive by Cully Rickard in a 9-4 win over Pittsburgh. A Priest administers last rites in the clubhouse and Reiser spends 10 days in the hospital, but he later returns to action.

1964— Sandy Koufax twirls his third no-hitter, and only one on the road, 3-0 over Philadelphia as Frank Howard's homer provides all the Dodger runs. Sandy fans 12, walks one.

1968— Don Drysdale hurls a record sixth straight shutout, 5-0 over the Pirates at Dodger Stadium, and extends his string of runless innings to 54.

1972— In pre-game ceremonies that all three attend, Dodgers retire the numbers of Sandy Koufax (32), Roy Campanella (39) and Jackie Robinson (42). Bob Gibson of the Cards throws a 4-0 shutout in the game following.

June 5

1926— When the *New York Sun* complains that leading pitcher Jesse Petty isn't among top-salaried Brooklyn players, manager Wilbert Robinson phones his objection to them. Henceforth, the *Sun* calls the team "Dodgers," never again the then-popular "Robins."

1934— Dodger Buzz Boyle's hitting streak of 25 games comes to an end in the second game of a doubleheader loss, 11-10, 5-4 to the Phils, as he pinch-hits for Hack Wilson and strikes out. Boyle raps out four hits in the first contest.

1977— On Oldtimer's Day, 23-year Dodgers manager Walt Alston's number 24 is retired. Doug Rau then beats San Diego, 4-2.

June 6

1918— Traded by the Dodgers in the off-season, Casey Stengel makes his return to Ebbets Field unforgettable! In his first at-bat, Casey calls time, steps out of the batter's box, doffs his cap—and a bird flies out as the crowd breaks into laughter. Dodgers nip the Pirates 1-0, Hy Myers scoring from third on a double steal.

1957— The Chicago at Brooklyn game is called off after an inning because of fog.

June 7

1896— When Bill Barnie is fired as Dodgers' manager, outfielder Mike Griffin is put in charge. He quits in disgust four days later so owner Charles Ebbets—tall silk hat and all—takes over on the bench the remainder of the season, turning over business affairs to an associate.

1982— A Dodger Stadium crowd of 44,714 gives Steve Garvey a one-minute standing ovation as he plays in his 1,000th consecutive game. But Garv goes 0-for-4 and the Braves win 4-3 on Dale Murphy's three-run homer in the seventh.

June 8

1896— The ninth-place Dodgers suffer their third shutout loss in a row, 9-0 to Pittsburgh, as lefty Frank Killen outduels Brickyard Kennedy.

1940— Not a good day for Dodger pitcher Carl Doyle. In four innings of relief he hits four Cincinnati batters, gives up 16 hits, and allows 14 runs in a 27-hit, 23-2 Reds' victory.

1944— Dodgers trade left-handed pitcher Bob Chipman for Eddie Stanky, a reserve infielder with the Cubs.

1955— Southpaw hurler Tom Lasorda is optioned to Montreal after eight big league games and 13 innings (0-0 record) to make room for bonus baby Sandy Koufax coming off the 30-day disabled list after injuring his ankle.

1968— Don Drysdale surpasses Walter Johnson's major league record of 56 as he runs his streak of scoreless pitched innings to 58⅔ innings before Howie Bedell of Philadelphia drives home Tony Taylor in the fifth inning of a 5-3 Dodgers' win at Los Angeles.

June 9

1926— Dazzy Vance fans 14 Reds but doesn't get credit for the triumph as he's lifted for a pinch-hitter in the ninth inning and the Dodgers win 4-3 in the 10th.

1945— Following a hectic 8-7 Dodgers' win over the Phils, Brooklyn fan John Christian, 21, swears out a warrant for the arrest of manager Leo Durocher and Ebbets Field special policeman Joe Moore claiming they beat him with a blunt instrument under the stands after he'd harassed Durocher from his seat in the upper stands. Charges are later dropped when Christian admits in court he received a $6,750 payoff from the Dodgers for the injuries he sustained.

1971— During a 9-4 loss at Philadelphia, shortstop Bill Russell joins Jackie Robinson as the only Dodgers ever to strike out five times in one game. Russell throws his bat and draws a $100 fine after the fifth whiff.

June 10

1915— The Dodgers and Cincinnati play a 14-inning 2-2 tie, called by darkness. The following day they go 15 innings, the Reds winning 1-0.

June 11

1957— Charlie Neal takes over at shortstop as both 15-year regular Pee Wee Reese and Don Zimmer are injured. He has a homer, a triple, and four RBI's in an 11-9 victory over Milwaukee.

1963— Nick Willhite becomes the first Los Angeles Dodger to toss a shutout in his first major league game, 2-0 over Chicago.

1969— Dodgers trade outfielder Ron Fairly and infielder Paul Popovich for shortstop Maury Wills and outfielder Manny Mota of Montreal.

1972— It's inside-the-park homer day at Dodger Stadium, as Manny Mota gets his second since becoming a Dodger in the third inning and Willie Davis his Dodger-record fourth in the fifth frame. But the Pirates win, 7-5.

1981— Fernando Valenzuela loses 2-1 to St. Louis, but the Dodgers finish one-half game ahead of Cincinnati to clinch a spot in the post-season division playoffs as the players' strike begins.

1983— In his first game since returning from his father's funeral in Kansas, Dodger shortstop Bill Russell hits a two-run homer "for dad" in the ninth frame that beats Frank Pastore and the Reds 3-2 in Cincinnati.

June 12

1890— The Dodgers' Darby O'Brien, coaching at third base, fakes like he is a baserunner, drawing a throw and causing the first big Dodgers-Giants rhubarb in only their eighth National League contest. Brooklyn wins 12-6 behind Tom Lovett at Washington Park.

1940— Dodgers give cash plus outfielder Ernie Koy, pitchers Carl Doyle and Sam Nahem, and utilityman Bert Haas to St. Louis for outfielder Joe Medwick and pitcher Curt Davis.

1955— After racking up a 10-0 record, Dodgers pitcher Don Newcombe suffers defeat as the Cubs bat three homers in a 9-5 victory at Ebbets.

1962— For their first time, the Aaron brothers—Hank and Tommie—hit homers in the same game during a 15-2 Braves win over the Dodgers at Milwaukee.

1976— Dodger catcher Steve Yeager is married on the steps of Los Angeles City Hall, mayor Tom Bradley serving as best man.

June 13

1957— Shortstop Johnny Logan and Dodgers pitcher Don Drysdale are banished for fighting after a Drysdale pitch hits Logan in the ribs during an 8-5 Braves' win. Clem Labine loses for the first time in 10 months and 38 relief appearances as he fails to quell an eighth-inning Milwaukee rally.

1973— The Dodgers' infield—Garvey, Lopes, Russell, and Cey—that will set a major league record for longevity, 8 1/2 years, plays together for the first time in a 16-3 loss in Philadelphia.

June 14

1890— Tom Lovett of Brooklyn pitches the first shutout in the Dodgers-Giants rivalry, a 16-0 win.

1906— Pittsburgh wins 6-1, but the Dodgers have as many assists as putouts, 27, an unprecedented happenstance.

June 15

1918— Charlie Deal of Chicago races home from third with the go-ahead run during a 6-1 Cubs' victory as Dodgers pitcher Jack Coombs drops the ball while winding up and it rolls toward second base.

1938— Night baseball debuts in New York City before 38,748 at Ebbets Field as Cincinnati's Johnny Vander Meer makes history with his second no-hitter in four days, 6-0 over the Dodgers. Leo Durocher is the final out.

1942— Dodgers play the first twilight game in the majors before 15,159 at Ebbets as the Cubs behind Claude Passeau win 6-0.

June 16

1946— Dodgers trade second baseman Billy Herman, hitting .296, to the Braves for catcher Stu Hofferth who is shipped to the minors.

1983—Longtime Dodger concessionaire Danny Goodman dies after a lengthy illness.

June 17

1885— Bad day for the Smiths (not related) of Brooklyn! Pitcher Phenomenal Smith makes his only Dodgers' start an 18-6 loser as he gives up 12 hits to St. Louis

Don Drysdale ran his streak of scoreless pitched innings to 58 2/3 before the Phillies' Howie Bedell singled off him.

at Washington Park and is non-supported with 14 errors. Seven are by shortstop Germany Smith, a major league record.

1905— The police make a test case of Sunday baseball play in Brooklyn by arresting Dodgers president Charles Ebbets and manager Patsy Donovan plus Cincinnati manager Ned Hanton and the game's starting pitchers, Chick Fraser (Reds) and Mal Eason. It's later dismissed on grounds the law doesn't cover the "contribution plan" of receipts on Sunday.

1908— Cincinnati's Andy Coakley shuts out the Dodgers 2-0 on two hits, both by John Hummel.

1916— Jeff Pfeffer of the Dodgers pitches all 19 innings and the Cubs' Zip Zabel sets a record for relief longevity, 18⅔ innings, as Chicago wins 4-3 on second baseman George Cutshaw's error.

1983—Bob Welch's first major league homer wins his own game, 1-0 over Mario (Speedwagon) Soto of the Reds at Dodger Stadium.

June 18

1940— Dodgers outfielder Joe Medwick is beaned by former teammate Bob Bowman, causing a near-riot at Ebbets Field in the second game of a showdown series won 7-5 by the Cardinals in 11 innings.

1962— Sandy Koufax and Bob Gibson of the Cards duel for eight-plus shutout innings before Tommy Davis' homer wins for the Dodgers 1-0 in the bottom of the ninth.

June 19

1938— Babe Ruth, signed two days earlier, takes batting practice and coaches at third base for the first time in a Dodgers' uniform during a doubleheader at Ebbets against the Cubs. Dodgers win the opener 6-2, lose the nightcap, 4-3.

1940— St. Louis' "Mr. Shortstop," Marty Marion, makes three errors in the seventh inning to tie a league record as the Dodgers win 8-3.

1952— A walk to opposing relief pitcher Willard Ramsdell ruins an otherwise perfect but rain-interrupted game as Carl Erskine gets his first no-hitter, 5-0 over Chicago at Ebbets Field.

June 21

1900— National League president Ned Young discusses the possibility of transferring the Brooklyn franchise to Washington, D.C. due to an average attendance of only 1,000 per game other than holidays—this despite the fact the Superbas (Dodgers) are leading the league and will win their second straight NL title.

1901— Wee Willie Keeler has five of the 26 hits off Cincinnati pitcher Doc Parker and scores five runs in a 21-3 Dodgers' win.

1910— Dodger outfielder Jack Dalton's second big league game is impressive as he singles four times off Christy Mathewson, but the Giants win 21-1.

1922— The Dodgers win 15-14, getting 25 hits to Pittsburgh's 19.

June 22

1947— A Crosley Field crowd of 31,204 sits stunned as the Reds' Ewell (The Whip) Blackwell has a second straight no-hitter that would equal Johnny Vander Meer in the works until Eddie Stanky of the Dodgers singles through the pitcher's box with one out in the ninth inning. Al Gionfriddo then flies out before Jackie Robinson gets the final hit in a 4-0 Cincy win.

June 23

1910— Giants' third baseman Art Devlin and two teammates are carted off to jail after the third inning for punching a Washington Park fan who'd been shouting abuse, but the Dodgers still lose, 8-2.

1930— Dodgers get 12 consecutive hits—10 in one inning, the sixth, when they score eight runs—en route to 28 safeties and a 19-6 triumph at Pittsburgh. Babe Herman homers twice.

1968— An NL season-high crowd of 56,738 in New York City shows up as the Mets beat the Dodgers 5-4 behind Nolan Ryan's pitching and Cleon Jones' three-run homer.

1973— Steve Garvey's turning-point day! After singling as a pinch-hitter during the first game, Garvey replaces Bill Buckner as a starter at first base in the second and gets two hits in a 5-1 win over Cincinnati at Dodger Stadium. Thereafter, he's a regular.

1976— Dodgers send relief pitcher Mike Marshall to Atlanta for the waiver price of $20,000.

June 24

1901— Catcher Deacon McGuire catches five Cubs' runners off base as the Dodgers win 2-1 on Bill Dahlen's sacrifice fly which scores Wee Willie Keeler who has singled.

1947— Jackie Robinson steals home for the first of 19 times in his Dodgers' career at Pittsburgh off lefty Fritz Ostermueller in a 4-2 Brooklyn win.

June 25

1936— Dodgers pitcher Van Lingle Mungo equals a major league record (since broken) by striking out seven straight batters in the first game, but the Reds win twice, 5-4 and 5-1.

June 26

1916— Giants whip the Dodgers 11-8 with 18 of the game's 19 runs scoring after two are out—including all eight of Brooklyn's in the fifth inning. Dodgers win the nightcap, 2-1, in 12.

1944— A crowd of 50,000 at the Polo Grounds watches the Dodgers, Giants, and Yankees all in action against each other in a six-inning contest to raise funds for war bonds. Each team plays successive innings against the other two then sits out an inning. Final score: Dodgers 5, Yanks 1, Giants 0.

June 27

1939— At the same site of their record 26-inning 1-1 tie of 1920—in Boston—the Dodgers and Braves go 23 innings and tie again, 2-2. Whit Wyatt hurls the first 16 for Brooklyn.

1960— The Dodgers' Jerry Reuss hurls the season's only no-hitter, 4-0 over the Giants at Candlestick Park. Only shortstop Bill Russell's error prevents a perfect game.

June 28

1969— Highlighted by the first 10-run inning in Los Angeles history, the third frame, Dodgers pound out 17 hits behind Don Drysdale in a 19-0 victory at San Diego that ties a league mark for "biggest shutout."

1983— Pedro Guerrero's first grand slam homer highlights the Dodgers' biggest inning since September 25, 1979 (Giants) as they score eight runs in the fourth to beat the Padres 9-5 despite five errors.

June 29

1923— Jack Fournier has six hits in six trips as the Dodgers get 25 in a 14-5 triumph at Philadelphia. Four other Dodgers have three safeties each.

June 30

1893— Dodgers strand 16 runners and Pittsburgh 14—a majors' record for two clubs—as the Dodgers have a nine-run sixth inning and win 22-16 while getting 18 hits and allowing 19.

1923— After being out once, Jimmy Johnston strokes eight straight hits—homer, three doubles, four singles—at Philadelphia as the Dodgers split a twin bill, winning 10-4, then losing 6-2. It gives him 24 hits in his last 34 trips. But the next day he's 0-for-2 against the Giants.

1959— Sam (Toothpick) Jones of the Giants winds up with a 2-0 one-hitter over the Dodgers at the Coliseum as the official scorer gives Jim Gilliam a controversial hit on a bounder that slips out of the hand of shortstop Andre Rogers.

1962— Sandy Koufax strikes out the side on nine pitches in the first inning and goes on to pitch his first no-hitter, 5-0 over the Phils at Dodger Stadium. He walks five, fans 13.

JULY

July 1

1917— Dodgers beat the Phils 3-2 in the first Sunday game in Brooklyn with admission charge.

1919— First baseman Ed Konetchy raps out his 10th straight hit, a major league record, as he goes 5-for-5 in a 9-4 victory over Philadelphia.

1948— Rookie Roy Campanella debuts catching pitcher Ralph Branca. Campy doubles in his first at-bat, has two singles, but the Dodgers lose 6-4 to the Giants.

1951— Pee Wee Reese's triple in the third inning drives in two mates who'd walked and the Dodgers—with one hit—nip Russ Meyer and Philadelphia 2-1.

1958— Norm Larker, 10 years in the minors, replaces an injured Gil Hodges at first base and promptly blasts two homers and a double for four RBI's in a 9-3 Dodgers win at St. Louis.

1968— A first-inning wild pitch allows Len Gabrielson to score, thus breaking Cardinal pitcher Bob Gibson's string of scoreless innings (48⅔) that threatened the Dodgers' Don Drysdale's record of 58⅔. Cards win the game, 5-1.

1975— Dodger catcher Joe Ferguson's season comes to an abrupt end as he breaks his forearm during the wild melee of a 10-1 loss in San Diego. The incident is touched off when Willie Crawford charges Padres pitcher Bill Grief after a "too close" pitch.

1978— Catcher Joe Ferguson is reunited with his former teammates as the Dodgers get him on waivers from Houston.

July 2

1930— Those Daffy Dodgers! Babe Herman asks, so manager Wilbert Robinson allows his star outfielder to make out the team's starting lineup. The considerable changes result in a 6-5 win over St. Louis that puts Brooklyn back into the league lead, at least temporarily.

1939— Dodger shortstop-manager Leo Durocher and Giant's first baseman Zeke Bonura wrestle in right field to the delight of 51,435 at the Polo Grounds after Durocher steps on Bonura's foot while passing first as the second out of a rally-killing double play. Both are ejected as the Dodgers drop this second contest of a twin bill, 6-4, after winning the opener, 3-2.

1958— Dodgers, with 1,016,285 in 35 games, surpass one million at the gate for the first time since coming West and they nip St. Louis 3-2 before 66,485 after losing 4-2 in the opening game.

1962— Johnny Podres sets a major league record (since topped) as he strikes out eight straight Phils in a 5-1 victory. Dodgers also win the second game, 4-0, behind Stan Williams to take a one-game league lead.

July 3

1912— Rube Marquard pitches a record 19th straight victory as he outduels Dodger Nap Rucker 2-1 and the Giants extend their team winning streak to 15—then 16 by winning the second game of a twin bill.

1917— Dodgers' pitcher Jack Coombs is finally beaten by the Giants, 8-0 in the nightcap of a twin bill, after having set them back 11 straight times.

1940— Pee Wee Reese's grand slam settles the issue, 7-3, after the Dodgers have tied the Giants at 3-3 in the ninth inning at the Polo Grounds. Reese's long blast strikes the foul pole in left field and falls back fair.

1951— At 37, a despondent former Dodgers relief pitcher Hugh Casey kills himself in Atlanta with a shotgun blast to the neck.

1974— Mike Marshall relieves for the 13th straight game in a 4-1 win over Cincinnati, but the record appearances string is broken in the day's second game won 6-0 by the Reds.

July 4

1902— With right field resembling a miniature lake from rain water that backed into the sewers in Pittsburgh, the Pirates blank the Dodgers 3-0 and 4-0 in a morning-afternoon doubleheader. Adopted ground rules allow one base on a fair ball hit into the lagoon.

1914— The later-named "Miracle Braves" lose twice, 7-5, 4-3, to the Dodgers and drop into last place, 15 games behind the league-leading Giants. Jake Daubert is knocked unconscious sliding into home with the winning run in the second game's ninth inning.

1951— Dodgers open a 6½-game lead over the Giants with 6-5, 4-2 wins in their traditional holiday twin bill. Afterwards, manager Chuck Dressen says, "The Giants are through. They'll never bother us again."

1959— Maury Wills takes over permanently from Don Zimmer at shortstop as the Dodgers split in Chicago, losing 2-1, winning 5-2.

1977— Ron Cey's bid for a major-league-record 10th consecutive hit during three games is foiled as he's called out on strikes in the ninth inning while trying to stop his swing. He'd collected three safeties in the 4-0 win at San Francisco and five straight the day before.

1980— Don Sutton pitches his Dodger-record 52nd and final career shutout, 4-0 over the Giants at Dodger Stadium before 47,846, as Reggie Smith strokes the 7,000th National League homer in Dodger history.

July 5

1935— Brothers on opposing teams hit homers in the same game for the first time in modern major league history—Tony Cuccinello for the Dodgers and Al Cuccinello for the Giants. Dodgers win 14-4 at the Polo Grounds.

1946— "Nice guys finish last" is born as Dodgers manager Leo Durocher responds to the needling of announcer Red Barber and is talking about Giants' pilot Mel Ott. But the Giants win 7-6 as ex-Dodger Goody Rosen drives home the winning run.

July 6

1912— Cornerstone for the new Ebbets Field is laid. Among items put in it is a telegram from Admiral Robert E. Peary to the Arctic Club describing how he raised the flag at the North Pole.

1933— Second baseman Tony Cuccinello is the lone Dodgers player named for the first-ever All-Star Game in Chicago. He fans as a pinch-hitter for Carl Hubbell in the ninth inning.

1938— Shortstop Leo Durocher becomes the first Dodger to start in the All-Star Game, at Cincinnati. He gets a "bunt home run" in the seventh inning when his sacrifice is tossed into right field and a series of throwing errors follow.

1942— Leo Durocher is the first Dodger to manage in the All-Star game. Only Dodger catcher Mickey Owen's homer prevents an American League shutout as they win 3-1.

1952— Ben Wade becomes the first Dodger pitcher to hit two homers in the same game—in the third and fourth innings off Warren Spahn—as Brooklyn beats the Braves, 8-2 in Boston, for the 13th straight time. Wade gets credit for the win, but is relieved by Joe Black in the seventh.

1955— In the second game of a doubleheader in Pittsburgh, Sandy Koufax makes his first major league start—allowing three hits, walking eight, and fanning four in 4⅔ innings of no-decision. Dodgers then lose, 4-1.

1979— Dodgers buy the contract of pitcher Fernando Valenzuela from Puebla of the Mexican League for $120,000 and ship him to Lodi of the California League.

1980— Duke Snider's No.4 is retired at an Oldtimers Day attended by former Dodger sluggers Babe Herman and Dolph Camilli. Giants win the main attraction, 7-4.

July 7

1915— Shufflin Phil Douglas of the Dodgers and Bill James and George Davis of Boston hook up in a nightcap 0-0 16 inning pitching duel called by darkness. Dodgers win the opener 4-3.

1921— Ray Schmandt's 10th-inning inside-the-park homer nips the Giants 7-6 as the Dodgers also rap out five triples.

1937— Pitcher Van Lingle Mungo becomes the first Dodger to play in two All-Star Games, allowing two hits and a pair of runs in two innings of relief. AL tops the NL, 8-3.

1959— The Dodgers' Don Drysdale retires all nine batters who face him as he makes his first All-Star Game start in Pittsburgh in a 5-4 NL victory.

July 8

1907— Angered at Washington Park fans throwing pop bottles at his club, Chicago manager Frank Chance begins tossing them back, cutting one fan in the leg. The Cubs win 5-0 and Chance leaves the park in an armored car and escorted by three policemen to escape the Brooklyn mob.

1941— Whit Wyatt is the first Dodger pitcher to start an All-Star Game as he hurls two innings of scoreless ball but the NL loses 7-5. Five other Dodgers also play in the contest, including starters Cookie Lavagetto at third, Pete Reiser in center field, and Mickey Owen at catcher.

1945— Brooklyn's Babe—Herman—returns, at age 42, for the first time in 14 years in a Dodger uniform. He singles his first at-bat as a pinch-hitter against the Cards at Ebbets, but falls flat on his face rounding first base and barely scrambles back safely. Dodgers lose 6-4.

1949— For the first time in modern major league history a negro batter, the Giants' Hank Thompson, faces a negro pitcher, Don Newcombe of the Dodgers. Thompson goes hitless as the Dodgers win 4-3.

1980— A capacity crowd of 56,088 is on hand for the first-ever Dodger Stadium All-Star Game and the debut of the new Dodger Diamond Vision matrix board. National League wins, 4-2, as Dodger Bob Welch hurls three innings and Jerry Reuss one.

July 9

1918— Larry Cheney of Brooklyn throws a record five wild pitches as the Cards also get 12 hits and beat the Dodgers 6-4.

1959— Roger (The Dodger) Craig throws only 88 pitches during the final 11 innings of a superb three-hit relief performance as the Dodgers nip the Braves 4-3 in Milwaukee and move into second place. Norm Larker's homer in the third ties the game at 3-3 and Rip Repulski drives home Wally Moon, who'd doubled, with the decider in the 13th.

1968— Don Drysdale of the Dodgers ties a National League record by starting his fifth All-Star Game as pitcher while making his eighth appearance in a 1-0 NL victory at the Astrodome.

1969— Manny Mota belts out three hits to go with his eight during the previous day's doubleheader in a 3-1 win over the Braves, but he falls one short of equalling the major league record of 12 in three games set by the Dodgers' Milt Stock in 1925.

July 10

1921— Dodger pitcher Burleigh Grimes wins his eighth straight, 7-3 over the Pirates at Ebbets.

1935— The Dodgers play their first-ever night game, losing at Cincinnati 15-2.

1943— Mutiny in the ranks! Led by Arky Vaughan, some Dodgers players threaten to turn in their uniforms in protest of Leo Durocher's suspension of pitcher Bobo Newsome. After tempers are calmed, Dodgers take the field 10 minutes late and maul Pittsburgh 23-6 at Ebbets. Newsome is traded several days later.

1962— Before a hometown Washington, D.C. crowd and President Kennedy, Maury Wills of the Dodgers steals one base, singles, and scores twice in the year's first of two All-Star Games.

1963— Johnny Podres hurls his third 1-0 victory of the season, beating the Mets on John Roseboro's homer.

July 11

1978— Steve Garvey of the Dodgers is named Most Valuable Player of the All-Star Game for the second time in four years. He has a pair of hits and two RBI's at San Diego Stadium.

1980— Dodgers sell pitcher Charlie Hough to the Rangers.

July 12

1938— After dropping 10 straight to the Giants, the Dodgers win 13-5 at Ebbets behind the pitching of Bill Posedel and the three hits of Packy Rogers, making his big league debut. But that night, after being taunted about his team, Dodger fan Robert Joyce murders two people in a Brooklyn cafe.

1949— Three Dodger blacks—Jackie Robinson, Roy Campanella, and Don Newcombe —make their initial appearance in the first-ever All-Star Game at Ebbets Field. Robby doubles his first at-bat, but the AL wins 11-7.

1966— The Dodgers' Sandy Koufax makes his only All-Star Game pitching start, in 106-degree St. Louis heat, as he hurls three innings of one-run, one-hit, one-strikeout ball. The NL wins 2-1.

July 13

1926— Subbing for Babe Herman, the rookie who has stolen his job, 32-year-old first baseman Jack Fournier becomes the first Dodger to hit three homers in a game as he totals five hits and five RBI's in a 12-10 loss to St. Louis.

1954— The Dodgers' rookie manager Walt Alston makes his first of a record nine appearances as National League All-Star Game pilot, but loses to Casey Stengel and the AL, 11-9.

July 14

1935— Casey at the barber! Dodgers lose twice in Cincinnati, 9-4, 4-2, and the following morning manager Casey Stengel tells the hotel barber—so goes the story—"I'll take a shave, but don't cut my throat; I want to do that myself."

1953— After being hitless in his first seven All-Star Games, Dodgers shortstop Pee Wee Reese gets a pair in his final appearance and helps the NL to a 5-1 victory.

1962— History is re-enacted when Ralph Branca trudges in from the bullpen to again pitch to Bobby Thomson—whose homer beat him in the famous 1951 Dodgers-Giants playoff game—during the New York Mets' first Oldtimers Day. This time Thomson flies out to center field. Dodgers win the regular game, 17-0.

1978— Umpire Doug Harvey ejects Dodger pitcher Don Sutton in the seventh inning at St. Louis for defacing the ball in a 4-1 Los Angeles loss. Sutton threatens suit and is later let off with a warning from league president Chub Feeney.

July 15

1922— Dodgers make five double plays, but lose 3-2 to Pittsburgh.

1942— As part of a wild beanball war at Wrigley Field in Chicago, Cub hurler Hi Bithorn fires the ball at Dodger manager Leo Durocher in the dugout as he is being relieved during the fifth inning. Dodgers win 10-5 behind the pitching of Kirby Higbe and Billy Herman's homer.

1955— Dodgers call up Don Bessent and Roger Craig to bolster a pitching staff plagued by arm troubles.

July 16

1913— The Dodgers tip Chicago 4-3 as second baseman George Cutshaw handles 14 chances without error.

1944— The Dodgers break their longest-ever losing streak, 16 games, on eight unearned runs over the Braves 8-5, Curt Davis beating Al Javery. But the Bums then follow with five more straight losses to hit the National League cellar.

1948— Mel Ott is fired as Giants' manager and Leo Durocher of the Dodgers moves across town to replace him. Burt Shotton, who piloted Brooklyn during Leo's season-long suspension, returns for a second season.

1974— Willie Davis—wearing a Montreal uniform—returns to Dodger Stadium and gets five hits in an 8-7 Expos triumph.

July 17

1900— In his major league debut—as a fifth-inning relief twirler—the Giants' Christy Mathewson walks two batters and hits three others as the Dodgers score five runs in the fifth and win 13-7 at Washington Park.

1962— In Cincinnati, Dodgers pitcher Sandy Koufax retires after an inning and is out for two months with a numbness in his left hand defined later as Reynaud's Phenomenon, a circulatory ailment. Dodgers lose 7-5.

1964— Baseball debuts on Pay-TV when Subscription Television screens the Dodgers-Cubs in Los Angeles. Don Drysdale whiffs 10 in a 3-2 Dodger win.

1974— Tommy John, with a 13-3 record, ruptures a ligament in his left (pitching) elbow in a 5-4 L.A. loss to Montreal at Dodger Stadium. He has successful surgery September 25 as the tendon from his right forearm is used to recon-struct the elbow.

1976— Walt Alston gets his 2,000th win as Dodgers manager while pitcher Rick Rhoden runs his season's record to 9-0 with a 5-4 win over the Cubs at Dodger Stadium.

July 18

1916— Dodgers win a forfeit as with the score tied 4-4 in the 10th inning Chicago manager Joe Tinker refuses to leave the field when ordered to do so. Tinker had questioned the umpire calling a ball against his pitcher for delaying his delivery with Brooklyn runners on base.

1949— Dodger second baseman Jackie Robinson makes headlines as he testifies before the House Un-American Activities Committee. Then, that evening, he steals home and scores also on Gene Hermanski's triple as the Dodgers top the Cubs 3-0.

1971— Joe Ferguson, fresh up from Spokane, hits a ninth-inning homer to ruin Luke Walker's attempt at being the first Pirate to pitch a no-hitter in Pittsburgh. Dodgers lose 7-1.

July 19

1940— A fight erupts in the eighth inning at Wrigley Field when Cubs' pitcher Claude Passeau throws his bat at Hugh Casey who has hit him in the ribs with a pitch. The Dodgers' Joe Gallagher and Passeau are tossed out but Chicago wins, 11-4.

1942— Dodger outfielder Pete Reiser suffers a concussion and is never quite the same again as he crashes into the fence at Sportsman's Park in St. Louis chasing down an 11th inning drive by Enos Slaughter in the second game of a twin bill. Upon impact, Reiser drops the ball and Slaughter's inside-the-park homer wins a key game, 7-6.

1957— On "Gil Hodges Night" at Ebbets the Dodger first baseman drives home his 1,000th career run in the first inning in a 3-0 victory over Chicago. John Roseboro's first majors' homer wins the first game, 5-3.

July 17, 1974—Tommy John, with 13-3 record at the time, ruptures a ligament in his left (pitching) elbow in a 5-4 loss to Montreal at Dodger Stadium. He had successful surgery on September 25, 1974, as the tendon from his right forearm was used to reconstruct his elbow.

1977— The Dodgers' Steve Garvey is the leading vote-getter, with 4,277,735, but teammate Don Sutton starts on the mound at Yankee Stadium, hurls three scoreless innings, and is named MVP of the All-Star Game won 7-5 by the NL. Garvey homers in the third frame.

July 20

1905— Dodgers' shortstop Phil Lewis handles 13 of 18 chances safely as he gets six putouts and seven assists but he also makes five errors in a 2-1 win over Cincinnati at Washington Park.

1906— Mal Eason tosses the first modern-day (since 1900) Dodgers no-hitter, 2-0 over St. Louis as he walks three and strikes out five. On May 1 Eason was the opposing pitcher when John Lush no-hit the Dodgers.

1925— Dazzy Vance strikes out 17 batters—15 in the first nine innings—as the Dodgers nip the Cards 4-3 in the 10th.

1957— Duke Snider hits his 300th homer as a Dodger in a 7-5 win over the Cubs at Ebbets, pitcher Don Drysdale needing help from Clem Labine.

1965— Sandy Koufax equals the Los Angeles Dodgers record of 11 straight wins (since topped) co-held by himself, 1964, and Don Drysdale, 1962, as he beats Houston 3-2. Sandy fans 10, gives up only three hits, and singles across the winning run in the ninth.

1970— Only 12,454 are on hand at Dodger Stadium as Bill Singer, recently recovered from hepatitis, pitches the Dodgers' first post-Koufax no-hitter, 5-0 over the Phils.

1983—Second baseman Steve Sax tosses away a double play ball in a 7-3 loss to Pittsburgh, his 26th error and the team's 108th. Sax commits 30 for the season, before going his final 57 games errorless.

July 21

1956— Big night for figures! Pee Wee Reese joins the 2,000-hit club with a pair of singles while Jim Gilliam's 12 assists at second base ties a major league record set in 1892 by a Dodger, Monte Ward. But St. Louis wins, 13-6.

July 22

1908— Dodgers first sacker Tim Jordan blasts the first over-the-fence homer in nine years in Pittsburgh but the Pirates win, 2-1.

1955— A crowd of 33,003 in Brooklyn showers 36-year-old shortstop Pee Wee Reese with gifts and sings "Happy Birthday" to him halfway through the game as a huge cake is wheeled on to the field and the lights turned out. He doubles twice in an 8-4 victory over Milwaukee.

1979— Charlie Hough and his knuckleball are inserted into the starting rotation after his string of eight straight runless relief appearances. Dodgers beat the Mets 4-3 as Lerrin LaGrow relieves Hough.

July 23

1943— The Dodgers' outfield ties a major league record with 18 putouts in a 2-0 win at Cincinnati as Luis Olmo in left field makes eight catches and Frenchy Bordagaray in right field seven. Whit Wyatt twirls a four-hitter.

1974— Dodger Steve Garvey makes the All-Star Game team as a write-in candidate, then strokes two key hits to win his first MVP award in a 7-2 NL victory.

1975— Willie Crawford and Lee Lacy tie a majors' record as they stroke pinch-hit homers in the same inning, the ninth, though the Cardinals win, 5-4. Dodgers Frank Howard and Bill Skowron also did it in 1963.

July 24

1886— Adonis Terry pitches his first of two no-hitters—and the Dodger team's second in history—1-0 over St. Louis at Washington Park.

1931— Babe Herman becomes the only Dodger to twice hit for the cycle and they're within 10 weeks of each other (May 18 was the first). However, Brooklyn loses 8-7 when Pirates' pitcher Larry French quells a ninth-inning rally.

1956— State legislation creating the Brooklyn Sports Authority is approved. It's designed to clear the way for leveling of the site at Atlantic and Flatbush avenues that Dodger owner Walter O'Malley is seeking for his new ballpark. However, the deal never materializes.

July 26

1948— Leo Durocher makes his first visit to Ebbets Field since becoming manager of the "Jints" a winner as the Dodgers fall 13-4 before a turnaway crowd.

1980— After getting three hits and taking the league lead in batting (.322) the night before, Reggie Smith hurts his shoulder and is out for the year as the Cubs win 5-3 at Dodger Stadium.

July 27

1918— Assigned to the Brooklyn Naval Yard, former Dodgers minor leaguer Harry Heitman starts the second game of a twin bill and is shelled for four quick hits and three runs before exiting to return for good to the Navy. The Cards win, 22-7.

1933— Joe Hutcheson debuts as a Dodger rookie with a pair of homers at the Polo Grounds. But the Giants win 5-3, 4-3 as "Hutch" misjudges key drives to the outfield in both contests.

July 28

1909— The Dodgers' Jim Pastorius tosses a 4-0 one-hitter over the Phils, ruined only by pinch-hitter Marty Martel's triple with one out in the ninth inning.

1944— Walter Alston gets his first managing job in the Dodgers' organization, with Trenton, N.J.

1973— The largest regular-season crowd in Dodger Stadium history, 55,185 on a Saturday afternoon, watches the Giants win 5-0.

July 29

1915— In drizzling Pittsburgh weather, Honus Wagner connects for a bases-loaded homer to deep center off the Dodgers' Jeff Pfeffer, making him the oldest—at 41—ever to hit a grand slam in the majors. Pirates win, 8-2.

1956— Don Newcombe registers his 100th victory, a 1-0 five-hitter over Chicago.

1959— One year to the day they were in last place their first season in Los Angeles the Dodgers move into first on Roger Craig's six-hit, 2-0 win. Joe Pignatano and Don Zimmer hit homers.

1962— Big Frank Howard drives in his 47th run since June 28th as the Dodgers top San Francisco 11-1.

July 30

1968— Dodger first baseman Wes Parker is charged with his only error in 1,009 chances for the season on a bad hop at the Astrodome. But the Dodgers and Bill Singer win, 3-2.

1982— In Atlanta, the Dodgers win twice, 10-9, 8-2, and make a race out of what had become a Braves' runaway. Ron Roenicke's bases-loaded single settles the opener and Bob Welch wins his 11th in the nightcap.

July 31

1891— Amos Rusie of the Giants, winning 6-0, throws the first-ever no-hitter against the Dodgers. But it's the second no-hitter within two months in the rivalry, the Dodgers' Tom Lovett having stopped New York June 22, 4-0.

1944— Dodgers are dubbed "Goats of the Gowanus" by a New York newspaper as they are in the NL cellar 31½ games behind after winning only five games during July. However, this day they beat Mort Cooper and the Cards, 6-1.

1950— On Brooklyn's first "Ladies Night" the Dodgers lose 8-5 to the Cubs.

1954— Joe Adcock rips four homers and a double for a major league record 18 total bases off four Dodgers pitchers in a 15-7 Braves' win at Ebbets. The Dodgers hit three of the game's total of 10 home runs.

1956— Jackie Robinson has all three RBI's in a 3-2 win over the Braves at Jersey City as he comes off the bench to start at third base, his third infield position since joining the Dodgers.

1973— Two men on third! When Manny Mota singles to center, Dodger third base coach Tommy Lasorda holds up Bill Russell coming from second. Davey Lopes, coming from first, isn't looking and he steams into third joining Russell and where he's tagged out. Dodgers lose 3-2 at Houston.

1983— Former Dodgers manager Walter Alston is inducted into the Hall of Fame but is unable to attend ceremonies at Cooperstown because of a heart attack he suffered in April. His grandson, Ron Ogle, accepts for him.

Jackie Robinson shown above in action; below Jackie contemplates his future after having the National League's Most Valuable Player award in 1949—a year after he hit a spectacular .342.

AUGUST

August 1

1890— Oyster Burns is the first Dodger to hit for the cycle as he collects four hits in the second game of a double bill, won 20-1 over Pittsburgh. The game is called after 7⅓ innings by darkness.

1906— The Dodgers' Harry McIntire no-hits the Pirates for 10⅔ innings, then allows one safety plus three more in the 13th to lose 1-0.

1924— Dazzy Vance fans seven consecutive batters, a majors' record since broken, as he blanks Chicago 4-0 in a game in which there are only three assists—two by Vance. Most of the Cub outs are flyouts.

1925— Percy Jones of the Cubs is the 10th lefthanded pitcher in 11 games to start against the Dodgers, who this game break the jinx and belt out 17 hits in a 7-1 victory. Zach Wheat gets five.

1954— Beanball battle! The Braves' Joe Adcock is skulled in the fourth inning by Clem Labine and Jackie Robinson of the Dodgers is knocked down by Gene Conley in the sixth. Milwaukee wins its 10th straight, 14-6, as Robinson and Eddie Mathews also scuffle.

1971— Manny Mota steals home in the 11th inning to beat the Reds 5-4 at Dodger Stadium.

August 2

1938— Dodger general manager Larry McPhail's "stitched lemon," the yellow ball, is used for the first time as the Dodgers trim the Cubs 6-2 at Ebbets. Supposedly easier to see, it's used twice more before fading into obscurity to await Charlie Finley's orange-colored baseballs.

1961— Dodgers nemesis Juan Marichal ends an eight-game Los Angeles winning streak and knocks the Dodgers out of first place with a 6-0 shutout at the Coliseum as Tommy Davis gets the only hit off him.

1971— Steve Garvey hits a three-run homer in the ninth to beat the Giants, 5-4, his "biggest thrill (then) in baseball."

1972— Bill Russell's fourth hit of the night, a ninth-inning homer, beats the Giants 12-11 and stops a five-game Dodgers losing streak.

1982— Former Dodger Jackie Robinson becomes the first baseball player ever depicted on a U.S. postage stamp called "Black Heritage."

August 3

1903— The Dodgers get win number 1,000 since joining the National League as Henry Schmidt stops the Phils 7-4 on a five-hitter. Jack Doyle gets three hits and Jimmy Sheckard homers.

1911— For the first time, three Dodgers all hit homers in the same inning, the fifth, in a 5-3 win at Chicago: Ed Zimmerman, Tex Erwin, and Zach Wheat.

1929— Cubs batters complain that Dodger pitcher Dazzy Vance's ragged shirtsleeve distracts their vision, but they still rap out a 12-1 victory at Wrigley Field.

1953— Perturbed by "racial insults," catcher Roy Campanella charges Milwaukee pitcher Lew Burdette on the mound but is restrained by Braves players and the umpire in a 1-0 Dodgers' win.

1959— The American League belts starter Don Drysdale from the Dodgers for three runs and a 5-3 triumph in the first-ever All-Star Game in Los Angeles, at the Coliseum.

1962— Don Drysdale gets his 20th victory on the earliest date for any National League hurler since 1918, 8-3 over Chicago at Dodger Stadium.

August 4

1941— Catcher Mickey Owen becomes the first to catch three foul flies in one inning, the third, as the Dodgers score a total of nine runs in the sixth and seventh innings to beat the Giants 11-6 at Ebbets.

1953— Johnny Podres and Larry Sherry share a 4-0 one-hitter over Houston that was a Podres no-hitter until Johnny Temple spoils it in the top of the ninth inning and Podres then hits the next batter, Bob Aspromonte.

August 5

1926— End of the Wheat Era! In an 11-9 Cardinal's win at Ebbets, Zach Wheat hits his final Dodger home run but near second base his injured leg gives out and he sits there, refusing a pinch-runner for several minutes before limping home.

1978— Rookie Bob Welch blanks the Giants 2-0 at Candlestick to stop a San Francisco winning streak and get the Dodgers back in the pennant race. Burt Hooton then wins the next day, 5-1.

August 6

1892— Jack Stivetts of Boston no-hits the Dodgers 11-0, Ed Stein losing.

1908— Johnny Lush becomes the only pitcher to twice no-hit the Dodgers, this one 2-0 in a six-inning affair halted by rain. Brooklyn first sacker Tim Jordan muffs a fly with the bases loaded.

1969— Pittsburgh's Willie Stargell hits the reputed longest-ever homer at Dodger Stadium, off Alan Foster. It travels over the right field pavillion, landing 506 feet, 6 inches from home plate, as the Pirates' win, 11-3.

August 7

1939— Dixie Walker starts his love affair with Brooklyn fans as he singles home the winning (7-6) run in the 10th inning over Boston in his first-ever game at Ebbets.

1952— On "Leo Durocher Night" at the Polo Grounds, the Dodgers and Giants split a twi-night doubleheader of two nine-inning games that total 6 hours, 36 minutes. Giants win the first 8-2, the Dodgers the second, 7-5, as Roy Campanella hits a grand slam.

August 8

1903— "Iron Man" McGinnity of the Giants trims the Dodgers two complete games in one day at the Polo Grounds, 6-1, 4-3, one of three twin bills he'll win in the same (August) month.

1934— Former Dodgers manager Wilbert Robinson suffers a stroke of apoplexy near his home in Atlanta and dies at 71.

1942— The Dodgers' Whit Wyatt and Manny Salvo of the Braves engage in a beanball-throwing contest—and subsequent fight—against each other that Boston wins, 2-0.

1954— Gil Hodges bats three times in one inning, the eighth, as the Dodgers score 13 runs in a 20-7 victory over Cincinnati at Ebbets Field. Twelve of the runs are unearned.

1965— The home-team Cincinnati bats boom out 20 hits—10 for extra bases—as the Los Angeles Dodgers suffer their largest margin of defeat, 18-0, with the Reds' Jim Maloney fashioning a four-hitter. A total of five Dodger pitchers allow runs, with the biggest victims being starter Don Drysdale, six in two innings; and Nick Willhite and Mike Kekich, both five in one inning each.

1972— Four different Dodger southpaw pitchers fan a total of 22 Reds, but Cincinnati still wins 2-1 in 19 innings as righthander Pete Mikkelsen gets the loss and L.A. catcher Steve Yeager sets league records with 24 chances and 22 putouts. Tommy John (13) and Jim Brewer (6) contribute the most strikeouts.

1982— Ken Landreaux scores twice and Bob Welch hurls a 2-0 shutout at Dodger Stadium as the challenging Dodgers hand leading Atlanta its 10th loss in 11 games and move to within 1½ games of the top.

August 9

1906— Chicago pitcher Jack Taylor beats the Dodgers 5-3, his 187th consecutive complete game, a major league record. But the Dodgers end the streak August 13 when he's relieved in the third inning against them.

1915— George Cutshaw of the Dodgers becomes the first National Leaguer since 1899 to get six hits in a game. He scores twice, has an RBI, and a stolen base in a 13-0 win at Chicago.

1975— Dodgers' Davey Lopes steals his 32nd consecutive base, breaking the major league record held by Max Carey, as he also gets two hits and scores both runs, 2-0 over the Mets in New York. The record theft is off pitcher Jerry Koosman.

1976— John Candalaria, in Pittsburgh, throws the first-ever no-hitter against the Los Angeles Dodgers, 2-0 over Doug Rau.

1979— Dodgers' Chairman of the Board Walter O'Malley, chief owner since 1950 and the man who moved the club West, dies at age 75 at the Mayo Clinic in Rochester, Minn.

1981— An All-Star Game record crowd of 72,086 in Cleveland sees Dodgers rookie Fernando Valenzuela make his first start in the game, pitching one inning and allowing two hits and no runs.

Sandy Koufax, shown here with Baseball Commissioner Bowie Kuhn, was inducted into baseball's Hall of Fame on August 7, 1972.

August 10

1897— Pitchers Harley Payne of the Dodgers and Joe Corbett of Baltimore hook up in their second 3-3 tie of the season, this one going eight innings before rain whereas the first, May 3, lasted 11 frames.

1966— Chuck Dressen, former Dodgers coach and manager, dies at 67 in Detroit.

1978— In his second big league start, Bob Welch puts the Dodgers into a tie for first place as he beats Vida Blue and the Giants 12-2.

1979— Don Sutton's 9-0 triumph at San Francisco is his 50th shutout, moving him ahead of Don Drysdale as the No.1 Dodger.

1981— Jerry Reuss blanks Cincinnati 4-0 as the players'-strike-interrupted "second season" begins.

1982— Dodgers move into the National League lead, a half-game up on Atlanta, as they beat Cincinnati 11-3 for their eighth straight victory.

August 11

1926— Rookie Babe Herman singles and doubles his first two at-bats giving him nine straight hits during three games as the Dodgers trim Pittsburgh 4-2 at Ebbets. However, Herman falls one hit short of the major league record of 10 straight as he flies out in the sixth inning to Kiki Cuyler—co-holder of the mark with ex-Dodger Ed Konetchy.

1941— Pitcher Kirby Higbe helps win his own game as he gets three singles and a double for four RBI's in a 15-7 win over the Giants.

1950— Vern Bickford of Boston no-hits the Dodgers 7-0 with four walks and three strikeouts, Carl Erskine being the loser.

1962— Dodgers protest the wet conditions of the field at Candlestick Park—designed, they say, to slow down the speedy Maury Wills on the basepaths—as the Giants hand Don Drysdale his first loss after 11 straight victories and capture the second game of a crucial series, 5-4. The wetting tactics earn Giants' manager Alvin Dark the nickname of the "Swamp Fox."

1969— The Dodgers' "last link to Brooklyn," pitcher Don Drysdale, announces his retirement at 33 after suffering most of the season with a deep-seated muscle tear in his right shoulder.

1983— On the night that "Mr. Potato Head" is born, Greg Brock's three-run first-inning homer keys a 4-3 Dodgers' victory in Cincinnati which will spark 30 wins in the next 49 games for the division crown. A silly-looking bald-headed doll, "Mr. Potato Head" goes to the most valuable player after each Dodger triumph. The award's initiation comes the day following manager Tommy Lasorda's closed-clubhouse tirade in Cincinnati and three days after the Atlanta Constitution's headline proclaiming "It's Over!" (Braves leading by 5 1/2 games).

August 12

1929— Rookie Johnny Frederick hits his 17th homer and second in as many days as the Dodgers beat Pittsburgh 4-2 in 10 innings.

August 13

1910— Baseball's most amazing tie game! Every total in the box score is the same as the Dodgers and Pirates play an 8-8 deadlock called after nine innings by darkness. Each team has 38 at-bats, 13 hits, 12 assists, two errors, five strike-outs, three walks, a hit batsman, and a passed ball.

1926— Dodgers purchase Max Carey from the Pirates after refusing to waive on him.

1932— Hollis (Sloppy) Thurston gives up six homers, but he also gets four hits as the Dodgers wallop the Giants 18-9 in the first of a twin bill. Giants win the second, 4-3.

1951— On one of Ebbets Field's zanier promotions, Music Depreciation Night, every fan with a musical instrument is admitted free and 2,000 take advantage, including one guy with a piano. Dodgers edge the Braves, 7-6.

1982— Steve Sax steals his 41st base, breaking Rudy Law's Dodger rookie record, as Los Angeles tops the Giants 6-1 to lead by 2½ over Atlanta.

August 14

1946— The Dodgers draw 57,224 and beat the Giants 8-4, 2-1 in the first afternoon-night doubleheader in major league history where separate admissions are charged.

1956— Ex-Giant Sal Maglie holds his former team scoreless for seven innings before being lifted for a pinch-hitter, after which Willie Mays hits a two-run homer off Dodger Clem Labine for the 3-1 win.

1958— The smallest crowd ever to see a regular-season game in Los Angeles, 6,195, turns out at the Coliseum to watch the seventh-place Dodgers turn back the Cubs 7-3 as Don Drysdale gets the win (with help from three relievers) and Duke Snider and Jim Gilliam hit homers. The smallest Dodger Stadium crowd, 6,559, is for a September 13, 1976 game.

1973— Ken McMullen's two-out, two-run homer in the bottom of the ninth inning beats Montreal 4-3, and later McMullen reveals he almost quit baseball in May when his wife had an operation for cancer.

August 15

1910— Dodgers get 11 hits, but Three Finger Brown of the Cubs still twirls a 14-0 shutout.

1914— First baseman Jake Daubert has an injured ankle and can't run, so he lays down a record six sacrifice bunts—including four in the second game—as the Dodgers trip the Phils 8-4 and 13-5 at Ebbets Field.

1926— Three men on third base! In one of baseball's most storied incidents, the Dodgers' Babe Herman tries to stretch a bases-loaded drive to right field into a triple. However, ahead of him Dazzy Vance who'd been on second retreats back to third after deciding he can't score and Chick Fewster—from first—is trying to make third after seeing Vance round the bag and initially head for home. All three wind up standing on third together with Fewster and Herman eventually tagged out. Dodgers win the first game of the twin bill over the Braves at Ebbets, 4-1, and also take the nightcap, 11-3, as Herman drives in three runs.

1951— The Giants' Willie Mays makes one of baseball history's great plays, flagging down Dodger Carl Furillo's 330-foot drive in center field, then spinning toward home in the same motion and firing a one-bounce liner to catcher Wes Westrum who puts out a stunned Billy Cox tagging up from third base. Giants win 3-1 at the Polo Grounds.

1959— Larry Sherry puts on practically a one-man show as he hurls scoreless ball after relieving Johnny Podres in the first inning, meanwhile driving in three runs on two singles and a homer in a 4-3 Dodgers victory at St. Louis.

August 16

1952— Dodgers put an all-right-handed hitting lineup on the field, and one of the replacements—Dick Williams—gets three hits as Billy Loes shuts out the Phils 15-0 in a 6½ inning game.

1961— A record twilight double header mob of 72,140 show up at the Coliseum only to see the Dodgers fall 6-0 and 8-0 to Cincinnati's Jim O'Toole and Bob Purkey.

August 17

1902— Dodgers play their longest (since broken) game, an 18-inning 7-7 tie with the Cards.

1904— Kid Nichols pitches St. Louis to a 17-inning, 4-3 win over the Dodgers at Washington Park.

1982— The Dodgers and Cubs play 17 innings in Chicago to a 1-1 tie, temporarily halted by darkness after five hours, five minutes . The next day, in the 21st inning, Steve Sax scores on Dusty Baker's sacrifice fly for the 2-1 victory—the longest-ever L.A. Dodger game.

August 19

1983— Dodgers ink Kenny Landreaux to a four-year, $2.4 million contract the same day as they get pitcher Rick Honeycutt (and Ricky Wright) from the Texas Rangers in exchange for reliever Dave Stewart. Honeycutt is signed to a five-year contract worth $3.5 million.

August 18

1897— Following consecutive-day 12-3 and 6-2 losses to Baltimore, the Dodgers are in their lowest place ever—tied for 10th with Washington in the 12-team (then) National League. The next day the Dodgers climb to 10th alone with a 13-5 win vs. St. Louis at Eastern Park.

1977— Don Sutton blanks the Giants 7-0 with a National League record-tying fifth one-hitter as Marc Hill gets the lone safety with two out in the eighth inning.

August 20

1886— The Metropolitans of New York nip Brooklyn 5-4 in 10 innings at Staten Island.

1945— Tommy Brown of the Dodgers becomes the youngest ever to hit a homer in the majors—four months shy of his 18th birthday—but Preacher Roe and the Pirates win 11-1 at Ebbets as the home club commits seven errors.

1953— Dodgers win their 13th in a row as Carl Erskine throws a 10-0 shutout, the seventh straight win over the Giants. Pittsburgh ends the streak the next day.

1974— Davey Lopes smacks three homers, a double, and a single for a Los Angeles Dodger record of 15 total bases in a 24-hit, 18-8 victory at Chicago. The team total of 48 bases sets an all-time Dodgers record.

1978— Steve Garvey takes exception to Don Sutton's newspaper comments about his All-American "facade" and the two scuffle in the clubhouse at Shea Stadium before a Met's game won 5-4 by the Dodgers.

August 22

1917— Dodgers get 28 hits in a marathon 22-inning 6-5 win over Pittsburgh, the longest (since topped) game in the team's history.

1925— The Dodgers and Cubs "exchange compliments," each winning one game of a doubleheader 9-2.

1948— Dodgers pull off a triple steal with Jackie Robinson on the front end in the fifth inning and total eight for the game, but the Braves win 4-3 at Ebbets with a homer in the eighth inning.

1965— A 14 minute free-for-all erupts in the third inning at Candlestick Park after Giants pitcher Juan Marichal hits catcher John Roseboro over the head with a bat, claiming he was deliberately whizzing throws back to the pitcher past his head while he (Marichal) batted. Roseboro is wounded, though not seriously, and both are taken out of the game. When play resumes, Willie Mays quickly hits a three-run homer off Sandy Koufax as the Giants win, 4-3. Marichal is later fined $1,750 and suspended eight playing days.

August 23

1958— Gil Hodges hits his National League record (since topped) 14th career grand slam and Don Drysdale belts his seventh homer of the season, tying Don Newcombe's league mark for a pitcher, as the Dodgers beat Milwaukee 10-1 at the Coliseum.

August 24

1906— After the Dodgers win the opener 6-4 behind Jim Pastorius, the Red's Jake Weimer no-hits them in the second contest of seven innings, 1-0, Cincy getting a run in the seventh.

1919— Dodgers win 10-1 over St. Louis with 21 hits, every batter in the lineup getting at least one and Jimmy Johnston collecting four.

1941— A pickup band of musicians, later to become famous as the Dodger Symphony, attracts attention at Ebbets as the Dodgers and Cards split a double-header. Whit Wyatt drives in the winner, 3-2, in the nightcap after the Dodgers lose 7-3.

1957— Dodgers use eight pitchers against the Braves to tie a league record as Johnny Podres is chased with three homers in the fourth inning and seven relievers follow. Braves win 13-7.

1961— Dodgers suffer their 10th straight loss, a Los Angeles record, 10-1 in St. Louis as six pitchers are bombed for 16 hits. The slump ends the following day with a 7-2 win at Cincinnati as Sandy Koufax registers his 50th NL victory.

1974— Davey Lopes steals five bases to tie a league one-game mark, while the team total of eight ties a Dodgers' record during a 3-0 Don Sutton win over the Cards.

1975— After extending his majors' record to 38 straight steals in the seventh inning, Davey Lopes is caught in the 12th by the Expos' catcher Gary Carter at second base. Montreal wins 5-2 with three runs in the 14th off Mike Marshall.

August 25

1979— A Dodger Stadium crowd of 47,244 sees television's Robin Williams run the bases clockwise, like they do on the Planet Ork, during a three-inning Hollywood Stars-Media fray which preceeds the main event—a 5-4 Dodgers' loss to the Cardinals.

1980— Shortstop Bill Russell is ejected during a fight with Phil's relief pitcher Tug McGraw as the Dodgers win 8-4 thanks in part to Joe Ferguson who slaps a two-run single while being intentionally passed.

August 26

1939— Bucky Walters of the Reds beats the Dodgers 5-2 in the first baseball game ever to be televised, from Ebbets Field and with Red Barber at the mike. NBC puts one set in the press box and the other at the RCA Pavillion in New York City which attracts a turnaway crowd.

1942— Whit Wyatt and Mort Cooper of the Cardinals have the year's top pitching duel, the Dodgers losing in the 14th inning 2-1 when catcher Walker Cooper drives in the winning tally.

1947— Dan Bankhead, the Dodgers' second black player, hits a homer in his first at-bat. But he's also shelled for 10 hits and eight runs in a 16-3 Pittsburgh win.

1950— Roy Campanella hits three home runs off Ken Raffensberger, each with Gil Hodges on base, as the Dodgers win 7-5 at Cincinnati.

August 27

1936— Following a four-error, 6-3 Dodgers' loss in Pittsburgh, pitcher Van Lingle Mungo jumps the club, returns to Brooklyn, and talks out his displeasure over the team's support of him with club president Steve McKeever. Mungo later rejoins.

1937— Fred Frankhouse no-hits the Reds 5-0 at Ebbets in a game halted by rain with two outs in the eighth inning.

1951— Dodgers pitcher Ralph Branca has a no-hitter into the ninth inning, thanks to Carl Furillo's throw from right field that robs Mel Queen of a single. Branca then winds up with a 5-0 two-hitter over the Pirates at Ebbets.

1955— Sandy Koufax blanks the Cubs 7-0 in his second major league start, fanning 14 while allowing two hits and walking five.

1961— With Gene Freese's three-run homer the key blow, the Reds rally to take the first game, 6-5, and then the nightcap, 8-3, to restore their 3½ game lead over the threatening Dodgers at Cincinnati.

August 28

1945— At a three-hour first meeting in the Dodgers offices, club president Branch

Rickey tells 26-year-old Jackie Robinson he has been chosen to become, possibly, the first black to play in the modern major leagues but the road ahead will be difficult.

1977— Steve Garvey has three doubles and a pair of homers—one a grand slam—for 14 total bases in an 11-0 Don Sutton win over St. Louis at Dodger Stadium.

August 29

1948— Jackie Robinson hits for the cycle and also scores three times, drives in two runs, and steals third base as the Dodgers whip the Cards 12-7 before 33,826 at St. Louis and then also win the second contest, 6-4, to move into first place three percentage points over the Braves.

August 30

1918— The Dodgers' now-second-fastest nine-inning game—but then a majors' record— takes 57 minutes, Jack Coombs losing 1-0 as the Giants score in the home half of the ninth.

August 31

1900— Brickyard Kennedy of the Dodgers walks a record six consecutive batters in the second inning, bringing in two runs. An error by shortstop Bill Dahlen lets in two more and the Phils go on to win 9-4 at Washington Park.

1919— Umpire Bill Klem clears the Brooklyn bench in the seventh inning—leaving only manager Wilbert Robinson and the bat boy—as the Giants score three runs over the argumentative Dodgers and win 4-3 in their final meeting of a short, 140-game season. Dodgers pitcher Burleigh Grimes is spiked while covering first base and sidelined the remainder of the year.

1946— A fight erupts between them when Goody Rosen of the Giants spikes Eddie Stanky sliding into second as the Dodgers lose 2-1 at the Polo Grounds.

1950— Gil Hodges has the biggest day at bat of any Dodger ever: four homers and a single for 17 total bases with nine RBI's. The Dodgers get 21 hits in the 19-3 win over Boston at Ebbets.

1959— Sandy Koufax sends 14 Giants down swinging as he strikes out 18 at the Coliseum to tie Bob Feller's major league record in a 5-2 victory capped by Wally Moon's ninth-inning three-run homer.

SEPTEMBER
September 1

1890— Dodgers win the first of three tripleheaders ever played in the majors, 10-9 in the morning, 3-2 and 8-4 in the afternoon. Bob Caruthers, Tom Lovett, and Adonis Terry all pitch complete games over Pittsburgh at Washington Park.

1957— Giants win the final game at Ebbets Field between the longtime New York rivals 7-5 as 18,000 watch. The same day, the Dodgers sell their ex-Giants pitcher, Sal Maglie, to the Yankees for cash and two minor leaguers.

September 2

1918— The Phils win the opener 4-2 and the Dodgers the nightcap 5-3 as the season ends a month early because of the government's "work or fight order" embracing men of draft age. Zach Wheat wins the league batting crown with .335.

1971— Second baseman Jim Lefebvre and rightfielder Bill Buckner of the Dodgers collide in the fifth inning as Cesar Cedeno's 200-foot fly ball off Claude Osteen falls for a grand slam homer and home-team Houston wins, 9-3.

1972— Doug Rau debuts by beating St. Louis 3-1 with a three-hitter and hitting a triple in his first at-bat.

1979— Manny Mota gets his major-league-record 145th career pinch-hit in the eighth inning and Davey Lopes' grand slam in the ninth caps a five-run rally as the Dodgers win 6-2 over Chicago at Dodger Stadium.

September 3

1906— Dodgers batter the Phils 18-0, their largest (since topped) shutout margin.

1975— After missing two games with the flu, Steve Garvey returns to the lineup and starts his record consecutive-games playing streak in Cincinnati as the Dodgers lose 13-2.

September 4

1889— Before a crowd of 2,500 at Washington Park, Tom Lovett twirls a seven-hitter but also connects for a homer off Cincinnati's Elmer Smith thus making Lovett the first Dodger pitcher to hit a grand slam. It comes in the fourth inning of a 12-1 victory.

1902— Alex Hardy of the Cubs is the first in modern history to hurl a shutout his first majors' game, 1-0 over Brooklyn.

1920— Dodgers beat Boston 10-0 in a game featuring seven double plays, four by Brooklyn, as Hy Myers gets five RBI's.

1924— The Dodgers capture their fourth twin bill in as many days, a league record (since tied), as Dazzy Vance and Dutch Reuther beat the Braves 4-1, 9-1. Brooklyn had trimmed the Phils in consecutive double headers September 1, 2, and 3.

1955— Jim Gilliam's two-run homer in the eighth inning gives the Dodgers a 6-5 win over Pittsburgh on the first Camera Day for fans at Ebbets Field.

1966— A Cincinnati crowd of 18,670 sees Jim Lefebvre's two-run homer beat the Reds 8-6 as the Dodgers become the first team in baseball history to draw 2 million both at home and on the road in the same season.

1969— Willie Davis' Dodger-record batting streak ends at 31 consecutive games in a 3-0 loss at San Diego with former Dodger Al Ferrara driving in all three tallies.

1972— Dodgers set a Los Angeles record of seven errors in one game as they lose 8-4 to Cincinnati but win the first of a double bill at Dodger Stadium 6-5 on Manny Mota's ninth-frame double.

September 5

1908— Nap Rucker no-hits Boston 6-0 at Ebbets as he strikes out 14 and walks none. Dodgers commit three errors.

September 6

1924— The Dodgers' winning streak reaches a club-record 15 with a 1-0 Bill Doak shutout at Boston. But in the second game, the suddenly-first-place Dodgers fall to third behind the Giants and Pirates by losing 5-4 as the Braves' Casey Stengel drives in the tying run.

1945— Manager Leo Durocher is kicked out of the game in a 17-5 Dodgers' loss in Pittsburgh and the Kings County Grand Jury holds him for alleged felonious assault against a fan at Ebbets Field.

1950— After three-hitting the Phils' "Whiz Kids" 2-0 in the opener, Don Newcombe's bid to pitch and win a twin bill falls short as he retires for a pinch-hitter after seven innings of the nightcap trailing 2-0. However, the Dodgers rally in the ninth for a 3-2 triumph that goes to reliever Dan Bankhead.

1953— The league's leading hitter, Carl Furillo at .344, suffers a broken finger as he grapples on the ground with Giants' manager Leo Durocher during the second inning of a 6-3 Dodgers' win at the Polo Grounds. Durocher intercepted when Furillo charged the New York dugout after being taunted while on first base by Giant players.

1962— Harvey Kuehn's three-run double in the ninth inning beats the Dodgers 9-6 as the Giants move within 1½ games of the lead in the final contest of a crucial "pennant" series. The Dodger Stadium crowd of 54,263 makes a season's mark of 2,287,772, breaking Cleveland's major league record of 2,260,627 in 1948.

1976— Dodgers' Steve Yeager nearly suffers serious injury when the loose end of a bat broken by Bill Russell strikes him in the neck as he awaits in the on-deck circle. Dodgers win 4-1 at San Diego.

1977— Reggie Smith homers in a 3-2 win at San Diego, giving him the feat of homering in every park except expansion Toronto and Seattle.

1981— Fernando Valenzuela's seventh ties a National League mark for shutouts by a rookie as he beats St. Louis 5-0 for his 12th victory.

September 7

1889— Baseball by candlelight? Dodgers win 9-0 by forfeit at their Washington Park when the St. Louis Browns, leading 4-2, seek to have the game called by darkness after eight innings. St. Louis protests the umpire's decision to continue, first by lighting candles in front of their bench and then by leaving the field and thus forfeiting.

1903— Dodgers and Giants split a Labor Day double header, the Dodgers losing 6-4 before 9,300 at Washington Park in the a.m. and winning 3-0 before 23,628 at the Polo Grounds in the p.m. Five errors in the eighth inning beats Brooklyn in the opener.

1908— Dodgers pitcher Jim Pastorius loses 1-0—on a walk, a sacrifice, and the lone hit he allows the Braves at Washington Park.

1916— Giants beat Nap Rucker and the Dodgers 4-1 to launch their major league record 26-game winning streak.

1924— The wildest day in the history of Ebbets Field! On a Sunday, the Giants in first place, the Dodgers one-half game behind, thousands of fans arrive early, bearing crowbars and tearing the heavy gates off their hinges as 40 patrolmen are sent to quell the mob and 150 more are later needed. An estimated 7,000 get in with no tickets as the Giants win 8-7 despite a three-run Dodgers' ninth-inning rally that almost ties the contest.

1931— Van Lingle Mungo of the Dodgers beats Boston 2-0 in his first major league start, fanning 12 and also batting in both runs with a single and a triple.

1936— Van Lingle Mungo strikes out a league-leading 14, but he gives up eight hits and loses 4-1 in the second game of a twin bill at Boston. Dodgers win the opener 2-1.

1962— Maury Wills steals a personal high of four bases to run his total to 82 and set a National League record, but the Dodgers lose 10-1 to Pittsburgh at Dodger Stadium.

September 8

1925— Nelson (Chicken) Hawks of the Phils singles in the second inning, but is caught stealing, the only base-runner off Dodgers pitcher Dazzy Vance who wins it 1-0.

1952— Feud time at the Polo Grounds! Dodgers beat the Giants 10-2 in the matinee of a day-night double header marked by constant beanballs and Gil Hodges gashing Giant second baseman Bill Rigney's leg on a slide into second. The Giants then win the nightcap 3-2, but Brooklyn stays five games ahead in first place.

1955— On the earliest date in history the Dodgers—with a 17-game lead—clinch the pennant with a 10-2 win at Milwaukee.

1957— Giants nip the Dodgers 3-2 in their final-ever meeting at the Polo Grounds, Willie Mays' triple being the final hit.

1982— After nine straight losses to the Dodgers, Atlanta regains the league lead with a 12-11 win as Dale Murphy singles home Claudell Washington. Braves win 10-3 the following day to go 1½ games up.

September 9

1915— Lefty Tyler of Boston holds the Dodgers to one hit, but Brooklyn wins 1-0 on a walk to Hy Myers, Gus Getz's single, and a double steal followed by a sacrifice fly. Jeff Pfeffer limits the Braves to two hits.

1926— Dodgers send up five pinch-hitters and all of them deliver, including Dick Cox who sets a record by getting two hits (plus two RBI's and two runs) during a nine-run ninth inning that tops the Phils 12-6.

1948— Rex Barney throws the first no-hitter against the Giants since 1915 as Gil Hodges and Carl Furillo get RBI's in a 2-0 Dodgers victory at New York.

1954— Joe Adcock homers in the first inning, but otherwise Billy Loes throws a 2-1 Dodgers one-hitter over Milwaukee in a game called by rain after five frames.

1965— Sandy Koufax makes his fourth and record-setting no-hitter "perfect" as he sets down 27 straight Cubs batters—14 by strikeout—in a 1-0 tingler before 29,139 at Dodger Stadium. Chicago's Bob Hendley gives up only one hit, a bloop double by Lou Johnson in the seventh inning. Johnson also scores the lone run in the fifth by walking, getting second on a sacrifice, stealing third and continuing home on a wild throw by catcher Chris Krug.

1981— Ron Cey suffers a fractured left forearm when struck by a Tom Griffin pitch at Dodger Stadium in a 6-3, 11-inning Giants' victory. He's sidelined, then, until the first game of the Championship Series (Oct. 13) against Montreal.

September 11

1909— Zach Wheat debuts, going hitless against Christy Mathewson in a 4-0 opener of a twin bill loss to the Giants but getting two hits off Bugs Raymond in a 10-1 nightcap Dodgers' win.

1946— The Dodgers and Reds hook up in the longest scoreless tie in major league history, at Ebbets and lasting 19 innings and four hours, 40 minutes until called by darkness. Dodgers later win the playoff, 5-3.

1947— Ralph Branca at age 21 becomes the youngest-ever Dodgers' 20-game winner as he beats the Cardinals 4-3 in the first game of a showdown series in St. Louis.

1959— Wally Moon's three-run homer at the Coliseum is a decisive blow as the Dodgers hand Pirates' relief ace Elroy Face his first loss of the season, 5-4, after he'd gone 17-0.

1966— Sandy Koufax, by 4-0, and Larry Miller, by 1-0, shut out Houston twice, the fourth Dodgers' shutout in three days as Los Angeles moves into first place for keeps.

1983— Rookie R.J. Reynolds squeezes home Pedro Guerrero with the decider as the Dodgers win 7-6 over Atlanta to go three-up on the Braves in a 101-degree pennant crucial at Dodger Stadium. Mike Marshall's two-run double helps bring the Dodgers from three runs behind in the ninth inning of the lengthy (3 hours, 48 minutes) contest.

September 12

1932— Johnny Frederick smacks his major league record sixth pinch-hit homer of the season with Glenn Wright aboard in the ninth inning as the Dodgers nip the Cubs 4-3 at Ebbets.

1942— The Cardinal's Max Lanier, with a 2-1 victory, follows up teammate Mort Cooper's shutout of the previous day as St. Louis moves into a tie with the Dodgers for the league lead. The next day the Cards take the lead for good.

1947— Dodgers first baseman Jackie Robinson is named Rookie of the Year by the *Sporting News.*

1963— John Roseboro drives in all five runs—four on a first-inning grand slam—as the Dodgers beat Pittsburgh 5-3.

1966— Relief pitcher Ron Perranoski ties a league record as he strikes out six straight St. Louis batters during the fifth and sixth innings of a 3-2 Dodgers' win.

September 13

1897— Dodgers and Giants players insist on continuing, but when the fielders can no longer see the ball their game is called after seven innings tied 8-8. Bleacher occupants at Eastern Park hold firebrands made of rolled paper so they can watch.

1925— Dazzy Vance sets a record (since broken) for least hits in two consecutive games as he no-hits the Phils 10-1 at Ebbets five days after one-hitting them. Dodgers lose the nightcap 7-3 as visiting left fielder George Harper is showered with pop bottles after his collision with first baseman Charlie Hargreaves.

1941— The Dodgers' Whit Wyatt outhurls Mort Cooper 1-0 in a pennant-drive showdown at St. Louis. Cooper's no-hitter is spoiled in the eighth inning when Dixie Walker doubles, then relays a stolen sign to Billy Herman who singles him home.

1977— Dusty Baker drives in a Dodger-record five runs in one inning, the second, in an 18-4 victory over San Diego as the Dodgers lead their division by 13½ games.

September 14

1945— Near-disaster strikes the Dodgers when following a 7-3, 6-1 double header win in St. Louis their past-midnight train to Chicago wrecks and burns, killing the engineer, though all the Dodgers survive. That afternoon (Sept. 15) the Cubs win twice, 12-5 and 7-6.

1946— Ralph Branca is intended as a decoy so the Cardinals will use their left-handed hitting lineup and the Dodgers can insert lefty Vic Lombardi on the mound. But Branca looks sharp, stays in, and he wins 5-0 as the Dodgers move 1½ games out.

September 15

1924— Jim Bottomley drives in a major league record 12 runs as the Cardinals bombard the Dodgers 17-3 at Ebbets.

1941— Dodgers score five runs in the top of the 17th inning to whip Cincinnati 5-1 after the teams had played 16 scoreless frames. Johnny Allen hurls the first 15, but Hugh Casey gets the win in relief.

1974— Jimmy Wynn's grand slam is the key blow as the Dodgers turn back the Reds, 7-1, after they'd closed within 1 1/2 games of L.A.'s lead.

1978— Dodgers hit 3,011,368 with a crowd of 47,188 as they become the first team to surpass 3 million in attendance for a season. Meanwhile, Don Sutton shuts out Altanta 5-0 and Lee Lacy hits a two-run homer.

September 16

1916— Zach Wheat's club-record hitting streak of 29 games (since bettered) is stopped in the nightcap of a twin bill by Cincinnati's Fred Toney as the teams tie 1-1 in 12 innings.

1930— Andy High doubles, then scores in the tenth, as the Cards nip Dazzy Vance 1-0 to move into a tie for the league lead then sweep a series that knocks the Dodgers out of the race.

1940— After Cincinnati wins 4-3 in 10 innings on a disputed call, hundreds of fans swarm onto the field at Ebbets and one of them floors 6ft. 3in., 245-pound umpire George Magerkurth with a punch. The 198 pound fan is arraigned for assault.

1957— The Los Angeles City Council okays the proposed contract with the Dodgers, whereby the city will sell 300 acres in Chavez Ravine to the baseball club. In return, the Dodgers will deed Wrigley Field—then valued at about $4 million— to the city and set aside 40 acres in the Ravine for playground facilities furnished by them.

September 17

1912— Casey Stengel makes his Dodgers and major league debut, getting four singles and a walk in a 7-3 win at Pittsburgh.

1935— Dodgers outfielder Len Koenecke is killed when hit in the head with a fire extinguisher by the pilot of an airplane he'd been bothering while in flight over Toronto.

1963— Sandy Koufax's four-hitter beats St. Louis, 4-0, giving him a team-record 11 shutouts for the season.

1979— Five Dodgers knock out 20-or-more homers in a season for the first time when Joe Ferguson's 20th helps the Dodgers trim Atlanta 9-4. Already over the top: Ron Cey, Dusty Baker, Steve Garvey, and Davey Lopes.

September 18

1898— Giants beat Brickyard Kennedy and the Dodgers 7-3 in their first-ever Sunday game, played before 4,000 at Weehawken, N.J. because Sunday baseball is outlawed in New York.

1917— Spittin' Bill Doak of St. Louis becomes the second pitcher in two weeks to beat the Dodgers twice in one day, 2-0, 12-4 (a 12-hitter), following the Phils' Grover Alexander (Sept. 3).

1963— Dick Nen's only hit as a Dodger, a ninth-inning score-tying homer, helps the Dodgers win 6-5 in 13 frames and sweep a series in St. Louis that buries the threatening Cardinals.

September 19

1982— Fernando Valenzuela wins his 19th as the Dodgers nip Houston 5-4 on Pedro Guerrero's 10-inning two-run double and head for San Diego with a three-game lead.

September 20

1907— Fred Clarke of Pittsburgh gets the game's only hits as Nick Maddox no-hits the Dodgers and Elmer Stricklett two-hits the Pirates who win 2-1. Dodgers score on wild throws by Maddox and Hans Wagner.

1937— Bert Haas hits his third straight pinch-hit double, worth two runs, in a four-run ninth-inning rally, but the Dodgers fall short 5-4 in Chicago.

1946— Dodgers win the replay of their 19-inning scoreless tie with the Reds, 5-3, as Dixie Walker hits a three-run homer.

1959— Dodgers sweep a crucial three-game series at San Francisco and move into the league lead as Johnny Podres tops Sam Jones 8-2. Maury Wills is 7-for-13 during the visit.

1961— Ron Fairly singles home Wally Moon in the 13th inning for a 3-2 Dodger win in the final game at the Coliseum before only 12,068. Dodgers drew over 8 million customers and had a 173-140 won-lost there in four seasons.

September 21

1897— Dodgers score 12 runs in the first inning and win 22-5 as Boston catcher Charlie Ganzel loses two foul flies. A Boston newspaper calls the game "yellow (lost in the sun) ball."

1919— Dodgers beat the Reds 3-1 in 55 minutes, a club record for a shortest-in-time nine-inning game, as Slim Sallee of Cincinnati also sets a league record by throwing only 65 pitches.

1934— Dodgers set a record for fewest hits in a double header as Dizzy Dean of St. Louis three-hits them 13-0 and his brother Paul no-hits them 3-0 in the second game at Ebbets Field.

1957— Duke Snider hits his 39th and 40th home runs tying a National League record for 40-or-more home runs in five straight seasons, as the Dodgers hand Robin Roberts of Philadelphia his 22nd defeat, 7-3.

September 22

1916— Jimmy Johnston becomes the first Dodger to steal second, third, and home in the same game as Rube Marquard throws a six-hit, 11-1 win over the Cards at Ebbets.

1925— Dodgers pitcher Burleigh Grimes hits into two double plays and one triple play as the Cubs win 3-2 in 12 innings at Wrigley Field.

1954— Southpaw Karl Spooner sets major league first-game records as he blanks the Giants 3-0 while striking out 15—including six straight in the seventh and eighth innings.

1976— Don Sutton of the Dodgers becomes a 20-game winner for the first time, tossing a 3-1 six-hitter in San Francisco.

September 23

1939— As Cookie Lavagetto gets six hits and Jimmy Ripple three doubles, the Dodgers set a Brooklyn record of 46 total bases in a 22-4 win at Philadelphia during which they bang out 27 hits, including three triples and three homers.

1942— Dodger pitcher Larry French's 6-0 one-hitter over the Phils at Ebbets is almost overshadowed by a stunning announcement: that 52-year-old club president for the past five years Larry MacPhail is resigning effective at the end of the season to reenter the Army. "I don't think I'll have another baseball association other than Brooklyn," a tearful MacPhail says, recalling happy days. French's 27-batter masterpiece—the only baserunner, Nick Etten, is wiped out by a double play—is his last-ever game in the majors, as he, too, then joins the military.

1947— Dodgers whip the Giants 6-1 on Jackie Robinson Day, also one day after they've clinched their first pennant in six years.

1952— Dodgers clinch the flag with a 5-4 win over Philadelphia.

1962— Maury Wills steals his 97th base, breaking Ty Cobb's modern major league mark, but the Cardinals win 12-2.

September 24

1901— Jimmy Sheckard hits a grand slam for the second consecutive game—a major league record—in a 16-2 Dodgers victory that the Reds concede after the fourth inning. At Cincinnati the day before both Sheckard and Joe Kelley hit grand slams in a 25-6 romp that equalled a Dodgers' runs-scored high.

1957— Organist Gladys Gooding plays "Auld Lang Syne" and Danny McDevitt shuts out the Pirates 2-0 before 6,702 in the Dodgers' last-ever game at Ebbets.

1974— Al Downing becomes the third Los Angeles Dodgers lefty, following Sandy Koufax and Claude Osteen, to win 20 games as he beats the Braves in Atlanta 2-0.

1978— Bob Welch trims the Padres 4-0 on a five-hitter as the Dodgers clinch their second straight National League West title.

1980— Dodgers surpass 3 million in attendance for the second time in three seasons in a 5-4 12-inning win over the Giants as the re-activated Manny Mota gets his 148th career pinch-hit.

September 25

1941— A wild celebration on the train back to New York follows Whit Wyatt's 6-0 five-hitter in Boston that clinches the Dodgers' first pennant in 21 years, Pete Reiser homering for two runs and Dixie Walker tripling for three.

1946— Dodgers suffer a bitter defeat as the Phils score five in the ninth inning to win 11-9 and "force" an eventual Brooklyn tie for the pennant with the Cardinals.

1956— Sal Maglie, aged 39, no-hits the Phils 5-0 to keep the Dodgers in the thick of a three-team pennant chase with Milwaukee and Cincinnati.

1962— Relief pitcher Ed Roebuck suffers his first setback, 3-2 to Houston in 10 innings, after 60 appearances over a two-year span.

September 26

1891— Amos Rusie of the Giants beats the Dodgers both ends, 10-4, 13-5, in the rivalry's first-ever double header. Darkness halts the second game after six innings.

1908— The Cubs' Ed Reulback becomes the only pitcher in major league history to twirl a double bill shutout, 5-0, 3-0, over the Dodgers at Washington Park.

1920— Rube Marquard scores his final victory as a Dodger, a 4-2 five-hitter over his former Giant mates. The next day the Giants also lose in Boston and the Dodgers clinch the pennant.

1954— Karl Spooner makes it two shutouts in two big league appearances, 1-0 over Pittsburgh, as his 12 strikeouts also gives him 27 for two games.

1975— Burt Hooton beats Houston and J.R. Richard 3-2 at Dodger Stadium for his 12th straight win, a Los Angeles Dodgers mark for starting pitchers.

1981— Nolan Ryan fires his record fifth no-hitter, 5-0 over the Dodgers at Houston's Astrodome.

September 27

1931— Dodgers beat the Giants 12-3 in the opener and the second game at Ebbets is called by darkness after three innings at 0-0 in what turns out to be the final meeting between managers Wilbert Robinson and John J. McGraw. Final tally: 197-190 in favor of the Giants' McGraw with five ties.

1951— Dodgers' rookie Bill Sharman gains a singular distinction—the only player kicked out of a major league game though he never played in one. It happens when umpire Frank Drascoli clears the bench following a violent protest of his call at home that gives Boston a critical 4-3 win on Bob Addie's score.

1959— The Dodgers top the Cubs 7-1 but the Braves trim the Phils 5-2, Los Angeles and Milwaukee thus tying for the National League crown.

1961— Sandy Koufax breaks Christy Mathewson's National League record of 267 strikeouts for a season as he whiffs seven for his 269th during a 2-1 win over the Phils.

September 28

1963— Tommy Davis gets two hits in a 12-3 loss to Philadelphia to finish with .326 and become the youngest ever to win two consecutive National League batting crowns.

1966— Larry Jaster of the Cardinals ties a league record by hurling his fifth consecutive shutout over one team, the Dodgers, 2-0.

1974— Andy Messersmith of the Dodgers becomes the 14th player in majors' history to win 20 games in both leagues as he trims San Diego 5-2.

September 29

1941— An estimated million spectators cheer their "Bums" during a downtown Brooklyn parade to celebrate the team's first pennant since 1920.

1957— The Brooklyn Dodgers play their final game, losing 2-1 in Philadelphia as Roger Craig starts but Sandy Koufax relieves and Jim Gilliam scores the final run.

1959— The Los Angeles Dodgers win their first flag, 6-5 in a second playoff victory over the Braves at the Coliseum, as Carl Furillo drives home the winner in the 12th after L.A.'s three-run ninth inning rally ties the contest.

1975— Former Dodgers player, coach, manager—and opponent—Casey Stengel dies at age 85 in Glendale, CA.

1976— Tommy Lasorda is named to succeed Walt Alston, who retired two days earlier, as the Dodgers' manager.

September 30

1934— Dodger fans pack the Polo Grounds, as for the second day in a row the Flock wins, 8-5 in 10 innings, to knock the Giants out of the championship and remind their manager, Bill Terry, that Brooklyn, indeed, still is in the league.

1945— Eddie Stanky of the Dodgers sets a National League record as he draws his 148th walk—off Dick Barrett—for the year in a 4-1 Brooklyn win before 2,241 frostbitten fans at Philadelphia.

1951— Jackie Robinson's greatest game! His 12th inning diving catch at Shibe Park kills a Phils' rally and in the 14th his homer settles the issue, 9-8, as the Dodgers keep alive their hopes of tying the Giants for the pennant.

1956— Duke Snider and Sandy Amoros each stroke two homers and Don Newcombe wins his 27th of the season, 8-6 over Pittsburgh, as the Dodgers edge Milwaukee for the title.

1962— Gene Oliver's homer in the ninth inning gives the Cards a 1-0 victory at Dodger Stadium as the Giants beat the Astros 2-1 at Candlestick to force a Dodgers-Giants tie for the National League championship.

1965— Dodgers win their 13th straight, 4-0 over the Braves, to tie a Los Angeles record as they move into a two-game league lead on the strength of Don Drysdale's 23rd triumph. However, the Dodgers lose to the Braves the next day, 2-0.

1982— Steve Garvey plays his final game at Dodger Stadium as a Dodger, getting three hits in a 10-3 win over Atlanta and moving into third on the all-time list with 1,104 consecutive games played. The Dodgers' final attendance of 3,608,881 (46,111 average) is a major league record.

OCTOBER
October 1

1937— Two days before the season ends, the Dodgers beat the Giants 7-4 at Ebbets and end a 14-game losing streak, second longest in the club's history.

1941— At Yankee Stadium, the Dodgers play their first World Series game since 1920 but lose 3-2 as Joe Gordon's two RBI's beats starter Curt Davis.

1950— Dick Sisler's three-run homer in the 10th inning at Ebbets Field settles both a Robin Roberts-Don Newcombe pitching duel and the pennant as the Phils beat the Dodgers 4-1 on the final day of the season.

1952— Joe Black spaces six hits as the Dodgers beat the Yankees for the first time in a World Series opener, 4-2. Duke Snider's two-run homer in the sixth inning is the big blow.

1959— The Go Go Sox turn into the Bang Bang Sox as they rake five pitchers for an 11-0 victory at Chicago in the Los Angeles Dodgers' first-ever World Series game. White Sox slugger Ted Kluszewski has five RBI's and two homers. Starter Roger Craig lasts only two innings for L.A.

1974— Dodgers beat Houston 8-5 to clinch the National League West crown as Don Sutton gains his 19th win and Mike Marshall appears in his major-league-record 106th game. For the first time, The L.A. Dodgers surpass 100 victories in a season.

1975— Larry McPhail, who played a major role in turning the Dodgers into a winner as general manager from 1938 to 1942, dies at age 85 in Miami.

October 2

1941— Whit Wyatt pitches all nine innings as the Dodgers even the World Series at one game each and stop the Yankees' consecutive-games Series streak at 10 games with a 3-2 triumph. Dolph Camilli singles home Dixie Walker with the decider in the sixth inning.

1949— After blowing an earlier 5-0 lead, the visiting Dodgers nose out Philadelphia 9-7 in the 10th inning to protect a one-game lead and win the National League flag on the season's last day. Duke Snider's single drives in Pee Wee Reese and Luis Olmo's single drives in Snider for the deciding runs.

1953— Carl Erskine's 14 strikeouts sets a World Series one-game record and Roy Campanella's eighth inning homer turns the tide as the Dodgers beat the Yankees 3-2 at Ebbets Field in Game Three. Johnny Mize is the record-setting 14th victim.

1959— Charlie Neal's two homers, the second with Jim Gilliam aboard in the seventh inning, are the difference as the Los Angeles Dodgers gain their first-ever World Series game win, 4-3 in Chicago. Johnny Podres gets the victory and Larry Sherry his first save.

1963— Ten years to the day, Sandy Koufax breaks Carl Erskine's record as he fans 15 Yankees in a 5-2 World Series-opening Dodger victory in New York. John Roseboro's three-run homer in the second off Whitey Ford is the big hit.

1965— With two days rest, Sandy Koufax strikes out 15 Braves and runs his major league record season total to 382 as the Dodgers win 3-1 at Dodger Stadium to clinch the pennant over the contending Giants. Lou Johnson scores the winning run.

1966— Sandy Koufax's 27th win, 6-3 in the second game of a twin bill at Philadelphia, gives the Dodgers back-to-back pennants but it turns out to be Sandy's final triumph as a Dodger. Don Drysdale drops the day's first contest, 4-3.

1977— Dusty Baker's 30th homer in the sixth inning off J.R. Richard gets a standing ovation from 46,501 at Dodger Stadium as for the first time in major league history four players from one team hit 30-or-more homers—Ron Cey (30), Reggie Smith (32), and Steve Garvey (33) joining Baker. But Houston beats the Dodgers 6-3.

1983— Southpaw Sid Fernandez—billed once as either the "next Koufax" or "next Fernando"—makes what will be his only start for the Dodgers (before later being traded) in the season's final game, a 4-3 loss to the Giants. He walks six in his three innings, while at the turnstiles the Dodgers show a decrease of nearly 100,000 from the previous year's record attendance.

October 3

1905— Bill Scanlon becomes the only Dodger ever to pitch two wins in one day as he beats St. Louis 4-0 and 3-2 and allows 12 hits in the 18 innings he works. Dodgers win the second by scoring twice in the top of the eighth inning.

1916— An angry Giants manager John McGraw retires to the clubhouse in the fifth inning, claiming his players aren't trying, as the Dodgers clinch their first-ever World Series appearance with a 9-6 victory.

1946— The Cardinals beat the Dodgers 8-4 at Ebbets to make a clean sweep of the first tie-breaking playoffs in National League history. Dodgers score three in the ninth before fizzling.

1947— One out from pitching the first no-hitter in World Series history, Yankee pitcher Floyd Bevens is stunned by pinch-hitter Cookie Lavagetto's long double to right that scores two runners and gives the Dodgers a 3-2 fourth-game and Series-tying victory at Ebbets Field. Dodgers use four hurlers.

1951— Baseball's most fabled game! With two on in the bottom of the ninth inning at the Polo Grounds Bobby Thomson of the Giants hits his "shot heard 'round the world" off reliever Ralph Branca to beat the Dodgers 5-4, win the post-season playoffs two games to one, and send New York which had trailed the Dodgers by 13½ games in August to the World Series.

1962— The San Francisco Giants rally for four runs in the ninth inning at Dodger Stadium as they beat the Dodgers 6-4 in the third game of the tie-breaking playoffs and advance to the World Series. Maury Wills' three stolen bases give him 104 for the 165-game season and a new major league record.

1976— The "Walt Alston Era" ends as the Dodgers and Doug Rau lose 3-2 to the Padres at Dodger Stadium to finish 10 games behind Cincinnati in the NL West.

1982— Joe Morgan swats a three-run homer off Terry Forster, who relieved starting pitcher Fernando Valenzuela, as the Dodgers' hopes for tying Atlanta for the division title are squelched 5-3 in San Francisco. Steve Garvey strikes out on his final Dodger at-bat.

October 4

1884— A 31-year-old rookie, Sam Kimber, hurls the first Dodger no-hitter in history against Toledo, but the game is called at 0-0 after 10 innings because of darkness.

1913— First baseman Jake Daubert is named as the Dodgers' only winner of the Chalmers (a motor car) Award as the National League's Most Valuable Player.

1917— The Dodgers split a twin bill with Boston at Ebbets, winning 5-1, but losing 4-2 to become the only National League team ever to win the pennant one year and fall as deep as seventh the next. Casey Stengel has a run-scoring single in what will be his final games as a Dodger player.

1936— Dodgers announce that Casey Stengel with one year left on his contract has been fired as manager. Coaches Otto Miller and Zach Taylor are also released.

1941— Pitchers Johnny Russo of the Yanks and Fred Fitzsimmons of the Dodgers lock up in a 0-0 duel that takes a dramatic turn when Russo's hit in the seventh inning caroms off Fitz's kneecap, chipping a bone and forcing him out. The Yankees score twice in the eighth to win the first game of the inter-borough series ever played at Ebbets, 2-1, and take a 2-1 World Series lead.

1955— Johnny Podres throws an eight-hit shutout, Gil Hodges drives in two runs, Sandy Amoros makes a sensational running catch of Yogi Berra's drive down the left field line in the sixth inning and it's no longer "wait 'til next year" as Brooklyn captures its only world championship, 2-0 over the Yankees.

1959— Before the first of three straight 90,000-plus crowds at the Coliseum, Carl Furillo's pinch-hit single in the seventh inning drives in two runs as the Dodgers beat Chicago 3-1 in the first World Series game ever played in Los Angeles. Don Drysdale is the winner, with the save by Larry Sherry.

1981— Dave Goltz suffers his seventh straight loss dating back to August 19, a Los Angeles club record that surpasses Don Sutton's six in 1974, as the Dodgers end the second half of the strike-interrupted season six games behind Houston which wins this game 5-3.

October 5

1912— Pat Ragan toes the rubber for the Dodgers' final game at Washington Park— before the move to Ebbets—but the Giants win 1-0 before 10,000 spectators and Shannon's Regimental Band. Afterwards, much of the crowd stays, savoring a last look.

1914— The Dodgers' Pat Ragan relieves in the eighth inning of a double header's second game and promptly fans the side on nine pitches—doffing his cap and bowing to the Ebbets Field crowd after each strike. But the Braves score five runs off him in the ninth to win 9-5 after having won the opener, 15-2.

1937— Dodgers trade infielders Joe Stripp and Jimmy Bucher, outfielder Johnny Cooney, and pitcher Roy Henshaw to the Cardinals for shortstop Leo Durocher.

1941— Hugh Casey's third-strike sinking pitch with two outs in the ninth inning gets away from Dodgers catcher Mickey Owen, giving Tommy Heinrich and the Yankees life at first base as they then rally to win 7-4 and take a commanding 3-1 World Series lead.

1947— A record 38 players are used as the Dodger knot the World Series 3-3 before 74,065 at Yankee Stadium in an 8-6 victory highlighted by sub outfielder Al Gionfriddo's rail-leaping catch of Joe DiMaggio's 415-foot drive with two aboard in the sixth inning.

1953— Billy Martin's 12th hit of the Series drives in the winning run in the ninth as the Yankees beat the Dodgers 4-3 and annex manager Casey Stengel's record fifth straight championship. Dodger Carl Furillo's two-run homer in the top of the inning had tied the score.

1956— The Dodgers win their fifth straight World Series game at Ebbets Field—including the three in 1955—as they outscore the Yankees 13-8, both teams getting 12 hits. Duke Snider's three-run homer highlights a six-run second inning.

1974— Dodgers make their debut in National League Championship Series play a winner as Don Sutton throws a 3-0 four-hitter at Pittsburgh and Jerry Reuss.

1980— Ron Cey smashes a two-run homer in the eighth inning and the Dodgers beat the Astros 4-3 to sweep a season-closing three-game series at Dodger Stadium and tie for the National League West title. But it's for naught as the next day Houston wins a one-game playoff 7-1 to advance into championship play.

October 6

1920— Spitballer Burleigh Grimes wins his only World Series game, besting Cleveland's 31-game winner Jim Bagby 3-0 on a seven-hitter at Ebbets Field as the Dodgers even the count at 1-1.

1952— With two runs in the seventh and one on Mickey Mantle's homer in the eighth inning the Yankees beat the Dodgers 3-2 to deadlock the World Series at 3-each. Asked later what happened on Vic Rashi's ground ball in the seventh that he kicked, Dodger pitcher Bill Loes explains "I lost it in the sun."

1959— The largest World Series crowd in history, 92,650 at the Coliseum, sees three White Sox pitchers post a 1-0 shutout over the Dodgers and send the teams back to Chicago for Game Six with Los Angeles leading 3-2 in games.

1963— Sandy Koufax pitches a six-hitter and Frank Howard hits a Buyonesque homer into the loge (second) level in the fifth inning off Whitey Ford as the Dodgers beat the Yankees 2-1 at Dodger Stadium to complete their only four-game Series sweep. Jim Gilliam gets life on first baseman Joe Pepitone's error and scores the decider on Willie Davis' sacrifice fly in the seventh.

1966— Dodgers centerfielder Willie Davis sets a record as he muffs two flyballs and throws wild to third base in one inning, the fifth, while Baltimore's Jim Palmer tosses a 6-0 shutout as the Orioles go two-up in the World Series at Dodger Stadium. Sandy Koufax is the losing pitcher, his final game on the mound.

October 7

1916— Rube Marquard pitches as the Dodgers—or Robins as they're then often called—make their first-ever World Series game, in Boston, a loser, 6-5 to the Red Sox. The Dodgers have four runs in and the bases loaded in the ninth when Jake Daubert grounds out to end the game. Outfielder Casey Stengel is 3 for 4 and scores the first-ever Dodger World Series run in the fourth.

1978— Philadelphia centerfielder Garry Maddox drops Dusty Baker's soft liner in the 10th inning at Dodger Stadium and Bill Russell then follows with a two-out single to score Ron Cey and give the Dodgers their second straight National League West crown, 4-3.

October 8

1956— Yankee pitcher Don Larsen faces 27 Dodgers as he pitches the only perfect game in World Series history, 2-0 over Sal Maglie (a five-hitter) at Yankee Stadium. Pinch-hitter Dale Mitchell goes down "half-swinging" on a 2-2 pitch for the final out.

1959— Larry Sherry rescues Johnny Podres in the fourth inning and gets the win as he throws blanks the final five innings to clinch Los Angeles' first ever World Series title over Chicago 9-3 at Comiskey Park. Duke Snider, Wally Moon, and Chuck Essegian all homer as the Dodgers build up an early 8-0 lead.

1977— Dusty Baker hits a two-run homer and Tommy John throws a seven-hitter as the Dodgers beat Philadelphia 4-1 in the rain to advance to the World Series for their first time under manager Tommy Lasorda.

October 9

1916— Hi Myers hits a first-inning home run, but thereafter Boston lefthander Babe Ruth throws a shutout as he bests Dodger lefty Sherry Smith 2-1 in 14 innings, the longest-ever World Series game.

1965— Claude Osteen throws a five-hit, 5-0 shutout at Minnesota in his World Series debut at Dodger Stadium to narrow the Twins' lead in games to 2-1. John Roseboro's single drives in the first two runs in the fourth frame.

1966— Frank Robinson hits a fourth-inning home run off Don Drysdale for a 1-0 Baltimore victory and World Series sweep over the Dodgers who fail to score in the final 33 innings. Los Angeles bats .142 as a team, but the Orioles aren't much better at .200.

1974— Steve Garvey drives in four runs and Bill Russell three in a 12-1 Dodger triumph over Pittsburgh for the National League West title. Don Sutton hurls his second win in the three-games-to-one series.

October 10

1916— Ivy Olson's two-run triple in the fifth inning is the deciding margin as Jack Coombs and Jeff Pfeffer combine to beat the Red Sox 4-3 in the first-ever World Series game in Brooklyn.

1920— In one of the most famous World Series games ever, Cleveland second baseman Bill Wambsganss completes the classic's only unassisted triple play—spearing Clarence Mitchell's low liner on the fifth-inning hit-and-run play being executed by the Dodgers, tagging second for the forceout of the runner Pete Kilduff at that base, and then running down Otto Miller before he can get back to first. The Indians win 8-1, their hitting highlight being Elmer Smith's first-inning grand slam, the first in World Series history.

1956— The Dodgers go out a loser, 9-0, in what proves to be the final World Series game in Brooklyn as the Yankees win the classic four games to three. It's also Jackie Robinson's final appearance in a Dodger uniform.

1978— Two days after his sudden death, the number 19 of coach Jim Gilliam is retired by the Dodgers. He's the only Dodger to play on four World Series championship teams.

October 11

1920— Duster Mails, whose record as a Dodger pitcher during 1915-16 was 0-2, turns tiger against his former team and throws a three-hit 1-0 shutout in Cleveland as the Indians take a 4-2 lead in the best-of-nine World Series. Tris Speaker scores the lone run in the sixth inning.

1956— En route to Japan after the World Series, Dodger owner Walter O'Malley tells the *Los Angeles Times* the chances of his team moving West are slim. He cites the good Brooklyn attendance, progress on a new stadium there, and that the L.A. territory belongs to "my good friend Phil Wrigley" of the Chicago Cubs.

1978— Bob Welch strikes out Yankee Reggie Jackson in a classic ninth inning duel to preserve Burt Hooton's 4-3 victory as the Dodgers head for New York City with a 2-0 Series lead. Ron Cey drives in all four runs with a single and three-run homer off Catfish Hunter.

1981— Jerry Reuss's five-hitter beats the Astros 4-0 as the Dodgers complete a three-game sweep at Dodger Stadium to capture the National League West divisional playoffs.

October 12

1916— A Boston crowd of 42,620 is on hand as the Dodgers lose Game Five of the World Series, 4-1, and thus drop their first Series four games to one. The Brooks make three errors and get only three hits off Ernie Shore.

1920— Four years to the day, the Dodgers complete their second World Series a loser five games to two as Stan Coveleski beats them a third time—not allowing a runner past first in a 3-0 shutout. Dodger pitcher Rube Marquard is arrested for scalping tickets that morning in front of a Cleveland hotel and later fined $25.

October 13

1938— A year and a week after coming to the club in a trade, Leo Durocher succeeds Burleigh Grimes as Dodgers manager. He names Chuck Dressen as one of his coaches.

1978— Third baseman Graig Nettles makes four dazzling stops, preventing at least seven Dodger runs, as the Yankees win 5-1 at Yankee Stadium behind Ron Guidry and narrow the Los Angeles games' margin to 2-1.

October 14

1889— Adonis Terry tosses a five-hitter and gets two hits, one a triple, as the Dodgers close out the season with a 6-1 win over Columbus. Combined with St. Louis' 8-3 loss to Cincinnati, it gives Brooklyn its first-ever major league (American Association) championship.

1953— Dodgers announce that manager Chuck Dressen, who'd written a letter requesting a three-year contract, won't be rehired—that it's against their policy to grant pacts of more than one year.

1965— The Dodgers' fourth world championship is also Walt Alston's fourth—a National League record—as Sandy Koufax tosses his second shutout, 2-0, over the Twins in the seventh game of the World Series at Minnesota. Lou Johnson homers in the fourth inning.

1978— Shortstop Bill Russell's throw to first on an attempted double play ricochets off the hip of Yankee baserunner Reggie Jackson in the sixth inning, allowing a run and leading to a 4-3 10-inning Dodger defeat that ties the World Series at two games each.

October 16

1893— The Dodgers beat the Giants 12-2 at Eastern Park in the first game of a series of six the two teams have scheduled on their own account after the regular season.

October 17

1974— Oakland's A's capture their third consecutive World Series in five games over the Dodgers as Joe Rudi hits a tie-breaking seventh-inning homer off reliever Mike Marshall and Rollie Fingers earns his third save in the 3-2 victory. Play is halted for several minutes in the seventh to clear up Oakland fans' debris thrown at Dodger outfielder Bill Buckner for his disparaging remarks about their team.

1978— The Yankees win their fourth straight game, and the World Series, four games to two at Dodger Stadium as Catfish Hunter and Goose Gossage cool Dodger bats 7-2. It's New York's 22nd world crown and their seventh over the Dodgers.

1981— Steve Garvey's two-run homer in the eighth breaks a 1-1 tie as the Dodgers go on to beat Montreal 7-1 and even their Championship Series at two games each.

October 18

1886— Dodgers top the Giants 7-2 at Washington Park in the first of four post-season matches agreed upon by the two clubs of different leagues. They also have post-season contests in 1887.

1889— Dodgers score five runs in the first inning and beat the Giants 12-10 behind Adonis Terry to take a one-game lead at the Polo Grounds in the world championship series between the champions of the American Association (Dodgers) and National League. The game ends after eight innings when the players stall as darkness approaches and the fans wander onto the field.

1977— "Reggie! Reggie!" the New York fans chant as their star slugger Reggie Jackson ties Babe Ruth's record with three home runs—each on the first pitch—and drives in five runs for an 8-4 victory that sews up the World Series over the Dodgers in six games. Jackson's victims are Burt Hooton in the fourth, Elias Sosa in the fifth, and Charlie Hough in the eighth.

October 19

1889— The second in the Dodgers-Giants "world's championship" series attracts a crowd of 16,172 at Brooklyn's Washington Park—double that of the Polo Grounds —and the Dodgers win 6-2 in nine innings with Bob Caruthers pitching.

1959— The deal is legal, at last, as the U.S. Supreme Court upholds the validity of the contract between the Dodgers and the city of Los Angeles for the Chavez Ravine site where the new stadium is to be built.

1981— Rick Monday's home run in the top of the ninth off Steve Rogers breaks a tense pitcher's battle, 2-1, as the Dodgers beat Montreal to advance into the World Series. Fernando Valenzuela throws a three-hitter but needs help from Bob Welch getting the final out.

October 20

1890— Brooklyn, now of the National League, and Louisville of the American Association play a 7-7 tie as part of their world championship series that opened October 17 in Louisville. The playoffs go seven games, devoid of interest, and end three games each plus the tie. No attempt is made to decide a winner.

1951— Two weeks after having served up the "shot heard 'round the world" to the Giants' Bobby Thomson, Dodgers pitcher Ralph Branca marries Ann Mulvey— the grand-daughter of deceased club part-owner Steve McKeever—in an impressive society wedding.

1983— Dodger manager Tommy Lasorda inks a three-year, $1 million contract, breaking a long club tradition of one-season offerings in effect since Walter O'Malley assumed ownership in the 1950s. Four days later, the Associated Press names Lasorda NL "Manager of The Year" for the third time in seven years.

October 21

1968— Fresco Thompson, vice president and general manager and a onetime player for the Dodgers, dies at age 65.

October 22

1965— The Dodgers release outfielder Wally Moon and third baseman Jim Gilliam, with Gilliam then re-signed as a coach.

October 23

1931— After 18 years, Wilbert Robinson is released as Dodgers manager and Max Carey hired to replace him.

1945— The Montreal Royals, a Dodger triple-A farm club, announce they've signed Jack Roosevelt Robinson, 26, a negro infielder, for the 1946 season.

1957— A huge crowd—including key city officials—is on hand to greet owner Walter O'Malley and the vanguard of Dodger officals as they alight at International Airport, Los Angeles, and begin the move West from Brooklyn.

1981— Ron Cey homers and drives in three runs to aid Fernando Valenzuela who staggers to a 5-4 nine-hit, seven-walk win over the Yankees at Dodger Stadium as the Dodgers get back in the World Series after dropping two games in New York.

October 24

1972— In Stamford, Ct., Jackie Robinson dies at 53 afflicted by diabetes, a heart condition, and failing sight.

October 25

1943— Dodgers manager Leo Durocher signs his 1944 contract, it calling for a base pay of $20,000 and another $5,000 for every 100,000 in attendance over the 600,000 mark.

1981— At Palm Springs, CA. former Dodger outfielder Pete Reiser dies at 62 while at Dodger Stadium. Seventh inning home runs by Pedro Guerrero and Steve Yeager give the Dodgers a 2-1 victory and sweep of the Los Angeles segment of the World Series. Ron Cey is beaned in the eighth inning by a Goose Gossage pitch.

October 26

1946— In his syndicated column, Westbrook Pegler questions the off-field association of Dodgers manager Leo Durocher with actor George Raft and others allegedly associated with gamblers. It's the first of a series of incidents that will lead to Durocher being barred for the 1947 baseball season.

1950— At age 47, former club attorney Walter O'Malley becomes the new president and is the chief stockholder of the Dodgers, thus ending a long struggle for control with Branch Rickey. It's announced that Rickey is selling up to 25 per cent of his interest for a reported $1,050,000.

October 27

1890— The Dodgers ("Grooms"), champions of the National League their first season in it, lose 9-8 to Louisville of the American Association but only 300 "frozen" people show up for the world championship series game at Brooklyn. After one more game, the series—tied at three games apiece (including one 7-7 tie)—is called off because of cold weather.

October 28

1981— Pedro Guerrero pounds out two homers and drives in five runs as the Dodgers rake six Yankee pitchers for 13 hits to win their fourth straight game, 9-2, and the World Series—their first under manager Tommy Lasorda and their fourth since coming to Los Angeles. Guerrero, Ron Cey, and Steve Yeager are named Tri-Players of the Series.

October 29

1889— At the Polo Grounds, the Giants nip the Dodgers 3-2 before a crowd of 3,057 to annex the first official world championship series between the two of them, six games to three. Adonis Terry is the losing pitcher.

October 30

1956— The Dodgers announce that Ebbets Field has been sold to Marvin Kratter, a Brooklyn real estate operator, and that the property will become a housing development. But the Dodgers also sign a lease allowing them to stay on through 1959.

In 1955, Roy Campanella, above, shown with television star Jinx Falkenberg, presents a baseball to a youngster in New York's Childrens Hospital.

NOVEMBER

November 1

1942— With a five year contract, Branch Rickey—who built the St. Louis Cardinals' successful farm system—succeeds Larry McPhail as general manager of the Dodgers.

1944— At a press conference, Dodgers GM Branch Rickey announces that he and two associates, attorney Walter O'Malley and Brooklyn business man Andrew J. Schmitz, have purchased 25 per cent of the stock in the club originally held by Steve McKeever and sold by the executors of his estate.

1966— Sandy Koufax becomes the first pitcher to win the Cy Young Award three times.

November 2

1976— Dodgers purchase outfielder Pedro Guerrero from their Albuquerque farm team.

1983— Jerry Reuss signs a four-year, $4.25 million contract, richest-ever for a Dodger pitcher, only 24 hours before he would have been lost to free agency.

November 4

1907— With money borrowed from friends, president Charles Ebbets of the Brooklyn Baseball Club purchases the stock of disgruntled shareholders F.A. Abel and Ed Hanlon and the estate of the late Harry Van Der Horst. It places Ebbets in the capacity of majority stockholder.

1966— During their barnstorming tour of Japan, Maury Wills leaves the Dodgers at Osaka saying the injured right knee that caused him trouble all season requires immediate treatment. Several days later he is discovered playing banjo at a nightclub in Hawaii and December I is traded to Pittsburgh for third baseman Bob Bailey and shortstop Gene Michael by owner Walter O'Malley.

November 5

1936— Former Dodger pitcher Burleigh Grimes is named manager, succeeding Casey Stengel fired in October at the World Series.

November 6

1982— "Born to be a Dodger" Steve Garvey becomes an ex-Dodger when, following an "intense" three-hour final negotiating session, he and the team's owner, Peter O'Malley, fail to come to terms. Later (December 21), the day before his 34th birthday, Garvey signs a $6.6 million five-year pact with the Padres, said to be 25 percent more than the Dodgers' apparent final offer of $5 million for four seasons.

November 7

1917— Dodgers sign Wilbert Robinson, who took over in 1914, to his second contract as manager.

1974— Mike Marshall becomes the first relief pitcher to win the Cy Young Award. Another Dodgers' hurler, Andy Messersmith, is second in the voting.

November 9

1926— The Dodgers' first "iron man," infielder George Pinckney, dies at age 64 in Peoria, Ill. He held the major leagues' record for consecutive games played, 577 between 1885 and 1890, until the Boston Red Sox's Everett Scott surpassed him in 1920. Lou Gehrig broke Scott's mark.

November 11

1940— Dodgers purchase pitcher Kirby Higbe from Philadelphia for a reported $100,000.

1981— At age 21, Fernando Valenzuela becomes the first rookie pitcher to win the Cy Young Award.

1982— Dodgers announce that Tommy Lasorda has signed his seventh one-year contract as manager and all his coaches have been retained, except Danny Ozark.

November 14

1889— At the Fifth Avenue Hotel in Manhattan, Dodgers owner Charles Byrne announces he is resigning his franchise in the American Association and joining the National League. Cincinnati also joins the same day.

November 15

1929— Iron Man (Joe) McGinnity, a 29-game winner for Brooklyn in 1900 and who pitched in various leagues until 54, dies after a long illness at age 56.

1979— Dave Goltz, first player ever selected by the maximum 13 teams in the first round of the free agent draft, signs a six-year Dodger contract worth an estimated $3 million. Two days later the Dodgers sign a second pitcher from the re-entry draft, Don Stanhouse, for $2.1 million.

November 16

1966— Dodgers suffer their fourth straight defeat and finish their tour of Japan at 9-8-1, worst-ever record by an American major league team. The Dodgers of 1956 had lost four games in Japan.

November 17

1913— Dodgers release Bill Dahlen and name Wilbert Robinson, pitching coach of John McGraw's New York Giants, as their new manager for 1914.

1975— Dodgers trade outfielders Jimmy Wynn and Tom Paciorek plus infielders Lee Lacy and Jerry Royster to Atlanta for outfielder Dusty Baker and infielder Ed Goodson.

November 18

1966— Pitcher Sandy Koufax announces that rather than risk permanent damage to his arthritic left elbow, he is retiring from baseball.

1977— Dodgers sign southpaw pitcher Terry Forster to a contract as their first free agent.

November 22

1954— Pirates draft Roberto Clemente, a .257 hitter and infrequent player spotted by former Brooklyn coach Clyde Sukeforth, from the Dodgers' Montreal farm club.

1982— Narrowly defeating Pittsburgh's Johnny Ray, Dodger second baseman Steve Sax becomes the fourth Dodger in a row to be chosen National League Rookie of the Year. He follows a trio of hurlers, Rick Sutcliffe, 1979; Steve Howe, 1980; and Fernando Valenzuela, 1981.

November 23

1907— Former Dodger pitcher Henry Schmidt—21-13 in 1903—is arrested in the Ruby Theater, Nashville, Tenn., after slashing the neck of Mrs. Alice Applewhite with a razor; they were to be married as soon as she secured a divorce. In court later Schmidt is fined $20 for assault and $50 for carrying a concealed weapon.

1962— Dodgers complete a sweep of major post-season awards as shortstop Maury Wills is named the National League's Most Valuable Player following Don Drysdale's November 15 selection as the Cy Young Award winner.

November 24

1953— After both shortstop Pee Wee Reese and vice president Fresco Thompson reportedly turned down offers, Walter ("Who's he?") Alston is named as the new Dodgers manager, succeeding Chuck Dressen. Alston piloted Dodger minor league teams at St. Paul and Montreal.

November 28

1956— Dodger pitcher Don Newcombe wins the first-ever Cy Young Award voted by the Baseball Writers Association. It follows his selection November 21 as the National League's Most Valuable Player.

1972— In their biggest swap with the crosstown California Angels, Dodgers trade outfielder Frank Robinson, infielders Billy Grabarkewitz and Bobby Valentine, and pitchers Bill Singer and Mike Strahler for pitcher Andy Messersmith and third baseman Ken McMullen.

DECEMBER

December 1

1916— Dodgers release pitcher Nap Rucker.

December 3

1941— The last of the name "Daffy Dodgers," Van Lingle Mungo, is released to Montreal.

1958— Dodgers trade outfielder Gino Cimoli and pitcher Phil Paine to St. Louis for outfielder Wally Moon.

December 5

1908— Dodgers owner Charles Ebbets presents National League president John Pulliam with an extensive collection of baseball literature for the library Pulliam is establishing.

1973— Dodgers trade outfielder Willie Davis to Montreal for relief hurler Mike Marshall.

December 6

1947— The Dodgers sign Leo Durocher as their manager for 1948 after he's sat out 1947 by order of commissioner Happy Chandler.

December 8

1947— Dodgers trade outfielder Dixie Walker and pitchers Vic Lombardi and Hal

Gregg to Pittsburgh for third baseman Billy Cox and pitcher Preacher Roe.

1955— Dodgers catcher Roy Campanella becomes the second player—following the Cardinal's Stan Musial—to win the National League's Most Valuable Player award three times. Duke Snider of Brooklyn is second in the close balloting.

1960— In New York City, the day after his approval as owner of the American League expansion franchise for Los Angeles, Gene Autry of the Angels agrees to a four-year lease of the Dodgers' ballpark with an option to renew for three.

1983— Dodgers trade pitcher Joe Beckwith to Kansas City for three minor leaguers on the same day as they swap promising minor league lefthander Sid Fernandez to the Mets for reliever Carlos Diaz and 32-year-old utility infielder Bob Bailor. One day later, outfielder Dusty Baker—with a no-trade clause in his contract—nixes a deal that would have sent him to Oakland for two minor leaguers.

December 9

1913— Charles Ebbets is elected to the Board of Directors of the National League, the same day as Brooklyn offers Cincinnati $35,000 for shortstop Joe Tinker.

1965— While giving a speech in Columbia, Mo. former Dodgers president and general manager Branch Rickey collapses and dies at age 83.

December 10

1924— At the annual National League meetings, Charles Ebbets proposes a plan for World Series games 1, 2, 6, and 7 to be played in the city that wins the 1925 National League pennant, with games 3, 4, and 5 in the American League city and this schedule rotating annually thereafter. The following day the American circuit approves Ebbets' idea.

December 11

1928— Dodgers trade pitcher Jesse Petty and second baseman Harry Riconda to Pittsburgh for shortstop Glenn Wright who injures himself playing handball in the off-season and is out most of 1929.

December 13

1956— Dodgers trade Jackie Robinson to the Giants for lefthanded pitcher Dick Littlefield and $35,000, a deal cancelled on January 5 when Robinson announces in a bylined national magazine article that he's retiring to go into private business.

December 14

1954— Dodgers sell pitcher Preacher Roe and infielder Billy Cox to Baltimore, and with room now on their roster offer lefthanded pitcher Sanford Koufax a bonus contract for $14,000.

December 15

1909— During a speech before a large gathering of the sport's leaders in New

York City, Dodgers president Charles Ebbets declares "baseball is still in its infancy."

1948— Dodgers trade outfielder Pete Reiser to the Braves for outfielder Mike McCormick.

1965— Dodgers trade infielder Dick Tracewski to Detroit for pitcher Phil Regan, who'd been farmed out to Syracuse most of the 1965 season.

1968— "Trader Al" Campanis of the Dodgers strikes again, dealing his own son, catcher Jimmy Campanis, to the Royals for two minor league players sent to Spokane.

1983— Bowie Kuhn suspends Dodger pitcher Steve Howe for one year, the baseball commissioner saying that for the "image of baseball" he cannot allow him to play until Howe demonstrates he is "drug-free." Nine days later, on Christmas Eve, it's revealed that Howe—having been fined $54,000 by the Dodgers earlier and out much of the season—has declared bankruptcy, listing debts of $340,900.

December 18

1958— Shortstop Pee Wee Reese, "the Captain," announces his retirement as a player after 16 seasons and is signed as a coach by the Los Angeles Dodgers.

December 19

1918— The so-called "oldest baseball fan in Brooklyn," 97-year-old William Brockinridge Cummings, dies. He's the father of William Arthur Cummings, credited with being the first to pitch the curve ball.

December 20

1978— Cartoonist Willard Mullin, who created the famed "Brooklyn Bum," dies at 76 in Corpus Christi, Tex. He got the idea one day in the late 1930s when he hailed a cab outside Ebbets Field and the driver asked, "How'd those bums do today?"

December 23

1958— Dodgers trade second baseman George (Sparky) Anderson—who never played a National League game for them—to the Phils for outfielder Rip Repulski and pitchers Gene Snyder and Jim Golden.

1975— In a landmark decision, pitchers Andy Messersmith of the Dodgers and Dave McNally of the Expos are granted free agency as Peter Seitz—chairman of baseball's three-man arbitration committee—rules in favor of the Major League Baseball Players Association and that clubs do not have the "perpetual right of renewal" (beyond one season) of contracts. Seitz's ruling, later upheld in the courts, opens the gates for a new era of gigantic player salaries but also leads to his dismissal by the owners.

December 27

1981— Fernando Valenzuela becomes the fifth Los Angeles Dodger to win Southern California Athlete of the Year honors, as presented by the First Interstate Bank Athletic Foundation. He joins Wally Moon and Larry Sherry, 1959; Sandy Koufax, 1963; and Steve Garvey, 1974.

TEAM AND MANAGER WON-LOSS RECORDS

WON-LOSS RECORDS
Where the Dodgers Finished, 1883 to Date

Year	W	L	Pct.	Pos.	Manager	Attendance
					Interstate League **(minor league)**	
1883	44	28	.611	1	George Taylor	
					American Association	
1884	40	64	.385	9	George Taylor	
1885	53	59	.473	5	Joe Doyle	
					Charlie Hackett	
					Charlie Byrne	
1886	76	61	.555	3	Charlie Byrne	
1887	60	74	.448	6	Charlie Byrne	
1888	88	52	.629	2	Bill McGunnigle	
1889	93	44	.679	1	Bill McGunnigle	
					National League	
1890	86	43	.667	1	Bill McGunnigle	
1891	61	76	.445	6	Monte Ward	
1892	95	59	.617	3	Monte Ward	
1893	65	63	.508	6	Dave Foutz	
1894	70	61	.534	5	Dave Foutz	
1895	71	60	.542	5	Dave Foutz	
1896	58	73	.443	9	Dave Foutz	
1897	61	71	.462	6	Bill Barnie	
1898	54	91	.372	10	Bill Barnie	
					Mike Griffin	
					Charles Ebbets	
1899	101	47	.682	1	Ned Hanlon	
1900	82	54	.603	1	Ned Hanlon	
1901	79	57	.581	3	Ned Hanlon	
1902	75	63	.543	2	Ned Hanlon	

Where the Dodgers Finished, 1883 to Date (Continued)

Year	W	L	Pct.	Pos.	Manager	Attendance
1903	70	66	.515	5	Ned Hanlon	
1904	56	97	.366	6	Ned Hanlon	
1905	48	104	.316	8	Ned Hanlon	
1906	66	86	.434	5	Patsy Donovan	
1907	65	83	.439	5	Patsy Donovan	
1908	53	101	.344	7	Patsy Donovan	
1909	55	98	.359	6	Harry Lumley	
1910	64	90	.416	6	Bill Dahlen	
1911	64	86	.427	7	Bill Dahlen	
1912	58	95	.379	7	Bill Dahlen	
1913	65	84	.436	6	Bill Dahlen	
1914	75	79	.487	5	Wilbert Robinson	
1915	80	72	.526	3	Wilbert Robinson	
1916	94	60	.610	1	Wilbert Robinson	
1917	70	81	.464	7	Wilbert Robinson	
1918	57	69	.452	5	Wilbert Robinson	
1919	69	71	.493	5	Wilbert Robinson	
1920	93	61	.604	1	Wilbert Robinson	
1921	77	75	.507	5	Wilbert Robinson	
1922	76	78	.494	6	Wilbert Robinson	
1923	76	78	.494	6	Wilbert Robinson	
1924	92	62	.597	2	Wilbert Robinson	
1925	68	85	.444	6	Wilbert Robinson	
1926	71	82	.464	6	Wilbert Robinson	
1927	65	88	.425	6	Wilbert Robinson	
1928	77	76	.503	6	Wilbert Robinson	
1929	70	83	.458	6	Wilbert Robinson	
1930	86	68	.558	4	Wilbert Robinson	1,097,473
1931	79	73	.520	4	Wilbert Robinson	753,760
1932	81	73	.526	3	Max Carey	682,188
1933	65	88	.425	6	Max Carey	527,020
1934	71	81	.467	6	Casey Stengel	434,437
1935	70	83	.458	5	Casey Stengel	471,114
1936	67	87	.435	7	Casey Stengel	489,720
1937	62	91	.405	6	Burleigh Grimes	482,569
1938	69	80	.463	7	Burleigh Grimes	750,132
1939	84	69	.549	3	Leo Durocher	1,007,759
1940	88	65	.575	2	Leo Durocher	977,093
1941	100	54	.649	1	Leo Durocher	1,215,772
1942	104	50	.675	2	Leo Durocher	1,087,860
1943	81	72	.529	3	Leo Durocher	688,633
1944	63	91	.409	7	Leo Durocher	618,193
1945	87	67	.565	3	Leo Durocher	1,059,160
1946	96	60	.615	2	Leo Durocher	1,796,824
1947	94	60	.610	1	Clyde Sukeforth (one game) Burt Shotton	1,807,526*
1948	84	70	.545	3	Leo Durocher Burt Shotton	1,398,967

One of Brooklyn's most illustrious sons, Charles Dillon Stengel (Casey), managed the Dodgers from 1934-1936. Casey is shown here with Baseball Commissioner Ford Frick (right) and Boston slugger Ted Williams.

Where the Dodgers Finished, 1883 to Date (Continued)

Year	W	L	Pct.	Pos.	Manager	Attendance
1949	97	57	.630	1	Burt Shotton	1,633,747
1950	89	65	.578	2	Burt Shotton	1,185,896
1951	97	60	.618	2	Charlie Dressen	1,282,628
1952	96	57	.627	1	Charlie Dressen	1,088,704
1953	105	49	.682	1	Charlie Dressen	1,163,419
1954	92	62	.597	2	Walter Alston	1,020,581
1955	98	55	.641	1	Walter Alston	1,033,589
1956	93	61	.604	1	Walter Alston	1,213,562
1957	84	70	.545	3	Walter Alston	1,028,258
1958**	71	83	.461	7	Walter Alston	1,845,556
1959	88	68	.564	1	Walter Alston	2,071,045
1960	82	72	.532	4	Walter Alston	2,253,887
1961	89	65	.578	2	Walter Alston	1,804,250
1962	102	63	.618	2	Walter Alston	2,755,184
1963	99	63	.611	1	Walter Alston	2,538,602
1964	80	82	.494	6	Walter Alston	2,228,751
1965	97	65	.599	1	Walter Alston	2,553,577
1966	95	67	.586	1	Walter Alston	2,617,029
1967	73	89	.451	8	Walter Alston	1,664,362
1968	76	86	.469	7	Walter Alston	1,581,093
1969***	85	77	.525	4	Walter Alston	1,784,527
1970	87	74	.540	2	Walter Alston	1,697,142
1971	89	73	.549	2	Walter Alston	2,064,594
1972	85	70	.548	3	Walter Alston	1,860,858
1973	95	66	.590	2	Walter Alston	2,136,192
1974	102	60	.630	1	Walter Alston	2,632,474
1975	88	74	.543	2	Walter Alston	2,539,349
1976	92	70	.568	2	Walter Alston	2,386,301
					Tommy Lasorda	
1977	98	64	.605	1	Tommy Lasorda	2,955,087
1978	95	67	.586	1	Tommy Lasorda	3,347,845****
1979	79	83	.488	3	Tommy Lasorda	2,860,954
1980	92	71	.564	2	Tommy Lasorda	3,249,287
1981	63	47	.573	1	Tommy Lasorda	2,381,292
(1st)	36	21	.632	1		
(2nd)	27	26	.509	4		
1982	88	74	.543	2	Tommy Lasorda	3,608,881*****
1983	91	71	.562	1	Tommy Lasorda	3,510,313

Notes: From 1892 through 1899 the National League had twelve teams. There were eight in all other years until 1962 when it was expanded to a ten-team circuit. Divisional play began in 1969 with six teams in each of the two divisions, the Dodgers being in the Western division. The 1981 season was shortened by a players' strike and divided into two halves, the Dodgers winning their first half to qualify for post-season divisional play.

*Brooklyn club record.
**Dodgers' first season in Los Angeles.
***Western Division Play began.
****First 3 million home attendance in Major League history.
*****Major League record.

Walt Alston, elected to baseball's Hall of Fame in 1983, managed the Dodgers for 23 years. Alston is shown above with Ed Goodson (left) and Dusty Baker (right). Below, Alston is shown throwing out the first ball in the fifth game of the 1977 World Series; Dodger President Peter O'Malley (right) is at his side.

Taking the managerial reins with four games left in the 1976 season, Tommy Lasorda has been one of the most successful and popular managers in Dodgers history.

Dodgers Managers Records

Manager		Years	Won	Lost	Pct.
George Taylor		(1884)	40	64	.385
Joe Doyle		(1885)	13	20	.394
Charlie Hackett		(1885)	15	25	.375
Charlie Byrne		(1885-1887)	161	149	.519
Bill McGunnigle		(1888-1890)	267	139	.658
Monte Ward		(1891-1892)	156	135	.536
Dave Foutz		(1893-1896)	264	257	.507
Bill Barnie		(1897-1898)	76	91	.455
Mike Griffin		(1898)	1	3	.250
Charles Ebbets		(1898)	38	68	.358
Ned Hanlon		(1899-1905)	511	488	.512
Patsy Donovan		(1906-1908)	184	270	.405
Harry Lumley		(1909)	55	98	.359
Bill Dahlen		(1910-1913)	251	355	.414
Wilbert Robinson		(1914-1931)	1375	1341	.506
Max Carey		(1932-1933)	146	161	.476
Casey Stengel		(1934-1936)	208	251	.453
Burleigh Grimes		(1937-1938)	131	171	.434
Leo Durocher	(1939-1946)	(1948)	739	565	.567
Clyde Sukeforth		(1947)	1	0	1.000
Burt Shotton	(1947)	(1948-1950)	327	215	.603
Charlie Dressen		(1951-1953)	298	166	.642
Walter Alston*		(1954-1976)	2040	1613	.558
Tommy Lasorda*		(1976-1983)	608	479	.559

*Lasorda credited with managing last four games of 1976.

3

BATTING RECORDS

BATTING AVERAGES
Leading Dodger Hitters, 1884 to Present

Year	Player	Batting Average	Year	Player	Batting Average
1884	Oscar Walker	.270	1914*	Jake Daubert	.329
1885	Bill Phillips	.302	1915	Jake Daubert	.301
1886	Ed Swartwood	.280	1916	Jake Daubert	.316
1887	Germany Smith	.294	1917	Zach Wheat	.312
1888	Dave Orr	.305	1918*	Zach Wheat	.335
1889	Oyster Burns	.304	1919	Hy Myers	.307
1890	Darby O'Brien	.314	1920	Zach Wheat	.328
1891	Oyster Burns	.285	1921	Jimmy Johnston	.325
1892*	Dan Brouthers	.335	1922	Zach Wheat	.335
1893	Mike Griffin	.293	1923	Zach Wheat	.375
1894	Mike Griffin	.365	1924	Zach Wheat	.375
1895	Mike Griffin	.335	1925	Zach Wheat	.359
1896	Fielder Jones	.353	1926	Babe Herman	.319
1897	John Anderson	.325	1927	Harvey Hendrick	.310
1898	Fielder Jones	.302	1928	Babe Herman	.340
1899	Willie Keeler	.377	1929	Babe Herman	.381
1900	Willie Keeler	.368	1930	Babe Herman	.393
1901	Jimmy Sheckard	.353	1931	Lefty O'Doul	.336
1902	Willie Keeler	.336	1932*	Lefty O'Doul	.368
1903	Jimmy Sheckard	.332	1933	Johnny Frederick	.308
1904	Doc Gessler	.290	1934	Sam Leslie	.332
1905	Harry Lumley	.293	1935	Sam Leslie	.308
1906	Harry Lumley	.324	1936	Babe Phelps	.367
1907	Tim Jordan	.274	1937	Heinie Manush	.333
1908	Tim Jordan	.247	1938	Ernie Koy	.299
1909	John Hummel	.280	1939	Cookie Lavagetto	.300
1910	Zach Wheat	.284	1940	Dixie Walker	.308
1911	Jake Daubert	.307	1941*	Pete Reiser	.343
1912	Jake Daubert	.308	1942	Pete Reiser	.310
1913*	Jake Daubert	.350	1943	Billy Herman	.330

Leading Dodger Hitters, 1884 to Present (Continued)

Year	Player	Batting Average	Year	Player	Batting Average
1944	Dixie Walker	.357	1964	Willie Davis	.294
1945	Goody Rosen	.325	1965	Maury Wills	.286
1946	Dixie Walker	.319	1966	Tommy Davis	.313
1947	Pete Reiser	.309	1967	Al Ferrara	.277
1948	Carl Furillo	.297	1968	Tom Haller	.285
1949*	Jackie Robinson	.342	1969	Willie Davis	.311
1950	Jackie Robinson	.328	1970	Wes Parker	.319
1951	Jackie Robinson	.338	1971	Willie Davis	.309
1952	Jackie Robinson	.308	1972	Manny Mota	.323
1953*	Carl Furillo	.344	1973	Steve Garvey	.304
1954	Duke Snider	.341	1974	Bill Buckner	.314
1955	Roy Campanella	.318	1975	Steve Garvey	.319
1956	Jim Gilliam	.300	1976	Steve Garvey	.317
1957	Carl Furillo	.306	1977	Reggie Smith	.307
1958	Duke Snider	.312	1978	Steve Garvey	.316
1959	Duke Snider	.308	1979	Steve Garvey	.315
1960	Norm Larker	.323	1980	Reggie Smith	.322
1961	Wally Moon	.328	1981	Dusty Baker	.320
1962*	Tommy Davis	.346	1982	Pedro Guerrero	.304
1963*	Tommy Davis	.326	1983	Pedro Guerrero	.298

*League Leader

(Note: Those batters with 300-or-more at-bats are listed as the leaders.)

Carl Furillo led the Dodgers in hitting in 1948, 1953 and 1957.

Dodgers .300 Hitters, 1884 to Date

Only those batters with at least 300 at-bats are listed.

Year	Player	Average	Year	Player	Average
1885	Bill Phillips	.302		Casey Stengel	.316
1888	Dave Orr	.305	1915	Jake Daubert	.301
1889	Oyster Burns	.304	1916	Jake Daubert	.316
	Darby O'Brien	.300		Zach Wheat	.312
1890	Darby O'Brien	.314	1917	Zach Wheat	.312
	George Pinckney	.309	1918	Zach Wheat	.335
	Dave Foutz	.303		Jake Daubert	.308
1892	Dan Brouthers	.335	1919	Hy Myers	.307
	Oyster Burns	.315	1920	Zach Wheat	.328
1894	Mike Griffin	.365		Ed Konetchy	.308
	Oyster Burns	.361		Hy Myers	.304
	Tom Daly	.341	1921	Jimmy Johnston	.325
	George Treadway	.328		Zach Wheat	.320
	Tommy Corcoran	.300		Tommy Griffith	.312
1895	Mike Griffin	.335		Ray Schmandt	.306
	Candy LaChance	.312	1922	Zach Wheat	.335
1896	Fielder Jones	.353		Jimmy Johnston	.319
	John Anderson	.314		Hy Myers	.317
	Mike Griffin	.314		Tommy Griffith	.316
1897	John Anderson	.325		Bert Griffith	.308
	Fielder Jones	.322	1923	Zach Wheat	.375
	Mike Griffin	.318		Jack Fournier	.351
	Candy LaChance	.308		Jimmy Johnston	.325
1898	Fielder Jones	.302	1924	Zach Wheat	.375
1899	Willie Keeler	.377		Jack Fournier	.334
	Joe Kelley	.330		Andy High	.328
	Tom Daly	.313		Eddie Brown	.308
1900	Willie Keeler	.368	1925	Zach Wheat	.359
	Joe Kelley	.319		Jack Fournier	.350
	Tom Daly	.312		Dick Cox	.329
	Fielder Jones	.309		Milt Stock	.328
1901	Willie Keeler	.355		Zach Taylor	.310
	Jimmy Sheckard	.353		Eddie Brown	.306
	Tom Daly	.315	1926	Babe Herman	.319
	Joe Kelley	.309	1927	Harvey Hendrick	.310
1902	Willie Keeler	.336	1928	Babe Herman	.340
1903	Jimmy Sheckard	.332		Del Bissonette	.320
	Jack Doyle	.313		Harvey Hendrick	.318
1906	Harry Lumley	.324	1929	Babe Herman	.381
	Jack McCarthy	.304		Harvey Hendrick	.354
1911	Jake Daubert	.307		Johnny Frederick	.328
1912	Jake Daubert	.308		Rube Bressler	.318
	Zach Wheat	.305		Wally Gilbert	.304
1913	Jake Daubert	.350	1930	Babe Herman	.393
	Zach Wheat	.301		Del Bissonnette	.336
1914	Jake Daubert	.329		Johnny Frederick	.334
	Jack Dalton	.319		Glenn Wright	.321
	Zach Wheat	.319		Al Lopez	.309

Dodgers .300 Hitters, 1884 to Date (Continued)

Year	Player	Average	Year	Player	Average
1931	Lefty O'Doul	.336	1952	Jackie Robinson	.308
	Babe Herman	.313		Duke Snider	.303
1932	Lefty O'Doul	.368	1953	Carl Furillo	.344
	Danny Taylor	.324		Duke Snider	.336
	Joe Stripp	.303		Jackie Robinson	.329
1933	Johnny Frederick	.308		Roy Campanella	.312
	Al Lopez	.301	1954	Duke Snider	.341
1934	Sam Leslie	.332		Jackie Robinson	.311
	Len Koenecke	.320		Pee Wee Reese	.309
	Joe Stripp	.315		Gil Hodges	.304
	Buzz Boyle	.305	1955	Roy Campanella	.318
1935	Sam Leslie	.308		Carl Furillo	.314
	Joe Stripp	.306		Duke Snider	.309
	Jim Bucher	.302	1956	Jim Gilliam	.300
1936	Babe Phelps	.367	1957	Carl Furillo	.306
	Joe Stripp	.317	1958	Duke Snider	.312
	Frenchy Bordagaray	.315	1959	Duke Snider	.308
	Bordagaray	.315		Wally Moon	.302
	Buddy Hassett	.310	1960	Norm Larker	.323
1937	Heinie Manush	.333	1961	Wally Moon	.328
	Babe Phelps	.313	1962	Tommy Davis	.346
	Buddy Hassett	.304	1963	Tommy Davis	.326
1939	Cookie Lavagetto	.300		Maury Wills	.302
1940	Dixie Walker	.308	1966	Tommy Davis	.313
	Joe Medwick	.300	1969	Willie Davis	.311
1941	Pete Reiser	.343	1970	Wes Parker	.319
	Joe Medwick	.318		Ted Sizemore	.306
	Dixie Walker	.311		Willie Davis	.305
1942	Pete Reiser	.310		Manny Mota	.305
	Joe Medwick	.300	1971	Willie Davis	.309
1943	Billy Herman	.330	1972	Manny Mota	.323
	Arky Vaughn	.305		Bill Buckner	.319
	Dixie Walker	.302	1973	Steve Garvey	.304
1944	Dixie Walker	.357	1974	Bill Buckner	.314
	Augie Galan	.318		Steve Garvey	.312
1945	Goody Rosen	.325	1975	Steve Garvey	.319
	Luis Olmo	.313		Lee Lacy	.314
	Augie Galan	.307	1976	Steve Garvey	.317
	Dixie Walker	.300		Bill Buckner	.301
1946	Dixie Walker	.319	1977	Reggie Smith	.307
1947	Pete Reiser	.309	1978	Steve Garvey	.316
	Dixie Walker	.306	1979	Steve Garvey	.315
1949	Jackie Robinson	.342	1980	Reggie Smith	.322
	Carl Furillo	.322		Steve Garvey	.304
1950	Jackie Robinson	.328	1981	Dusty Baker	.320
	Duke Snider	.321		Pedro Guerrero	.300
	Carl Furillo	.305	1982	Pedro Guerrero	.304
1951	Jackie Robinson	.338		Dusty Baker	.300
	Roy Campanella	.325			

.300 Lifetime Hitters (500-Game minimum)

Player	Years	Average
Willie Keeler	(1893; 1899-1902)	.360
Babe Herman	(1926-1931; 1945)	.339
Jack Fournier	(1923-1926)	.337
Zach Wheat	(1909-1926)	.317
Manny Mota	(1969-1980; 1982)	.315
Babe Phelps	(1935-1941)	.315
Fielder Jones	(1896-1900)	.314
Jackie Robinson	(1947-1956)	.311
Dixie Walker	(1939-1947)	.311
Johnny Frederick	(1929-1934)	.308
Mike Griffin	(1891-1898)	.308
Pete Reiser	(1940-1942; 1946-1948)	.306
Del Bissonette	(1928-1931; 1933)	.305
Jake Daubert	(1910-1918)	.305
Tommy Davis	(1959-1966)	.304
Pedro Guerrero	(1978-1983)	.302
Oyster Burns	(1888-1895)	.301
Augie Galan	(1941-1946)	.301
Duke Snider	(1947-1962)	.301
Steve Garvey	(1969-1982)	.301
Carl Furillo	(1946-1960)	.300

.290 Lifetime Hitters (500-Game minimum)

Player	Years	Average
Jimmy Sheckard	(1897-1898; 1900-1905)	.299
Jimmy Johnston	(1916-1925)	.298
Reggie Smith	(1976-1981)	.297
Joe Stripp	(1932-1937)	.295
Tom Daly	(1890-1896; 1898-1901)	.294

.280 Lifetime Hitters (500-Game minimum)

Player	Years	Average
Bill Buckner	(1969-1976)	.289
Wally Moon	(1959-1965)	.286
Frenchy Bordagaray	(1935-1936; 1942-1945)	.286
Tommy Griffith	(1919-1925)	.285
Dusty Baker	(1976-1982)	.284
Hy Myers	(1909; 1911; 1914-1922)	.282
Gene Hermanski	(1943; 1946-1951)	.281
Maury Wills	(1959-1966; 1969-1972)	.281
Dusty Baker	(1976-1983)	.281

.270 Lifetime Hitters (500-Game minimum)

Player	Years	Average
Al Lopez	(1928; 1930-1935)	.279
Willie Davis	(1960-1973)	.279
Darby O'Brien	(1888-1892)	.278
Roy Campanella	(1948-1957)	.276
Cookie Lavagetto	(1937-1941; 1946-1947)	.275
Harry Lumley	(1904-1910)	.274
Gil Hodges	(1943; 1947-1961)	.274
Bill Shindle	(1894-1898)	.273
Casey Stengel	(1912-1917)	.272
George Pinckney	(1885-1891)	.271
Tony Cuccinello	(1932-1935)	.271
Bill Dahlen	(1899-1903; 1910-1911)	.270
Dave Foutz	(1888-1896)	.270
Dolph Camilli	(1938-1943)	.270
Lee Lacy	(1972-1978)	.270

.260 Lifetime Hitters (500-Game minimum)

Player	Years	Average
Frank Howard	(1958-1964)	.269
Pee Wee Reese	(1940-1942; 1946-1958)	.269
Willie Crawford	(1964-1975)	.268
Wes Parker	(1964-1972)	.267
Hank DeBerry	(1922-1930)	.267
Jim Gilliam	(1953-1966)	.265
Charlie Neal	(1956-1961)	.265
Bill Russell	(1969-1983)	.264
Ron Cey	(1971-1982)	.264
Tim Jordan	(1906-1910)	.263
Eddie Stanky	(1944-1947)	.263
Davey Lopes	(1972-1981)	.262
Ivy Olson	(1915-1924)	.261
George Cutshaw	(1912-1917)	.260
Ron Fairly	(1958-1969)	.260

.250 Lifetime Hitters (500-Game minimum)

Player	Years	Average
Billy Cox	(1948-1954)	.259
Mickey Owen	(1941-1945)	.258
Derrel Thomas	(1979-1983)	.257
Rick Monday	(1977-1983)	.256
John Hummel	(1905-1915)	.253
John Roseboro	(1957-1967)	.251
Jim Lefebvre	(1965-1972)	.251

Tony Cuccinello, who came to the Dodgers from Cincinnati in a trade for the popular Babe Herman, hit a .271 average in his four years with the Dodgers.

.240 Lifetime Hitters (500-Game minimum)

Player	Years	Average
Otto Miller	(1910-1922)	.245
Joe Ferguson	(1970-1976; 1978-1981)	.245
Phil Lewis	(1905-1908)	.242

Below .240 Lifetime Hitters (500-Game minimum)

Player	Years	Average
Germany Smith	(1885-1890; 1897)	.233
Steve Yeager	(1972-1983)	.229
Bill Bergen	(1904-1911)	.163

The friendly confines of Ebbets Field in July 1940.

Batting Average by Position (Season)

Modern, Brooklyn

1B	Jack Fournier	1923	.351
2B	Jackie Robinson	1949	.342
SS	Glenn Wright	1930	.321
3B	Jimmy Johnston	1921-23	.325
OF	Babe Herman	1930	.393
OF	Zach Wheat	1923-24	.375
OF	Willie Keeler	1900	.368
	Lefty O'Doul	1932	.368
C	Babe Phelps	1936	.367

Los Angeles

1B	Norm Larker	1960	.323
2B	Ted Sizemore	1970	.306
SS	Maury Wills	1963	.302
3B	Pedro Guerrero	1983	.298
OF	Tommy Davis	1962	.346
OF	Wally Moon	1961	.328
OF	Manny Mota	1969-72	.323
C	John Roseboro	1964	.287

19th Century

1B	Dan Brouthers	1892	.335
2B	Tom Daly	1894	.341
SS	Tommy Corcoran	1894	.300
3B	George Pinckney	1890	.309
OF	Willie Keeler	1899	.377
OF	Mike Griffin	1894	.365
OF	Oyster Burns	1894	.361
C	John Grim	1895	.280

All-Time

1B	Jack Fournier	1923	.351
2B	Jackie Robinson	1949	.342
SS	Glenn Wright	1930	.321
3B	Jimmy Johnston	1921-23	.325
OF	Babe Herman	1930	.393
OF	Willie Keeler	1899	.377
OF	Zach Wheat	1923-24	.375
C	Babe Phelps	1936	.367

LEADERS IN HITS

Year-by-Year Leader in Base Hits

Year	Player	Total	Year	Player	Total
1884	John Cassidy	109	1930	Babe Herman	241
1885	Bill McClellan	124	1931	Babe Herman	191
	George Pinckney	124	1932	Lefty O'Doul	219
1886	Bill Phillips	160	1933	Johnny Frederick	171
1887	George Pinckney	155	1934	Sam Leslie	181
1888	Dave Foutz	156	1935	Sam Leslie	160
	George Pinckney	156	1936	Buddy Hassett	197
1889	Darby O'Brien	170	1937	Buddy Hassett	169
1890	Dave Foutz	154	1938	Ernie Koy	156
1891	Mike Griffin	139	1939	Cookie Lavagetto	176
1892*	Dan Brouthers	197	1940	Dixie Walker	171
1893	Dave Foutz	137	1941	Pete Reiser	184
1894	Oyster Burns	185	1942	Joe Medwick	166
1895	Mike Griffin	175	1943	Billy Herman	193
1896	Mike Griffin	155	1944	Dixie Walker	191
1897	Fielder Jones	178	1945	Goody Rosen	197
1898	Fielder Jones	181	1946	Dixie Walker	184
1899	Willie Keeler	215	1947	Jackie Robinson	175
1900*	Willie Keeler	208	1948	Jackie Robinson	170
1901	Willie Keeler	209	1949	Jackie Robinson	203
1902	Willie Keeler	188	1950*	Duke Snider	199
1903	Jimmy Sheckard	171	1951	Carl Furillo	197
1904	Harry Lumley	161	1952	Duke Snider	162
1905	Harry Lumley	148	1953	Duke Snider	198
1906	Harry Lumley	157	1954	Duke Snider	199
1907	Tim Jordan	133	1955	Duke Snider	166
1908	John Hummel	143	1956	Jim Gilliam	178
1909	Al Burch	163	1957	Gil Hodges	173
1910	Zach Wheat	172	1958	Jim Gilliam	145
1911	Jake Daubert	176	1959	Charlie Neal	177
1912	Jake Daubert	172	1960	Maury Wills	152
1913	Jake Daubert	178	1961	Maury Wills	173
1914	Zach Wheat	170	1962*	Tommy Davis	230
1915	Jake Daubert	164	1963	Tommy Davis	181
1916	Zach Wheat	177	1964	Willie Davis	180
1917	Ivy Olson	156	1965	Maury Wills	186
1918	Zach Wheat	137	1966	Willie Davis	177
1919*	Ivy Olson	164	1967	Willie Davis	146
1920	Zach Wheat	191	1968	Willie Davis	161
1921	Jimmy Johnston	203	1969	Ted Sizemore	160
1922	Zach Wheat	201	1970	Wes Parker	196
1923	Jimmy Johnston	203	1971	Willie Davis	198
1924	Zach Wheat	212	1972	Willie Davis	178
1925	Zach Wheat	221	1973	Willie Davis	171
1926	Babe Herman	158	1974	Steve Garvey	200
1927	Jay Partridge	149	1975	Steve Garvey	210
1928	Del Bissonette	188	1976	Steve Garvey	200
1929	Babe Herman	217	1977	Steve Garvey	192

Year-by-Year Leader in Base Hits (Continued)

Year	Player	Total	Year	Player	Total
1978*	Steve Garvey	202	1981	Dusty Baker	128
1979	Steve Garvey	204	1982	Steve Sax	180
1980*	Steve Garvey	200	1983	Steve Sax	175

*Led League

200 Base Hits on One Season

Year	Player	Total	Year	Player	Total
1899	Willie Keeler	215		Johnny Frederick	206
1900	Willie Keeler	208	1932	Lefty O'Doul	219
1901	Willie Keeler	209	1949	Jackie Robinson	203
1921	Jimmy Johnston	203	1962	Tommy Davis	230
1922	Zach Wheat	201		Maury Wills	208
1923	Jimmy Johnston	203	1974	Steve Garvey	200
1924	Zach Wheat	212	1975	Steve Garvey	210
1925	Zach Wheat	221	1976	Steve Garvey	200
	Milt Stock	202	1978	Steve Garvey	202
1929	Babe Herman	217	1979	Steve Garvey	204
1930	Babe Herman	241	1980	Steve Garvey	200

100-or-More Hits, Season

Year	Player	Total	Year	Player	Total
1884	John Cassidy	109	1889	Darby O'Brien	170
	Oscar Walker	103		Oyster Burns	153
1885	Bill McClellan	124		Dave Foutz	153
	George Pinckney	124		Hub Collins	149
	Bill Phillips	118		Pop Corkhill	134
	Germany Smith	108		George Pinckney	134
	Ed Swartwood	106		Germany Smith	103
1886	Bill Phillips	160	1890	Dave Foutz	154
	George Pinckney	156		George Pinckney	150
	Bill McClellan	152		Hub Collins	142
	Ed Swartwood	132		Oyster Burns	134
	Ernie Burch	119		Darby O'Brien	110
	Jim McTamany	106		Adonis Terry	101
	Germany Smith	105	1891	Mike Griffin	139
1887	George Pinckney	155		George Pinckney	137
	Bill McClellan	144		Oyster Burns	134
	Bill Phillips	142		Dave Foutz	134
	Jim McTamany	134		Monte Ward	122
	Germany Smith	128		Hub Collins	120
	Adonis Terry	103		Darby O'Brien	100
1888	Dave Foutz	156	1892	Dan Brouthers	197
	George Pinckney	156		Oyster Burns	171
	Darby O'Brien	149		Monte Ward	163
	Dave Orr	120		Tommy Corcoran	146

100-or-More Hits, Season (Continued)

Year	Player	Total	Year	Player	Total
	Mike Griffin	127	1901	Willie Keeler	209
	Darby O'Brien	119		Jimmy Sheckard	197
	Tom Daly	114		Tom Daly	164
1893	Dave Foutz	137		Joe Kelley	152
	Tom Daly	136		Bill Dahlen	134
	Tommy Corcoran	126	1902	Willie Keeler	188
	Oyster Burns	112		Cozy Dolan	166
	Mike Griffin	106		Bill Dahlen	139
1894	Oyster Burns	185		Jimmy Sheckard	131
	Tommy Corcoran	173		Charlie Irwin	125
	Tom Daly	168		Tom McCreery	105
	George Treadway	157		Tim Flood	104
	Mike Griffin	148	1903	Jimmy Sheckard	171
	Bill Shindle	141		Jack Doyle	164
1895	Mike Griffin	175		Sammy Strang	138
	Candy LaChance	167		Bill Dahlen	124
	Tommy Corcoran	150	1904	Harry Lumley	161
	Bill Shindle	135		Charlie Babb	138
	Tom Daly	128		Pop Dillon	132
	John Anderson	120		Jimmy Sheckard	121
1896	Mike Griffin	155	1905	Harry Lumley	148
	Tommy Corcoran	154		Emil Batch	143
	Bill Shindle	144		Jimmy Sheckard	140
	Fielder Jones	141		Doc Gessler	125
	John Anderson	135		John Dobbs	117
1897	Fielder Jones	178		Phil Lewis	110
	Mike Griffin	170	1906	Harry Lumley	157
	John Anderson	160		Doc Casey	133
	Candy LaChance	160		Billy Maloney	125
	Bill Shindle	154		Tim Jordan	118
1898	Fielder Jones	181		Whitey Alperman	111
	Mike Griffin	161		Phil Lewis	110
	Candy LaChance	130	1907	Tim Jordan	133
	Bob Hallman	124		Whitey Alperman	130
	Jimmy Sheckard	119		Doc Casey	122
	Bill Shindle	105		Harry Lumley	121
1899	Willie Keeler	215		Phil Lewis	118
	Joe Kelley	178		Billy Maloney	115
	Tom Daly	156	1908	John Hummel	143
	Doc Casey	143		Tim Jordan	127
	Bill Dahlen	121		Al Burch	111
	John Anderson	118		Tom Sheehan	100
	Fielder Jones	104	1909	Al Burch	163
1900	Willie Keeler	208		John Hummel	152
	Fielder Jones	172		Ed Lennox	114
	Joe Kelley	145		Whitey Alperman	104
	Bill Dahlen	125	1910	Zach Wheat	172
	Hughie Jennings	120		Jake Daubert	146
	Tom Daly	107		John Hummel	141

100-or-More Hits, Season (Continued)

Year	Player	Total	Year	Player	Total
	Bill Davidson	121		Zach Wheat	159
1911	Jake Daubert	176		Hy Myers	157
	Zach Wheat	153		Ed Konetchy	145
	John Hummel	129		Tommy Griffith	136
	Bob Coulson	122		Jimmy Johnston	114
1912	Jake Daubert	172	1920	Zach Wheat	191
	Herbie Moran	140		Jimmy Johnston	185
	Red Smith	139		Hy Myers	177
	Zach Wheat	138		Ivy Olson	162
	John Hummel	116		Ed Konetchy	153
	Hub Northen	116		Pete Kilduff	130
	George Cutshaw	100	1921	Jimmy Johnston	203
1913	Jake Daubert	178		Zach Wheat	182
	Zach Wheat	161		Ivy Olson	174
	Red Smith	160		Hy Myers	158
	George Cutshaw	158		Tommy Griffith	142
	Herbie Moran	137		Pete Kilduff	107
	Bobby Fisher	124		Ray Schmandt	107
	Casey Stengel	119	1922	Zach Wheat	201
1914	Zach Wheat	170		Hy Myers	196
	Jake Daubert	156		Jimmy Johnston	181
	George Cutshaw	150		Andy High	164
	Jack Dalton	141		Ivy Olson	150
	Casey Stengel	130		Ray Schmandt	106
1915	Jake Daubert	164		Tommy Griffith	104
	Hy Myers	150		Bert Griffith	100
	Ollie O'Mara	141	1923	Jimmy Johnston	203
	George Cutshaw	139		Jack Fournier	181
	Zach Wheat	136		Tommy Griffith	141
	Gus Getz	123		Zach Wheat	131
	Casey Stengel	109		Bernie Neis	122
1916	Zach Wheat	177		Andy High	115
	George Cutshaw	151		Gene Bailey	109
	Jake Daubert	151	1924	Zach Wheat	212
	Casey Stengel	129		Andy High	191
	Mike Mowrey	121		Jack Fournier	188
	Hy Myers	108		Eddie Brown	140
	Jimmy Johnston	107		Milt Stock	136
1917	Ivy Olson	156		Tommy Griffith	121
	Casey Stengel	141		Zach Taylor	100
	George Cutshaw	126	1925	Zach Wheat	221
	Hy Myers	126		Milt Stock	202
	Jake Daubert	122		Jack Fournier	191
	Zach Wheat	113		Eddie Brown	189
1918	Zach Wheat	137		Dick Cox	143
	Jimmy Johnston	136		Jimmy Johnston	128
	Jake Daubert	122		Zach Taylor	109
	Ivy Olson	121	1926	Babe Herman	158
	Hy Myers	104		Johnny Butler	135
1919	Ivy Olson	164		Gus Felix	121

100-or-More Hits, Season (Continued)

Year	Player	Total	Year	Player	Total
	Zach Wheat	119		Al Lopez	112
	Dick Cox	118		Sam Leslie	104
1926	Babe Herman	158		Danny Taylor	102
	Johnny Butler	135		Buzz Boyle	101
	Gus Felix	121	1934	Sam Leslie	181
	Zach Wheat	119		Len Koenecke	147
	Dick Cox	118		Buzz Boyle	144
1927	Jay Partridge	149		Lonny Frey	139
	Max Carey	143		Tony Cuccinello	138
	Harvey Hendrick	142		Joe Stripp	121
	Jigger Statz	139		Danny Taylor	121
	Johnny Butler	124		Al Lopez	120
	Gus Felix	118	1935	Sam Leslie	160
	Babe Herman	112		Jim Bucher	143
1928	Del Bissonette	188		Lonny Frey	135
	Babe Herman	165		Buzz Boyle	129
	Rube Bressler	148		Frenchy Bordagaray	119
	Harvey Hendrick	135		Joe Stripp	114
	Dave Bancroft	127		Tony Cuccinello	105
1929	Babe Herman	217		Danny Taylor	102
	Johnny Frederick	206	1936	Buddy Hassett	197
	Wally Gilbert	173		Lony Frey	146
	Rube Bressler	145		Johnny Cooney	143
	Harvey Hendrick	136		Joe Stripp	139
	Del Bissonette	121		Frenchy Bordagaray	117
	Eddie Moore	119		Babe Phelps	117
1930	Babe Herman	241	1937	Buddy Hasset	169
	Johnny Frederick	206		Heinie Manush	155
	Del Bissonette	192		Cookie Lavagetto	142
	Wally Gilbert	183		Babe Phelps	128
	Glenn Wright	171		Johnny Cooney	126
	Al Lopez	130		Gib Brack	102
	Rube Bressler	100	1938	Ernie Koy	156
1931	Babe Herman	191		Cookie Lavagetto	133
	Lefty O'Doul	172		Goody Rosen	133
	Del Bissonette	170		Johnny Hudson	130
	Johnny Frederick	165		Dolph Camilli	128
	Wally Gilbert	147		Leo Durocher	105
	Mickey Finn	113	1939	Cookie Lavagetto	176
1932	Lefty O'Doul	219		Dolph Camilli	164
	Tony Cuccinello	168		Ernie Koy	118
	Joe Stripp	162		Pete Coscarart	116
	Hack Wilson	143		Leo Durocher	108
	Danny Taylor	128	1940	Dixie Walker	171
	Glenn Wright	122		Dolph Camilli	147
	Johnny Frederick	115		Joe Medwick	127
	Al Lopez	111		Pete Coscarart	120
1933	Johnny Frederick	171		Cookie Lavagetto	115
	Joe Stripp	149		Joe Vosmick	114
	Tony Cuccinello	122		Babe Phelps	109

100-or-More Hits, Season (Continued)

Year	Player	Total	Year	Player	Total
1941	Pete Reiser	184		Gil Hodges	170
	Joe Medwick	171		Duke Snider	161
	Dixie Walker	165		Roy Campanella	125
	Billy Herman	156	1950	Duke Snider	199
	Dolph Camilli	151		Carl Furillo	189
	Pee Wee Reese	136		Jackie Robinson	170
	Cookie Lavagetto	122		Gil Hodges	159
1942	Joe Medwick	166		Pee Wee Reese	138
	Pete Reiser	149		Roy Campanella	123
	Billy Herman	146		Billy Cox	116
	Pee Wee Reese	144	1951	Carl Furillo	197
	Arky Vaughan	137		Jackie Robinson	185
	Dolph Camilli	132		Pee Wee Reese	176
	Dixie Walker	114		Duke Snider	168
	Mickey Owen	109		Roy Campanella	164
1943	Billy Herman	193		Gil Hodges	156
	Arky Vaughan	186		Billy Cox	127
	Dixie Walker	163	1952	Duke Snider	162
	Augie Galan	142		Andy Pafco	158
1944	Dixie Walker	191		Jackie Robinson	157
	Augie Galan	174		Pee Wee Reese	152
	Frenchy Bordagaray	141		Gil Hodges	129
	Luis Olmo	134		Roy Campanella	126
	Howie Schultz	134		Billy Cox	118
	Mickey Owen	126		Carl Furillo	105
1945	Goody Rosen	197	1953	Duke Snider	198
	Dixie Walker	182		Jim Gilliam	168
	Augie Galan	177		Carl Furillo	165
	Luis Olmo	174		Roy Campanella	162
	Eddie Stanky	143		Jackie Robinson	159
1946	Dixie Walker	184		Gil Hodges	157
	Pee Wee Reese	154		Pee Wee Reese	142
	Eddie Stanky	132	1954	Duke Snider	199
	Pete Reiser	117		Gil Hodges	176
1947	Jackie Robinson	175		Jim Gilliam	171
	Dixie Walker	162		Pee Wee Reese	171
	Eddie Stanky	141		Carl Furillo	161
	Bruce Edwards	139		Jackie Robinson	129
	Pee Wee Reese	135	1955	Duke Snider	166
	Carl Furillo	129		Carl Furillo	164
	Spider Jorgensen	121		Gil Hodges	158
	Pete Reiser	120		Pee Wee Reese	156
1948	Jackie Robinson	170		Roy Campanella	142
	Pee Wee Reese	155		Jim Gilliam	134
	Gil Hodges	120	1956	Jim Gilliam	178
	Gene Hermanski	116		Duke Snider	158
	Carl Furillo	108		Carl Furillo	151
1949	Jackie Robinson	203		Pee Wee Reese	147
	Carl Furillo	177		Gil Hodges	146
	Pee Wee Reese	172	1957	Gil Hodges	173

Jim Gilliam (above) was an outstanding hitter for the Dodgers—both in Brooklyn and in Los Angeles—for fourteen years. Pee Wee Reese (right) was a perennial all-star for the Dodgers for sixteen years.

100-or-More Hits, Season (Continued)

Year	Player	Total	Year	Player	Total
	Gino Cimoli	156		Lou Johnson	121
	Jim Gilliam	154		Jim Gilliam	104
	Duke Snider	139		John Roseboro	102
	Carl Furillo	121	1966	Willie Davis	177
	Charlie Neal	121		Maury Wills	162
1958	Jim Gilliam	145		Jim Lefebvre	149
	Gil Hodges	123		Lou Johnson	143
	Charlie Neal	120		John Roseboro	123
	Carl Furillo	119		Wes Parker	120
	Don Zimmer	119	1967	Willie Davis	146
	John Roseboro	104		Jim Lefebvre	129
	Duke Snider	102		Ron Fairly	107
1959	Charlie Neal	177		Ron Hunt	102
	Wally Moon	164		Wes Parker	102
	Jim Gilliam	156	1968	Willie Davis	161
	Gil Hodges	114		Tom Haller	135
	Duke Snider	114		Wes Parker	112
1960	Maury Wills	152		Ron Fairly	103
	Norm Larker	142	1969	Ted Sizemore	160
	Wally Moon	140		Willie Davis	155
	Jim Gilliam	138		Wes Parker	131
	Charlie Neal	122		Maury Wills	129
	Frank Howard	120		Tom Haller	117
1961	Maury Wills	173		Bill Sudakis	108
	Wally Moon	152		Andy Kosco	105
	Tommy Davis	128	1970	Wes Parker	196
	Jim Gilliam	107		Willie Davis	181
1962	Tommy Davis	230		Billy Grabarkewitz	153
	Maury Wills	208		Maury Wills	141
	Willie Davis	171		Manny Mota	127
	Jim Gilliam	159		Ted Sizemore	104
	Frank Howard	146	1971	Willie Davis	198
	Ron Fairly	128		Maury Wills	169
1963	Tommy Davis	181		Richie Allen	162
	Maury Wills	159		Wes Parker	146
	Jim Gilliam	148	1972	Willie Davis	178
	Ron Fairly	133		Bill Buckner	122
	Willie Davis	126		Manny Mota	120
	Frank Howard	114		Wes Parker	119
	John Roseboro	111		Bill Russell	118
1964	Willie Davis	180		Bobby Valentine	107
	Maury Wills	173	1973	Willie Davis	171
	Tommy Davis	163		Bill Russell	163
	John Roseboro	119		Bill Buckner	158
	Ron Fairly	116		Davey Lopes	147
1965	Maury Wills	186		Willie Crawford	135
	Ron Fairly	152		Joe Ferguson	128
	Jim Lefebvre	136		Ron Cey	124
	Willie Davis	133		Steve Garvey	106
	Wes Parker	129	1974	Steve Garvey	200

100-or-More Hits, Season (Continued)

Year	Player	Total	Year	Player	Total
	Bill Buckner	182		Davey Lopes	154
	Ron Cey	151		Dusty Baker	152
	Bill Russell	149		Ron Cey	137
	Jimmy Wynn	145		Derrel Thomas	104
	Davey Lopes	141	1980	Steve Garvey	200
	Willie Crawford	138		Dusty Baker	170
1975	Steve Garvey	210		Ron Cey	140
	Davey Lopes	162		Davey Lopes	139
	Ron Cey	160		Bill Russell	123
	Steve Yeager	103		Rudy Law	101
	Jimmy Wynn	102		Reggie Smith	100
1976	Steve Garvey	200	1981	Dusty Baker	128
	Bill Buckner	193		Steve Garvey	122
	Bill Russell	152		Pedro Guerrero	104
	Ron Cey	139	1982	Steve Sax	180
	Davey Lopes	103		Steve Garvey	176
1977	Steve Garvey	192		Pedro Guerrero	175
	Bill Russell	176		Dusty Baker	171
	Dusty Baker	155		Ron Cey	141
	Reggie Smith	150		Bill Russell	136
	Davey Lopes	142		Ken Landreaux	131
	Ron Cey	136	1983	Steve Sax	175
1978	Steve Garvey	202		Pedro Guerrero	174
	Bill Russell	179		Dusty Baker	138
	Davey Lopes	163		Ken Landreaux	135
	Ron Cey	150		Mike Marshall	132
	Dusty Baker	137		Bill Russell	111
	Reggie Smith	132		Greg Brock	102
1979	Steve Garvey	204			
	Bill Russell	170			

Base Hits by Position (Season)

Modern, Brooklyn

1B	Jake Daubert	1913	176
2B	Jackie Robinson	1949	203
SS	Pee Wee Reese	1951	176
3B	Jimmy Johnston	1921	203
OF	Babe Herman	1930	241
OF	Zach Wheat	1925	221
OF	Lefty O'Doul	1932	219
C	Roy Campanella	1951	164

Los Angeles

1B	Steve Garvey	1975	210
2B	Steve Sax	1982	180
SS	Maury Wills	1962	208
3B	Pedro Guerrero	1983	175
OF	Tommy Davis	1962	230
OF	Willie Davis	1971	198
OF	Bill Buckner	1976	193
C	Tom Haller	1968	135

19th Century

1B	Dan Brouthers	1892	197
2B	Tom Daly	1894	168
SS	Tommy Corcoran	1894	173
3B	George Pinckney	1886-88	156
OF	Willie Keeler	1899	215
OF	Oyster Burns	1894	185
OF	Fielder Jones	1898	181
C	John Grim	1895	92

All-Time

1B	Steve Garvey	1975	210
2B	Jackie Robinson	1949	203
SS	Maury Wills	1962	208
3B	Jimmy Johnston	1921	203
OF	Babe Herman	1930	241
OF	Tommy Davis	1962	230
OF	Zach Wheat	1925	221
C	Roy Campanella	1951	164

Career Leaders in Base Hits

Player	Total	Player	Total
Zach Wheat	2804	Fielder Jones	776
Pee Wee Reese	2170	Cookie Lavagetto	763
Willie Davis	2091	Joe Stripp	758
Duke Snider	1995	Jim Lefebvre	756
Steve Garvey	1968	Willie Crawford	748
Carl Furillo	1910	Tommy Griffith	731
Jim Gilliam	1889	Harry Lumley	728
Gil Hodges	1884	Steve Yeager	719
Bill Russell	1758	Germany Smith	708
Maury Wills	1732	Del Bissonette	699
Jackie Robinson	1518	Otto Miller	695
Jimmy Johnston	1440	Bill Shindle	679
Dixie Walker	1395	Pete Reiser	666
Jake Daubert	1387	Al Lopez	665
Ron Cey	1378	Billy Cox	659
Hy Myers	1253	Charlie Neal	659
Davy Lopes	1204	Steve Yeager	651
Tom Daly	1181	Wally Moon	649
Mike Griffin	1166	Darby O'Brien	648
Roy Campanella	1161	Casey Stengel	646
Dusty Baker	1144	Candy LaChance	645
Wes Parker	1110	Bill Dahlen	643
Ivy Olson	1100	Augie Galan	640
Babe Herman	1093	Jack Fournier	629
George Pinckney	1012	Manny Moto	605
Ron Fairly	1010	John Anderson	567
John Roseboro *	1009	Frank Howard	567
Jimmy Sheckard	977	Babe Phelps	561
John Hummel	973	Billy Herman	548
Johnny Frederick	954	Frenchy Bordagaray	542
Tommy Davis	912	Joe Medwick	535
Dave Foutz	901	Wally Gilbert	534
Willie Keeler	844	Tony Cuccinello	533
Bill Buckner	837	Pedro Guerrero	532
George Cutshaw	824	Reggie Smith	516
Dolph Camilli	809		

DOUBLES

Year-by-Year Leaders in Doubles

Year	Player	Total	Year	Player	Total
1884	Charlie Householder	15	1891*	Mike Griffin	36
1885	Germany Smith	17	1892	Dan Brouthers	30
1886	Bill McClellan	33	1893	Oyster Burns	22
1887	Bill Phillips	34	1894	Oyster Burns	32
1888	Darby O'Brien	27	1895	Mike Griffin	38
1889	Darby O'Brien	30	1896	Mike Griffin	27
1890	Hub Collins	32	1897	Bill Shindle	32

Year-by-Year Leaders in Doubles (Continued)

Year	Player	Total	Year	Player	Total
1898	Candy LaChance	23	1940	Dixie Walker	37
1899	Tom Daly	24	1941*	Pete Reiser	39
1900	Fielder Jones	26	1942	Joe Medwick	37
1901*	Tom Daly	38	1943	Billy Herman	41
1902	Bill Dahlen	26	1944	Augie Galan	43
1903	Jimmy Sheckard	29	1945	Dixie Walker	42
1904	Harry Lumley	23	1946	Dixie Walker	29
	Jimmy Sheckard	23	1947	Jackie Robinson	31
1905	John Dobbs	21		Dixie Walker	31
1906	Harry Lumley	23	1948	Jackie Robinson	38
1907	Whitey Alperman	23	1949	Jackie Robinson	38
	Harry Lumley	23	1950	Jackie Robinson	39
1908	Tim Jordan	18	1951	Roy Campanella	33
	Tom Sheehan	18		Jackie Robinson	33
1909	Al Burch	20	1952	Gil Hodges	27
	Tim Jordan	20	1953	Carl Furillo	38
1910	Zach Wheat	36		Duke Snider	38
1911	Zach Wheat	26	1954	Duke Snider	39
1912	Red Smith	28	1955	Duke Snider	34
	Zach Wheat	28	1956	Duke Snider	33
1913*	Red Smith	40	1957	Gil Hodges	28
1914	Zach Wheat	26	1958	Jim Gilliam	25
1915	Ollie O'Mara	26	1959	Charlie Neal	30
1916	Zach Wheat	32	1960	Norm Larker	26
1917	Casey Stengel	23	1961	Jim Gilliam	26
1918	Jimmy Johnston	16	1962	Tommy Davis	27
	Ivy Olson	16	1963	Jim Gilliam	27
1919	Ed Konetchy	24	1964	John Roseboro	24
1920	Hy Myers	36	1965	Ron Fairly	28
1921	Jimmy Johnston	41	1966	Willie Davis	31
1922	Zach Wheat	29	1967	Willie Davis	27
1923	Jack Fournier	30	1968	Tom Haller	27
1924	Zach Wheat	41	1969	Willie Davis	23
1925	Zach Wheat	42		Wes Parker	23
1926	Babe Herman	35	1970*	Wes Parker	47
1927	Max Carey	30	1971	Willie Davis	33
1928	Babe Herman	37	1972	Willie Davis	22
1929*	Johnny Frederick	52	1973	Willie Davis	29
1930	Babe Herman	48	1974	Steve Garvey	32
1931	Babe Herman	43	1975	Steve Garvey	38
1932	Hack Wilson	37	1976	Steve Garvey	37
1933	Tony Cuccinello	31	1977	Bill Russell	28
1934	Tony Cuccinello	32	1978	Steve Garvey	36
1935	Lonny Frey	35	1979	Steve Garvey	32
1936	Joe Stripp	31	1980	Steve Garvey	27
1937	Babe Phelps	37	1981	Steve Garvey	23
1938	Cookie Lavagetto	34	1982	Steve Garvey	35
1939	Ernie Koy	37	1983	Pedro Guerrero	28

*Led League

30-or-More Doubles in One Season

1886				**1927**	
Bill McClellan	33		Max Carey		30
1887				**1928**	
Bill Phillips	34		Babe Herman		37
1889			Del Bissonette		30
Darby O'Brien	30			**1929**	
1890			Johnny Frederick		52
Hub Collins	32		Babe Herman		42
1891			Wally Gilbert		31
Mike Griffin	36			**1930**	
1892			Babe Herman		48
Dan Brouthers	30		Johnny Frederick		44
1894			Wally Gilbert		34
Oyster Burns	32		Del Bissonette		33
1895				**1931**	
Mike Griffin	38		Babe Herman		43
1897			Johnny Frederick		34
Bill Shindle	32		Lefty O'Doul		32
1901				**1932**	
Tom Daly	38		Hack Wilson		37
Jimmy Sheckard	31		Joe Stripp		36
1910			Tonny Cucinello		32
Zach Wheat	36		Lefty O'Doul		32
1913			Glenn Wright		31
Red Smith	40			**1933**	
1916			Tony Cuccinello		31
Zach Wheat	32			**1934**	
1920			Tony Cuccinello		32
Hy Myers	36		Len Koenecke		31
1921				**1935**	
Jimmy Johnston	41		Lonny Frey		35
Zach Wheat	31		Sam Leslie		30
1923				**1936**	
Jack Fournier	30		Joe Stripp		31
1924				**1937**	
Zach Wheat	41		Babe Phelps		37
Eddie Brown	30		Buddy Hassett		31
1925				**1938**	
Zach Wheat	42		Cookie Lavagetto		34
Eddie Brown	39			**1939**	
1926			Ernie Koy		37
Babe Herman	35		Dolph Camilli		30
Zach Wheat	31			**1940**	
			Dixie Walker		37

30-or-More Doubles in One Season (Continued)

1941			
Pete Reiser	39	Duke Snider	38
Joe Medwick	33	Jackie Robinson	34
Dixie Walker	32	Jim Gilliam	31
Billy Herman	30	**1954**	
1942		Duke Snider	39
Joe Medwick	37	Pee Wee Reese	35
Billy Herman	34	**1955**	
Pete Reiser	33	Duke Snider	34
1943		**1956**	
Billy Herman	41	Duke Snider	33
Arky Vaughn	39	Carl Furillo	30
Dixie Walker	32	**1959**	
1944		Charlie Neal	30
Augie Galan	43		
Dixie Walker	37	**1966**	
Howie Shultz	32	Willie Davis	31
1945		**1970**	
Dixie Walker	42	Wes Parker	47
Augie Galan	36	**1971**	
1947		Willie Davis	33
Jackie Robinson	31	**1974**	
Dixie Walker	31	Steve Garvey	32
1948		Bill Buckner	30
Jackie Robinson	38	**1975**	
Pee Wee Reese	31	Steve Garvey	38
1949		**1976**	
Jackie Robinson	38	Steve Garvey	37
1950		**1978**	
Jackie Robinson	39	Steve Garvey	36
Duke Snider	31	Ron Cey	32
Carl Furillo	30	Bill Russell	32
1951		**1979**	
Roy Campanella	33	Steve Garvey	32
Jackie Robinson	33	**1982**	
1953		Steve Garvey	35
Carl Furillo	38		

Lifetime Leaders in Doubles

Player	Total	Player	Total
Zach Wheat	464	Willie Davis	321
Duke Snider	343	Jim Gilliam	304
Steve Garvey	333	Gil Hodges	294
Pee Wee Reese	330	Dixie Walker	274
Carl Furillo	324	Jackie Robinson	273

Lifetime Leaders in Doubles (Continued)

Player	Total	Player	Total
Bill Russell	264	Dave Foutz	132
Babe Herman	232	Joe Stripp	129
Ron Cey	223	John Hummel	127
Mike Griffin	210	Babe Phelps	127
Johnny Frederick	200	Jim Lefebvre	126
Wes Parker	194	Willie Crawford	125
Tom Daly	190	Bill Buckner	121
Jimmy Johnson	181	Del Bissonette	117
Dusty Baker	179	Darby O'Brien	117
Roy Campanella	178	Tony Cuccinello	115
Ron Fairly	168	George Cutshaw	115
Davey Lopes	165	Babe Herman	113
Jimmy Sheckard	162	Billy Cox	112
John Roseboro	162	Bill Shindle	110
Hy Myers	155	Harry Lumley	109
Dolph Camilli	151	Tommy Davis	109
Maury Wills	150	Germany Smith	108
Augie Galan	146	Steve Yeager	108
Cookie Lavagetto	143	Tommy Griffith	105
Jake Daubert	138	Joe Medwick	102
Pete Reiser	135	Casey Stengel	100
Ivy Olson	134		

Doubles by Position (Season)

Modern, Brooklyn

1B	Del Bissonette	1930	33
2B	Billy Herman	1943	41
SS	Lonny Frey	1935	35
	Pee Wee Reese	1954	35
3B	Jimmy Johnston	1921	41
OF	Johnny Frederick	1929	52
OF	Babe Herman	1930	48
OF	Augie Galan	1944	43
C	Babe Phelps	1937	37

Los Angeles

1B	Wes Parker	1970	47
2B	Charlie Neal	1959	30
SS	Bill Russell	1978	32
3B	Ron Cey	1978	32
OF	Willie Davis	1971	33
OF	Bill Buckner	1974	30
OF	Ron Fairly	1965	28
C	Tom Haller	1968	27

19th Century

1B	Bill Phillips	1887	34
2B	Bill McClellan	1886	33

Doubles by Position (Season) (Continued)

SS	Germany Smith	1889	22
	Bill Dahlen	1899	22
3B	Bill Shindle	1897	32
OF	Mike Griffin	1895	38
OF	Oyster Burns	1894	32
OF	Darby O'Brien	1889	30
C	John Grim	1895	17

All-Time

1B	Wes Parker	1970	47
2B	Billy Herman	1943	41
SS	Lonny Frey	1935	35
	Pee Wee Reese	1954	35
3B	Jimmy Johnston	1921	41
OF	Johnny Frederick	1929	52
OF	Babe Herman	1930	48
OF	Augie Galan	1944	43
C	Babe Phelps	1937	37

TRIPLES

Most Triples, Season

Year	Player	Total	Year	Player	Total
1884	Oscar Walker	8	1905	Emil Batch	11
1885	Bill Phillips	11		Jimmy Sheckard	11
	Germany Smith	11	1906	Harry Lumley	12
1886	Bill Phillips	15	1907*	Whitey Alperman	16
1887	Germany Smith	16	1908	John Hummel	12
1888	Dave Foutz	13		Harry Lumley	12
1889	Oyster Burns	13	1909	Whitey Alperman	12
1890	Dave Foutz	13	1910	Jake Daubert	15
	Oyster Burns	13		Zach Wheat	15
1891	Oyster Burns	13	1911	Zach Wheat	13
1892	Dan Brouthers	20	1912	Jake Daubert	16
1893	Tom Daly	14	1913	George Cutshaw	13
1894	George Treadway	26	1914	George Cutshaw	12
1895	John Anderson	14	1915	Casey Stengel	12
1896	John Anderson	17		Zach Wheat	12
1897	Candy LaChance	16	1916	Hy Myers	14
1898	Fielder Jones	9	1917	Casey Stengel	12
	Jimmy Sheckard	9	1918*	Jake Daubert	15
1899	Willie Keeler	14	1919*	Hy Myers	14
	Joe Kelley	14	1920*	Hy Myers	22
1900	Joe Kelley	17	1921	Jimmy Johnston	14
1901*	Jimmy Sheckard	19	1922	Zach Wheat	12
1902	Jimmy Sheckard	10	1923	Jack Fournier	13
1903	Bill Dahlen	9	1924	Andy High	13
	Jimmy Sheckard	9	1925	Jack Fournier	16
1904*	Harry Lumley	18	1926	Babe Herman	11

*Led League

Most Triples, Season (Continued)

Year	Player	Total	Year	Player	Total
1927	Harvey Hendrick	11		Charlie Neal	7
1928	Del Bissonette	13		Duke Snider	7
	Rube Bressler	13	1958	John Roseboro	9
1929	Babe Herman	13	1959*	Wally Moon	11
1930	Del Bissonette	13		Charlie Neal	11
1931	Babe Herman	16	1960	Wally Moon	6
1932	Joe Stripp	9	1961	Maury Wills	10
1933	Danny Taylor	9	1962*	Willie Davis	10
1934	Buzz Boyle	10		Maury Wills	10
1935	Lonny Frey	11	1963	Willie Davis	8
1936	Buddy Hassett	11	1964	Willie Davis	7
1937	Gib Brack	9	1965	Wes Parker	7
1938	Ernie Koy	13		Maury Wills	7
1939	Dolph Camilli	12	1966	Willie Davis	6
1940	Dolph Camilli	13	1967	Willie Davis	9
1941*	Pete Reiser	17	1968	Willie Davis	10
1942	Dolph Camilli	7	1969	Willie Davis	8
1943	Dolph Camilli	6		Maury Wills	8
	Arky Vaughn	6	1970*	Willie Davis	16
	Dixie Walker	6	1971	Willie Davis	10
1944	Augie Galan	9	1972	Willie Davis	7
1945*	Luis Olmo	13	1973	Willie Davis	9
1946	Pee Wee Reese	10	1974	Bill Russell	6
1947	Bruce Edwards	8	1975	Steve Garvey	6
	Spider Jorgensen	8		Davey Lopes	6
1948	Jackie Robinson	8	1976	Davey Lopes	7
1949	Jackie Robinson	12	1977	Bill Russell	6
1950	Duke Snider	10	1978	Steve Garvey	9
1951	Pee Wee Reese	8	1979	Davey Lopes	6
1952	Pee Wee Reese	8	1980	Dusty Baker	4
1953*	Jim Gilliam	17		Rudy Law	4
1954	Duke Snider	10	1981	Ken Landreaux	4
1955	Jim Gilliam	8	1982	Ken Landreaux	7
1956	Sandy Amoros	8		Steve Sax	7
	Jim Gilliam	8		Pedro Guerrero	6
1957	Gil Hodges	7		Derrel Thomas	6

*Led League

15-or-More Triples in One Season

Year	Player	Total	Year	Player	Total
1886	Bill Phillips	15	1907	Whitey Alperman	16
1887	Germany Smith	16	1910	Jake Daubert	15
1892	Dan Brouthers	20		Zach Wheat	15
	Oyster Burns	18	1912	Jake Daubert	16
1894	George Treadway	26	1918	Jake Daubert	15
	Tommy Corcoran	20	1920	Hy Myers	22
1896	John Anderson	17	1925	Jack Fournier	16
1897	Candy LaChance	16	1931	Babe Herman	16
1900	Joe Kelley	17	1941	Pete Reiser	17
1901	Jimmy Sheckard	19	1953	Jim Gilliam	17
	Willie Keeler	15	1970	Willie Davis	16
1904	Harry Lumley	18			

Lifetime Leaders in Triples

Player	Total
Zach Wheat	171
Willie Davis	110
Hy Myers	97
Jake Daubert	87
John Hummel	82
Duke Snider	82
Pee Wee Reese	80
Jimmy Sheckard	78
Tom Daly	76
Jimmy Johnston	73
Jim Gilliam	71
Harry Lumley	66
Babe Herman	66
Dave Foutz	65
Mike Griffin	64
John Anderson	57
Carl Furillo	56
Dixie Walker	56
Maury Wills	56
Dolph Camilli	55
Bill Russell	55
Jackie Robinson	54
Bill Russell	54
Willie Keeler	53
Candy LaChance	52
Germany Smith	51
Ivy Olson	51
Del Bissonette	50
Casey Stengel	50
Gil Hodges	48
John Roseboro	44
Bill Dahlen	44
Joe Kelley	43
Adonis Terry	41
Davey Lopes	39
Babe Phelps	37
Whitey Alperman	36
Tommy Griffith	36
Steve Garvey	35
Pete Reiser	35
Darby O'Brien	34
Rube Bressler	34
Andy High	33
Wes Parker	32
*Bill Shindle	30
Joe Stripp	30
Goody Rosen	30

Triples by Position (Season)

Modern, Brooklyn

1B	Jake Daubert	1912	16
	Jack Fournier	1925	16
2B	Jim Gilliam	1953	17
SS	Glenn Wright	1930	12
3B	Jimmy Johnston	1921	14
OF	Hy Myers	1920	22
OF	Jimmy Sheckard	1901	19
OF	Harry Lumley	1904	18
C	Bruce Edwards	1947	8

Los Angeles

1B	Steve Garvey	1978	9
2B	Charlie Neal	1959	11
SS	Maury Wills	1962	10
3B	Billy Grabarkewitz	1970	8
OF	Willie Davis	1970	16
OF	Wally Moon	1959	11
OF	Tommy Davis	1962	9
C	John Roseboro	1958	9

19th Century

1B	Dan Brouthers	1892	20
2B	Tom Daly	1893	14
SS	Tommy Corcoran	1894	20
3B	Bill Joyce	1892	12
OF	George Treadway	1894	26
OF	Oyster Burns	1892	18
OF	John Anderson	1896	17
C	Tom Kinslow	1892	11

All-Time

1B	Dan Brouthers	1892	20
2B	Jim Gilliam	1953	17
SS	Tommy Corcoran	1894	20
3B	Jimmy Johnston	1921	14
OF	George Treadway	1894	26
OF	Hy Myers	1920	22
OF	Jimmy Sheckard	1901	19
C	Tom Kinslow	1892	11

HOME RUNS
Year-by-Year Home Run Leaders

Year	Player	Total	Year	Player	Total
1884	Bill Greenwood	3	1925	Jack Fournier	22
	Charlie Householder	3	1926	Jack Fournier	11
	Jack Remsen	3		Babe Herman	11
1885	Germany Smith	4	1927	Babe Herman	14
1886	Jimmy Peoples	3	1928	Del Bissonette	25
	Ed Swartwood	3	1929	Johnny Frederick	24
1887	Germany Smith	4	1930	Babe Herman	35
1888	Bob Caruthers	5	1931	Babe Herman	18
1889	Pop Corkhill	8	1932	Hack Wilson	23
	Joe Visner	8	1933	Tony Cuccinello	9
1890	Oyster Burns	13		Danny Taylor	9
1891	Darby O'Brien	5		Hack Wilson	9
1892	Bill Joyce	6	1934	Tony Cuccinello	14
1893	Tom Daly	8		Len Koenecke	14
1894	Tom Daly	8	1935	Lonny Frey	11
1895	John Anderson	9	1936	Babe Phelps	5
1896	Candy LaChance	7	1937	Cookie Lavagetto	8
1897	John Anderson	4	1938	Dolph Camilli	24
	Candy LaChance	4	1939	Dolph Camilli	26
1898	Candy LaChance	5	1940	Dolph Camilli	23
1899	Joe Kelley	6	1941*	Dolph Camilli	34
1900	Joe Kelley	6	1942	Dolph Camilli	26
1901	Jimmy Sheckard	11	1943	Augie Galan	9
1902	Tom McCreery	4	1944	Dixie Walker	13
	Jimmy Sheckard	4	1945	Goody Rosen	12
1903*	Jimmy Sheckard	9	1946	Pete Reiser	11
1904*	Harry Lumley	9	1947	Pee Wee Reese	12
1905	Harry Lumley	7		Jackie Robinson	12
1906*	Tim Jordan	12	1948	Gene Hermanski	15
1907	Harry Lumley	9	1949	Gil Hodges	23
1908*	Tim Jordan	12		Duke Snider	23
1909	John Hummel	4	1950	Gil Hodges	32
1910	Jake Daubert	8	1951	Gil Hodges	40
1911	Tex Erwin	7	1952	Gil Hodges	32
1912	Zach Wheat	8	1953	Duke Snider	42
1913	George Cutshaw	7	1954	Gil Hodges	42
	Casey Stengel	7	1955	Duke Snider	42
	Zach Wheat	7	1956*	Duke Snider	43
1914	Zach Wheat	9	1957	Duke Snider	40
1915	Zach Wheat	5	1958	Gil Hodges	22
1916	Zach Wheat	9		Charlie Neal	22
1917	Dave Hickman	6	1959	Gil Hodges	25
	Casey Stengel	6	1960	Frank Howard	23
1918	Hy Myers	4	1961	John Roseboro	18
1919	Tommy Griffith	6	1962	Frank Howard	31
1920	Zach Wheat	9	1963	Frank Howard	28
1921	Zach Wheat	14	1964	Frank Howard	24
1922	Zach Wheat	16	1965	Lou Johnson	12
1923	Jack Fournier	22		Jim Lefebvre	12
1924*	Jack Fournier	27	1966	Jim Lefebvre	24

*Led League

Year-by-Year Home Run Leaders (Continued)

Year	Player	Total	Year	Player	Total
1967	Al Ferrara	16	1976	Ron Cey	23
1968	Len Gabrielson	10	1977	Steve Garvey	33
1969	Andy Kosco	19	1978	Reggie Smith	29
1970	Billy Grabarkewitz	17	1979	Ron Cey	28
1971	Richie Allen	23		Steve Garvey	28
1972	Willie Davis	19		Davey Lopes	28
	Frank Robinson	19	1980	Dusty Baker	29
1973	Joe Ferguson	25	1981	Ron Cey	13
1974	Jimmy Wynn	32	1982	Pedro Guerrero	32
1975	Ron Cey	25	1983	Pedro Guerrero	32
				*Led League	

20-or-More Home Runs, Season

Year	Player	HR	Year	Player	HR
1923	Jack Fournier	22		Roy Campanella	32
1924	Jack Fournier	27		Gil Hodges	27
1925	Jack Fournier	22		Carl Furillo	26
1928	Del Bissonette	25	1956	Duke Snider	43
1929	Johnny Frederick	24		Gil Hodges	32
	Babe Herman	21		Carl Furillo	21
1930	Babe Herman	35		Roy Campanella	20
	Glenn Wright	22	1957	Duke Snider	40
1932	Hack Wilson	23		Gil Hodges	27
	Lefty O'Doul	21	1958	Gil Hodges	22
1938	Dolph Camilli	24		Charlie Neal	22
1939	Dolph Camilli	26	1959	Gil Hodges	25
1940	Dolph Camilli	23		Duke Snider	23
1941	Dolph Camilli	34	1960	Frank Howard	23
1942	Dolph Camilli	26	1962	Frank Howard	31
1949	Gil Hodges	23		Tommy Davis	27
	Duke Snider	23		Willie Davis	21
	Roy Campanella	22	1963	Frank Howard	28
1950	Gil Hodges	32	1964	Frank Howard	24
	Roy Campanella	31	1966	Jim Lefebvre	24
	Duke Snider	31	1971	Richie Allen	23
1951	Gil Hodges	40	1973	Joe Ferguson	25
	Roy Campanella	33	1974	Jimmy Wynn	32
	Duke Snider	29		Steve Garvey	21
1952	Gil Hodges	32	1975	Ron Cey	25
	Roy Campanella	22	1976	Ron Cey	23
	Duke Snider	21	1977	Steve Garvey	33
1953	Duke Snider	42		Reggie Smith	32
	Roy Campanella	41		Ron Cey	30
	Gil Hodges	31		Dusty Baker	30
	Carl Furillo	21	1978	Reggie Smith	29
1954	Gil Hodges	42		Ron Cey	23
	Duke Snider	40		Steve Garvey	21
1955	Duke Snider	42	1979	Ron Cey	28

20-or-More Home Runs, Season (Continued)

Year	Player	HR	Year	Player	HR
	Steve Garvey	28		Steve Garvey	26
	Davey Lopes	28	1982	Pedro Guerrero	32
	Dusty Baker	23		Ron Cey	24
	Joe Ferguson	20		Dusty Baker	23
1980	Dusty Baker	29	1983	Pedro Guerrero	32
	Ron Cey	28		Dusty Baker	20

20-Homer Club, Lifetime

Player	Total	Player	Total
Duke Snider	389	Sandy Amoros	42
Gil Hodges	361	Lou Johnson	40
Roy Campanella	242	Hack Wilson	38
Ron Cey	228	Bill Buckner	38
Steve Garvey	211	Gene Hermanski	38
Carl Furillo	192	Joe Medwick	38
Willie Davis	154	Harry Lumley	38
Dusty Baker	144	Andy Pafco	37
Dolph Camilli	139	Jimmy Sheckard	36
Jackie Robinson	137	Danny Taylor	36
Zach Wheat	131	Cookie Lavagetto	35
Pee Wee Reese	126	Tommy Griffith	35
Frank Howard	123	Bruce Edwards	35
Babe Herman	112	Harvey Hendrick	34
Davey Lopes	99	Pete Reiser	34
Reggie Smith	97	Don Demeter	34
Steve Yeager	96	Bill Sudakis	34
John Roseboro	92	Otto Miller	33
Joe Ferguson	91	Jake Daubert	33
Ron Fairly	90	Lefty O'Doul	33
Tommy Davis	86	Augie Galan	33
Johnny Frederick	85	Tim Jordan	32
Pedro Guerrero	85	Hy Myers	29
Jack Fournier	82	Casey Stengel	29
Willie Crawford	74	Candy LaChance	29
Jim Lefebvre	74	John Hummel	29
Rick Monday	72	Lee Lacy	29
Charlie Neal	73	Mike Griffin	28
Dixie Walker	67	Andy Kosco	27
Del Bissonette	66	Dave Foutz	25
Jim Gilliam	65	Tom Haller	25
Wally Moon	64	Luis Olmo	24
Wes Parker	64	Shotgun Shuba	24
Jimmy Wynn	50	Al Ferrara	23
Billy Cox	46	Norm Larker	22
Bill Russell	46	Bobby Morgan	21
Tom Daly	44	Billy Grabarkewitz	21
Glenn Wright	44	Jimmy Johnston	20
Tony Cuccinello	43	Ernie Koy	20
Babe Phelps	43	Al Lopez	20
Don Zimmer	43	Greg Brock	20

Grand-Slam Home Runs
Modern Era (Since 1900)

Date		Player	Opponent
1900	April 28	Fielder Jones	Boston
	June 19	Tom Daly	at Boston
1901	Sept. 23	Joe Kelley	at Cincinnati
	Sept. 23	Jimmy Sheckard	at Cincinnati
	Sept. 24	Jimmy Sheckard	at Cincinnati
1903	Aug. 17	Jimmy Sheckard	St. Louis
1906	Aug. 15	Tim Jordan	at Chicago
1907	June 25	Harry Lumley	Philadelphia
1911	July 28	Tex Erwin	at Cincinnati
1914	Sept. 28	George Cutshaw	St. Louis
1916	Sept. 16	Zach Wheat	Cincinnati
1919	June 24	Tommy Griffith	New York
1925	May 13	Eddie Brown	St. Louis
	June 4	Zach Taylor	at Chicago
	August 24	Zach Wheat	Chicago
1927	Sept. 14	Max Carey	at Chicago
1928	June 16	Del Bissonette	St. Louis
1929	July 13	Babe Herman	St. Louis
	July 23	Billy Rhiel	at Pittsburgh
	Sept. 17	Babe Herman	at Chicago
1930	April 21	Del Bissonette	Boston
	July 9	Del Bissonette	Boston
1931	May 30	Gordon Slade	at New York
	June 29	Johnny Frederick	Cincinnati
1932	June 8	Hack Wilson	Chicago
	Sept. 25	Joe Stripp	Boston
1933	May 14*	Hack Wilson	Philadelphia
	June 23	Tony Cuccinello	Pittsburgh
1934	July 6	Sam Leslie	New York
1935	April 19	Dan Taylor	at Boston
	April 23	Lonny Frey	Philadelphia
	July 24	Dan Taylor	at Chicago
1937	Sept. 3	Jim Bucher	at New York
	Sept. 12	Eddie Wilson	Philadelphia
1938	June 12	Dolph Camilli	at Chicago
1939	May 28	Cookie Lavagetto	Boston
	Sept. 26	Cookie Lavagetto	at New York
1940	April 26	Cookie Lavagetto	at Philadelphia
	June 29	Dixie Walker	Boston
	July 3	Pee Wee Reese	at New York
	Sept. 6	Joe Medwick	at Philadelphia
	Sept. 18	Babe Phelps	St. Louis
1941	May 6	Dixie Walker	Pittsburgh
	May 25	Pete Reiser	Philadelphia
1942	May 31	Dixie Walker	Boston
	August 3	Dolph Camilli	at New York
	August 23	Dolph Camilli	New York
1943	July 5	Augie Galan	Chicago
	July 26	Arky Vaughan	at Pittsburgh
1944	May 17	Howie Schultz	at Pittsburgh

*Pinch Hit.

Grand-Slam Home Runs

Date		Player	Opponent
1945	May 18	Luis Olmo	Chicago
	May 26	Luis Olmo	at St. Louis
	July 8	Dixie Walker	St. Louis
1947	June 4	Pee Wee Reese	Pittsburgh
	June 22	Carl Furillo	at Cincinnati
	August 18	Bruce Edwards	St. Louis
1948	April 29	Preston Ward	New York
	May 9	Pee Wee Reese	at Pittsburgh
	June 24	Jackie Robinson	Pittsburgh
1949	May 14	Gil Hodges	at Boston
	June 12	Gil Hodges	Cincinnati
	July 2	Gene Hermanski	at New York
	July 28	Gene Hermanski	at Chicago
	August 7	Bruce Edwards	at Cincinnati
	Sept. 11	Carl Furillo	New York
1950	April 21	Roy Campanella	New York
	June 11	Roy Campanella	at Cincinnati
	June 20	Gil Hodges	Cincinnati
	June 24	Jackie Robinson	Pittsburgh
	Sept. 20	Gil Hodges	Pittsburgh
	Sept. 24	Erv Palica	at Philadelphia
1951	May 6	Pee Wee Reese	St. Louis
	May 15	Duke Snider	at Chicago
	May 22	Gil Hodges	at Pittsburgh
	May 23	Billy Cox	at Pittsburgh
	August 5	Roy Campanella	at Cincinnati
	Sept. 3	Roy Campanella	Boston
	Sept. 5	Gil Hodges	Philadelphia
1952	April 19	Carl Furillo	New York
	May 23	Roy Campanella	at Philadelphia
	June 8	Carl Furillo	at Cincinnati
	July 19	Pee Wee Reese	at Pittsburgh
	August 5	Gil Hodges	at New York
	August 7	Roy Campanella	at New York
	August 31	Gil Hodges	New York
	September 11	Andy Pafco	Chicago
1953	July 16	Gil Hodges	St. Louis
	July 17	Billy Cox	St. Louis
	July 18*	Wayne Belardi	St. Louis
	August 9	Duke Snider	at Cincinnati
	August 11	Duke Snider	at New York
	Sept. 9	Pee Wee Reese	at Cincinnati
1954	May 16	Gil Hodges	Cincinnati
	August 8	Don Hoak	Cincinnati
	August 14	Carl Furillo	New York
1955	May 8	Duke Snider	at Philadelphia
	May 14	Carl Furillo	at Cincinnati
	August 3	Gil Hodges	at Milwaukee
	Sept. 9	Don Zimmer	at Chicago
1956	May 13	Duke Snider	New York

Grand-Slam Home Runs

Date		Player	Opponent
	July 15	Carl Furillo	at Chicago
	August 4	Chico Fernandez	St. Louis
1957	July 18	Gil Hodges	St. Louis
	July 28	Carl Furillo	at Cincinnati
	August 1	Gil Hodges	at Chicago
1958**	August 23	Gil Hodges	Milwaukee
1960	April 29	John Roseboro	San Francisco
	May 17	Frank Howard	at Milwaukee
	May 31	Norm Sherry	St. Louis
	June 4	Wally Moon	Chicago
	July 28	Frank Howard	Cincinnati
	July 30	Tommy Davis	Milwaukee
1961	April 29	Frank Howard	at Chicago
	June 2	Tommy Davis	San Francisco
	July 26	Norm Larker	at Philadelphia
	August 9	Don Drysdale	Milwaukee
1962	July 2 (1st G)	Willie Davis	Philadelphia
	Sept. 10	Tommy Davis	Chicago
1963	July 4	Ken McMullin	St. Louis
	July 21 (2nd G)	Ron Fairly	at Milwaukee
	Sept. 12	John Roseboro	at Pittsburgh
1964	Sept. 9	Willie Davis	at San Francisco
1968	July 16	Ron Fairly	at Cincinnati
	Sept. 9	Bill Sudakis	at St. Louis
1969	April 15	Andy Kosco	San Diego
	August 16	Maury Wills	at Montreal
1970	July 22*	Tom Haller	Montreal
	August 5	Willie Davis	Atlanta
1971	July 27	Bill Buckner	Pittsburgh
1973	May 25	Willie Crawford	New York
1974	August 5	Steve Yeager	Cincinnati
	Sept. 15	Jimmy Wynn	Cincinnati
1975	April 16	Jimmy Wynn	Cincinnati
	April 24*	Ken McMullin	San Diego
	June 18	Ron Cey	Houston
	Sept. 27	Steve Yeager	Houston
1976	June 7	Ron Cey	Philadelphia
1977	April 24	Ron Cey	at Atlanta
	May 5	Ron Cey	New York
	June 22	Steve Garvey	St. Louis
	August 22	Steve Yeager	at St. Louis
	August 28	Steve Garvey	St. Louis
	Sept. 12	Dusty Baker	San Diego
	Oct. 4**	Ron Cey	Philadelphia
	Oct. 5**	Dusty Baker	Philadelphia
1978	June 12	Dusty Baker	Philadelphia
	July 6	Davey Lopes	Atlanta
	July 26	Steve Garvey	Chicago
	August 16	Reggie Smith	at Philadelphia
1979	April 6	Joe Ferguson	San Diego

**National League Playoffs.

Grand-Slam Home Runs

Date	Player		Opponent
	July 24	Dusty Baker	Philadelphia
	August 10	Derrel Thomas	at San Francisco
	September 2	Davey Lopes	Chicago
	September 25	Ron Cey	at San Francisco
	September 28	Steve Garvey	Houston
1982	June 30	Dusty Baker	San Diego
	Oct. 1	Rick Monday	at San Francisco
1983	May 18	Greg Brock	at Montreal
	June 28	Pedro Guerrero	at San Diego
	July 23	Ken Landreaux	at St. Louis
	September 7	Mike Marshall	Cincinnati

Three Consecutive Homers in One Inning

Date		Players	In.	Opponent	Site
1911	August 3	(Zimmerman, Erwin, Wheat)	5	Cubs	A
1952	April 19	(Campanella, Pafco, Snider)	7	Giants	H
1956	June 29	(Snider, Jackson, Hodges)	9	Phils	H

Four Home Runs in a Game

Date	Player	Opponent	Site
1950	August 31 Gil Hodges	Braves	Ebbets Field

Three Home Runs in a Game

1926	July 13	Jack Fournier	Cardinals	Sportsman's Park
1948	August 5	Gene Hermanski*	Cubs	Ebbets Field
1950	May 30—2nd-G Duke Snider*		Phils	Ebbets Field
	August 26 Roy Campanella*		Reds	Crosley Field
	Sept. 18	Tommy Brown*	Cubs	Ebbets Field
1955	June 1	Duke Snider	Braves	Ebbets Field
1959	April 21	Don Demeter	Giants	Coliseum (11 innings)
1974	May 11	Jimmy Wynn	Padres	San Diego Stadium
	August 20 Davey Lopes		Cubs	Wrigley Field

*Consecutive homers

World Series Home Runs

Date		Player	Game	In.	Pitcher	Team	Site
1916	Oct. 9	Hy Myers	2	1	Ruth	Red Sox	Braves Field
1941	Oct. 5	Pete Reiser	4	5	Donald	Yankees	Ebbets Field
1947	Oct. 1	Dixie Walker	2	4	Reynolds	Yankees	Yankee Stadium
1949	Oct. 7	Pee Wee Reese	3	4	Byrne	Yankees	Ebbets Field
	Oct. 7	Luis Olmo	3	9	Page	Yankees	Ebbets Field
	Oct. 7	Roy Campanella	3	9	Page	Yankees	Ebbets Field

World Series Home Runs (Continued)

Date		Player	Game	In.	Pitcher	Team	Site
	Oct. 9	Gil Hodges	5	7	Raschi	Yankees	Ebbets Field
1952	Oct. 1	Jackie Robinson	1	2	Reynolds	Yankees	Ebbets Field
	Oct. 1	Duke Snider	1	6	Reynolds	Yankees	Ebbets Field
	Oct. 1	Pee Wee Reese	1	8	Scarborough	Yankees	Ebbets Field
	Oct. 5	Duke Snider	5	5	Blackwell	Yankees	Yankee Stadium
	Oct. 6	Duke Snider	6	6	Raschi	Yankees	Ebbets Field
	Oct. 6	Duke Snider	6	8	Raschi	Yankees	Ebbets Field
1953	Sept. 30	Jim Gilliam	1	5	Reynolds	Yankees	Yankee Stadium
	Sept. 30	Gil Hodges	1	6	Reynolds	Yankees	Yankee Stadium
	Sept. 30	George Shuba	1	6	Reynolds	Yankees	Yankee Stadium
	Oct. 2	Roy Campanella	3	8	Raschi	Yankees	Ebbets Field
	Oct. 3	Duke Snider	4	6	Sain	Yankees	Ebbets Field
	Oct. 4	Billy Cox	5	8	McDonald	Yankees	Ebbets Field
	Oct. 4	Jim Gilliam	5	9	Kuzava	Yankees	Ebbets Field
	Oct. 5	Carl Furillo	6	9	Reynolds	Yankees	Yankee Stadium.
1955	Sept. 28	Carl Furillo	1	2	Ford	Yankees	Yankee Stadium
	Sept. 28	Duke Snider	1	3	Ford	Yankees	Yankee Stadium
	Sept. 30	Roy Campanella	3	1	Turley	Yankees	Ebbets Field
	Oct. 1	Roy Campanella	4	4	Larsen	Yankees	Ebbets Field
	Oct. 1	Gil Hodges	4	4	Larsen	Yankees	Ebbets Field
	Oct. 1	Duke Snider	4	5	Kucks	Yankees	Ebbets Field
	Oct. 2	Sandy Amoros	5	2	Grim	Yankees	Ebbets Field
	Oct. 2	Duke Snider	5	3	Grim	Yankees	Ebbets Field
	Oct. 2	Duke Snider	5	5	Grim	Yankees	Ebbets Field
1956	Oct. 3	Jackie Robinson	1	2	Ford	Yankees	Ebbets Field
	Oct. 3	Gil Hodges	1	3	Ford	Yankees	Ebbets Field
	Oct. 5	Duke Snider	2	2	Byrne	Yankees	Ebbets Field
1959	Oct. 2	Charlie Neal	2	5	Shaw	White Sox	Comiskey Park
	Oct. 2	Chuck Essegian	2	7	Shaw	White Sox	Comiskey Park
	Oct. 2	Charlie Neal	2	7	Shaw	White Sox	Comiskey Park
	Oct. 5	Gil Hodges	4	8	Staley	White Sox	Memorial Coliseum
	Oct. 8	Duke Snider	6	3	Wynn	White Sox	Comiskey Park
	Oct. 8	Wally Moon	6	4	Donovan	White Sox	Comiskey Park
	Oct. 8	Chuck Essegian	6	9	Moore	White Sox	Comiskey Park
1963	Oct. 2	John Roseboro	1	2	Ford	Yankees	Yankee Stadium

World Series Home Runs (Continued)

Date		Player	Game	In.	Pitcher	Team	Site
	Oct. 3	Bill Skowron	2	4	Downing	Yankees	Yankee Stadium
	Oct. 6	Frank Howard	4	5	Ford	Yankees	Dodger Stadium
1965	Oct. 6	Ron Fairly	1	2	Grant	Twins	Metropolitan Stadium
	Oct. 10	Wes Parker	4	4	Grant	Twins	Dodger Stadium
	Oct. 10	Lou Johnson	4	8	Pleis	Twins	Dodger Stadium
	Oct. 13	Ron Fairly	6	7	Grant	Twins	Metropolitan Stadium
	Oct. 14	Lou Johnson	7	4	Kaat	Twins	Metropolitan Stadium
1966	Oct. 5	Jim Lefebvre	1	2	McNally	Orioles	Dodger Stadium
1974	Oct.12	Jimmy Wynn	1	9	Fingers	A's	Dodger Stadium
	Oct. 13	Joe Ferguson	2	6	Blue	A's	Dodger Stadium
	Oct. 15	Bill Buckner	3	8	Hunter	A's	Oakland Coliseum
	Oct. 15	Willie Crawford	3	9	Fingers	A's	Oakland Coliseum
1977	Oct. 12	Ron Cey	2	1	Hunter	Yankees	Yankees Stadium
	Oct. 12	Steve Yeager	2	2	Hunter	Yankees	Yankee Stadium
	Oct. 12	Reggie Smith	2	3	Hunter	Yankees	Yankee Stadium
	Oct. 12	Steve Garvey	2	9	Lyle	Yankees	Yankee Stadium
	Oct. 14	Dusty Baker	3	3	Torrez	Yankees	Dodger Stadium
	Oct. 15	Davey Lopes	4	3	Guidry	Yankees	Dodger Stadium
	Oct. 16	Steve Yeager	5	4	Gullett	Yankees	Dodger Stadium
	Oct. 16	Reggie Smith	5	6	Tidrow	Yankees	Dodger Stadium
	Oct. 18	Reggie Smith	6	3	Torrez	Yankees	Yankee Stadium
1978	Oct. 10	Dusty Baker	1	2	Figueroa	Yankees	Dodger Stadium
	Oct. 10	Davey Lopes	1	2	Figueroa	Yankees	Dodger Stadium
	Oct. 10	Davey Lopes	1	4	Clay	Yankees	Dodger Stadium
	Oct. 11	Ron Cey	2	6	Hunter	Yankees	Dodger Stadium

World Series Home Runs (Continued)

Date		Player	Game	In.	Pitcher	Team	Site
	Oct. 14	Reggie Smith	4	5	Figueroa	Yankees	Yankee Stadium
	Oct. 17	Davey Lopes	6	1	Hunter	Yankees	Dodger Stadium
1981	Oct. 20	Steve Yeager	1	5	Guidry	Yankees	Yankee Stadium
	Oct. 23	Ron Cey	3	1	Righetti	Yankees	Dodger Stadium
	Oct. 24	Jay Johnstone	4	6	Davis	Yankees	Dodger Stadium
	Oct. 25	Pedro Guerrero	5	7	Guidry	Yankees	Dodger Stadium
	Oct. 25	Steve Yeager	5	7	Guidry	Yankees	Dodger Stadium
	Oct. 28	Pedro Guerrero	6	8	May	Yankees	Yankee Stadium

Dodgers All-Star Game Home Runs

Date		Player	In.	Pitcher	Site
1942	July 6	Mickey Owen	8	Benton	Polo Grounds (N.Y.)
1951	July 10	Gil Hodges	6	Hutchinson	Briggs Stadium (Det.)
1952	July 8	Jackie Robinson	1	Raschi	Shibe Park (Phil.)
1959	Aug. 3	Jim Gilliam	7-2ndG	O'Dell	Memorial Coliseum (L.A.)
1962	July 30	John Roseboro	9-2ndG	Pappas	Wrigley Field (Chicago)
1973	July 24	Willie Davis	6	Ryan	Royal Stadium (K.C.)
1975	July 15	Steve Garvey	2	Blue	County Stadium (Milw.)
1975	July 15	Jimmy Wynn	2	Blue	County Stadium (Milw.)
1977	July 19	Steve Garvey	3	Palmer	Yankee Stadium (N.Y.)

Most Home Runs by Position, One Season

Modern, Brooklyn

1B	Gil Hodges	1954	42
2B	Jackie Robinson	1951-52	19
SS	Glenn Wright	1930	22
3B	Cookie Lavagetto	1939	10
	Billy Cox	1953	10
OF	Duke Snider	1956	43
OF	Babe Herman	1930	35
OF	Carl Furillo	1955	26
C	Roy Campanella	1953	41

Los Angeles

1B	Steve Garvey	1977	33
2B	Davey Lopes	1979	28
SS	Bill Russell	1979	7
3B	Pedro Guerrero	1983	32
OF	Jimmy Wynn	1974	32
OF	Reggie Smith	1977	32
OF	Pedro Guerrero	1982	32
C	Joe Ferguson	1973	25

19th Century

1B	Candy LaChance	1895	8
2B	Tom Daly	1893-94	8
SS	Tommy Corcoran	1894	5
3B	George Pinckney	1890	7
OF	Oyster Burns	1890	13
OF	John Anderson	1895	9
OF	Pop Corkhill	1889	8
C	Joe Visner	1889	8

All-Time

1B	Gil Hodges	1954	42
2B	Davey Lopes	1979	28
SS	Glenn Wright	1930	22
3B	Pedro Guerrero	1983	32
OF	Duke Snider	1956	43
OF	Babe Herman	1930	35
OF	Jimmy Wynn	1974	32
	Reggie Smith	1977	32
	Pedro Guerrero	1982	32
C	Roy Campanella	1953	41

Home Run Frequency

Player	At Bats	Homers	Frequency
Steve Bilko	101	7	14.4
Wayne Belardi	185	11	16.8
Duke Snider	6640	389	17.1
Frank Howard	2108	123	17.1
Roy Campanella	4205	242	17.4
Gil Hodges	6881	361	19.1
Don Demeter	677	34	19.9
Rick Monday	1479	72	20.5
Pedro Guerrero	1759	85	20.7
Dolph Camilli	2992	139	21.5
Jack Fournier	1866	82	22.8
Ron Cey	5216	228	22.9
Greg Brock	472	20	23.6
Richie Allen	549	23	23.9
Al Ferrara	594	23	25.8
Mike Marshall	585	22	26.6
Hack Wilson	1013	38	26.7
Dusty Baker	4073	144	28.3
Babe Herman	3221	112	28.8
Sandy Amoros	1244	42	29.6
Steve Garvey	6543	211	31.0
Chuck Essegian	125	4	31.3
Ken McMullen	502	16	31.4
Lou Johnson	1324	40	33.1
Carl Furillo	6378	192	33.2
Charlie Neal	2491	73	34.1
Del Bissonette	2291	66	34.7
Tommy Davis	2999	86	34.9

Home Runs by Decades (Top Ten)

1880's
1. Germany Smith	16
2. George Pinckney	11
3. Dave Foutz	10
4. Pop Corkhill	8
5. Adonis Terry	8
6. Joe Visner	8
7. Oyster Burns	7
8. Bob Caruthers	7
9. Darby O'Brien	7
10. Jimmy Peoples	5
Bill Phillips	5

7. Tommy Corcoran	13
8. Bill Shindle	12
9. George Treadway	11
10. Fielder Jones	8
Tom Kinslow	8
Darby O'Brien	8

1890's
1. Tom Daly	37
2. Oyster Burns	33
3. Candy LaChance	29
4. Mike Griffin	28
5. John Anderson	18
6. Dave Foutz	15

1900's
1. Harry Lumley	38
2. Tim Jordan	31
3. Jimmy Sheckard	29
4. John Hummel	12
5. Joe Kelley	10
6. Bill Dahlen	8
7. Emil Batch	7
8. Tom Daly	7
9. Tom McCreery	7
10. Whitey Alperman	6
Willie Keeler	6

Home Runs by Decades (Top Ten) (Continued)

1910's			1950's	
1. Zach Wheat	51		1. Duke Snider	326
2. Jake Daubert	33		2. Gil Hodges	310
3. Casey Stengel	29		3. Roy Campanella	211
4. John Hummel	17		4. Carl Furillo	159
5. George Cutshaw	15		5. Jackie Robinson	97
6. Hy Myers	15		6. Pee Wee Reese	74
7. Red Smith	14		7. Charlie Neal	55
8. Tex Erwin	10		8. Sandy Amoros	42
9. Dave Hickman	7		9. Don Zimmer	42
10. Tommy Griffith	6		10. Jim Gilliam	41

1920's			1960's	
1. Jack Fournier	82		1. Frank Howard	121
2. Zach Wheat	80		2. Willie Davis	101
3. Babe Herman	58		3. Tommy Davis	86
4. Del Bissonette	37		4. Ron Fairly	84
5. Tommy Griffith	29		5. John Roseboro	66
6. Harvey Hendrick	29		6. Jim Lefebvre	53
7. Johnny Frederick	24		7. Wally Moon	45
8. Jimmy Johnston	18		8. Wes Parker	44
9. Bernie Neis	16		9. Lou Johnson	40
10. Andy High	15		10. Duke Snider	35

1930's			1970's	
1. Johnny Frederick	61		1. Ron Cey	163
2. Babe Herman	53		2. Steve Garvey	159
3. Dolph Camilli	50		3. Davey Lopes	84
4. Tony Cuccinello	43		4. Joe Ferguson	82
5. Glenn Wright	42		5. Reggie Smith	81
6. Hack Wilson	38		6. Steve Yeager	74
7. Danny Taylor	36		7. Dusty Baker	68
8. Lefty O'Doul	33		8. Willie Crawford	59
9. Del Bissonette	29		9. Willie Davis	53
10. Babe Phelps	28		10. Jimmy Wynn	50

1940's			1980's	
1. Dolph Camilli	79		1. Pedro Guerrero	83
2. Dixie Walker	65		2. Dusty Baker	66
3. Pee Wee Reese	52		3. Ron Cey	65
4. Peter Reiser	44		4. Steve Garvey	52
5. Jackie Robinson	40		5. Rick Monday	38
6. Joe Medwick	38		6. Ken Landreaux	31
7. Gil Hodges	35		7. Steve Yeager	22
8. Carl Furillo	33		8. Mike Marshall	22
9. Augie Galan	33		9. Greg Brock	20
10. Roy Campanella	31		10. Reggie Smith	16

EXTRA BASE HITS

Year-by-Year Leaders in Extra Base Hits

Year	Player	2B	3B	HR	Total
1884	Oscar Walker	12	8	2	22
1885	Germany Smith	17	11	4	32
1886	Bill McClellan	33	9	1	43
1887	Bill Phillips	34	11	2	47
1888	Dave Foutz	20	13	3	36
1889	Darby O'Brien	30	11	5	46
1890	Oyster Burns	22	13	13	48
1891	Mike Griffin	36	9	3	48
1892	Dan Brouthers	30	20	5	55
1893	Tom Daly	21	14	8	43
1894	Oyster Burns	32	14	5	51
1895	Mike Griffin	38	7	4	49
1896	John Anderson	23	17	1	41
1897	Candy LaChance	28	16	4	48
1898	Candy LaChance	23	7	5	35
1899	Joe Kelley	21	14	6	41
1900	Joe Kelley	23	17	6	46
1901	Jimmy Sheckard	31	19	11	61
1902	Bill Dahlen	26	7	2	35
1903	Jimmy Sheckard	29	9	9	47
1904	Harry Lumley	23	18	9	50
1905	Emil Batch (tie)	20	11	5	36
	Harry Lumley (tie)	19	10	7	36
1906	Harry Lumley	23	12	9	44
1907	Harry Lumley	23	11	9	43
1908	Tim Jordan	18	5	12	35
1909	Whitey Alperman	19	12	1	32
1910	Zach Wheat	36	15	2	53
1911	Zach Wheat	26	13	5	44
1912	Zach Wheat	28	7	8	43
1913	Red Smith	40	10	6	56
1914	Zach Wheat	26	9	9	44
1915	Casey Stengel	20	12	3	35
1916	Zach Wheat	32	13	9	54
1917	Casey Stengel	23	12	6	41
1918	Jake Daubert	12	15	2	29
1919	Hy Myers	23	14	5	42
1920	Hy Myers	36	22	4	62
1921	Jimmy Johnston	41	14	5	60
1922	Zach Wheat	29	12	16	57
1923	Jack Fournier	30	13	22	65
1924	Zach Wheat	41	8	14	63
1925	Zach Wheat	42	14	14	70
1926	Babe Herman	35	11	11	57
1927	Babe Herman	26	9	14	49
1928	Del Bissonette	30	13	25	68
1929	Johnny Frederick	52	6	24	82
1930	Babe Herman	48	11	35	94

Year-by-Year Leaders in Extra Base Hits (Continued)

Year	Player	2B	3B	HR	Total
1931	Babe Herman	43	16	18	77
1932	Hack Wilson	37	5	23	65
1933	Tony Cuccinello	31	4	9	44
1934	Len Koenecke	31	7	14	52
1935	Lonny Frey	35	11	11	57
1936	Buddy Hassett	29	11	3	43
1937	Babe Phelps	37	3	7	47
1938	Dolph Camilli	25	11	24	60
1939	Dolph Camilli	30	12	26	68
1940	Dolph Camilli	29	13	23	65
1941	Pete Reiser	39	17	14	70
1942	Dolph Camilli	23	7	26	56
1943	Arky Vaughan	39	6	5	50
1944	Augie Galan	43	9	12	64
1945	Dixie Walker	42	9	8	59
1946	Dixie Walker	29	9	9	47
1947	Jackie Robinson	31	5	12	48
1948	Jackie Robinson	38	8	12	58
1949	Jackie Robinson	38	12	16	66
1950	Duke Snider	31	10	31	72
1951	Gil Hodges	25	3	40	68
1952	Gil Hodges	27	1	32	60
1953	Duke Snider	38	4	42	84
1954	Duke Snider	39	10	40	89
1955	Duke Snider	34	6	42	82
1956	Duke Snider	33	2	43	78
1957	Duke Snider	25	7	40	72
1958	Carl Furillo	19	3	18	40
1959	Charlie Neal	30	11	19	60
1960	Frank Howard (tie)	15	2	23	40
	Wally Moon (tie)	21	6	13	40
1961	Wally Moon	25	3	17	45
1962	Tommy Davis	27	9	27	63
1963	Frank Howard	16	1	28	45
1964	Willie Davis	23	7	12	42
1965	Wes Parker	24	7	8	39
1966	Jim Lefebvre	23	3	24	50
1967	Willie Davis	27	9	6	42
1968	Willie Davis	24	10	7	41
1969	Willie Davis	23	8	11	42
1970	Wes Parker	47	4	10	61
1971	Willie Davis	33	10	10	53
1972	Willie Davis	22	7	19	48
1973	Willie Davis	29	9	16	54
1974	Steve Garvey	32	3	21	56
1975	Steve Garvey	38	6	18	62
1976	Steve Garvey	37	4	13	54
1977	Reggie Smith	27	4	32	63
1978	Steve Garvey	36	9	21	66
1979	Steve Garvey	32	1	28	61

Year-by-Year Leaders in Extra Base Hits (Continued)

Year	Player	2B	3B	HR	Total
1980	Dusty Baker	26	4	29	59
1981	Steve Garvey	23	1	10	34
1982	Pedro Guerrero	27	5	32	64
1983	Pedro Guerrero	28	6	32	66

50 Extra Base Hits in One Season

Player	2B	Date	3B	HR	Total
		1892			
Dan Brouthers	30		20	5	55
		1894			
Oyster Burns	32		14	5	51
		1901			
Jimmy Sheckard	31		19	11	61
Tom Daly	38		10	3	51
		1910			
Zach Wheat	36		15	2	53
		1913			
Red Smith	40		10	6	56
		1916			
Zach Wheat	32		13	9	54
		1920			
Hy Myers	36		22	4	62
		1921			
Jimmy Johnston	41		14	5	60
Zach Wheat	31		10	14	55
		1922			
Zach Wheat	29		12	16	57
		1923			
Jack Fournier	30		13	22	65
		1924			
Zach Wheat	41		8	14	63
Jack Fournier	25		4	27	56
		1925			
Zach Wheat	42		14	14	70
Jack Fournier	21		16	22	59
Eddie Brown	39		11	5	55
		1926			
Babe Herman	35		11	11	57
		1928			
Del Bissonette	30		13	25	68
Babe Herman	37		6	12	55
		1929			
Johnny Frederick	52		6	24	82
Babe Herman	42		13	21	76
Del Bissonette	28		10	12	50
		1930			
Babe Herman	48		11	35	94

50 Extra Base Hits in One Season (Continued)

Player	2B	Date	3B	HR	Total
Johnny Frederick	44		11	17	72
Del Bissonette	33		13	16	62
Glenn Wright	28		12	22	62
		1931			
Babe Herman	43		16	18	77
Johnny Frederick	34		8	17	59
Lefty O'Doul	32		11	7	50
		1932			
Hack Wilson	37		5	23	65
Lefty O'Doul	32		8	21	61
Joe Stripp	36		9	6	51
Tony Cuccinello	32		6	12	50
		1934			
Len Koenecke	31		7	14	52
		1935			
Lonny Frey	35		11	11	57
		1938			
Dolph Camilli	25		11	24	60
Ernie Koy	29		13	11	53
		1939			
Dolph Camilli	30		12	26	68
Ernie Koy	37		5	8	50
		1940			
Dolph Camilli	29		13	23	65
Dixie Walker	37		8	6	51
		1941			
Pete Reiser	39		17	14	70
Dolph Camilli	29		6	34	69
Joe Medwick	33		10	18	61
		1942			
Dolph Camilli	23		7	26	56
		1943			
Arky Vaughan	39		6	5	50
		1943			
Augie Galan	43		9	12	64
Dixie Walker	37		8	13	58
		1945			
Dixie Walker	42		9	8	59
Augie Galan	36		7	9	52
Luis Olmo	27		13	10	50
		1948			
Jackie Robinson	38		8	12	58
		1949			
Jackie Robinson	38		12	16	66
Duke Snider	28		7	23	58
Carl Furillo	27		10	18	55
Gil Hodges	23		4	23	50
		1950			
Duke Snider	31		10	31	72
Gil Hodges	26		2	32	60

50 Extra Base Hits in One Season (Continued)

Player	2B	Date	3B	HR	Total
Jackie Robinson	39		4	14	57
Carl Furillo	30		6	18	54
Roy Campanella	19		3	31	53
		1951			
Gil Hodges	25		3	40	68
Roy Campanella	33		1	33	67
Duke Snider	26		6	29	61
Jackie Robinson	33		7	19	59
Carl Furillo	32		4	16	52
		1952			
Gil Hodges	27		1	32	60
Duke Snider	25		7	21	53
		1953			
Duke Snider	38		4	42	84
Roy Campanella	26		3	41	70
Carl Furillo	38		6	21	65
Gil Hodges	22		7	31	60
Jim Gilliam	31		17	6	54
Jackie Robinson	34		7	12	53
		1954			
Duke Snider	39		10	40	89
Gil Hodges	23		5	42	70
Pee Wee Reese	35		8	10	53
		1955			
Duke Snider	34		6	42	82
Gil Hodges	24		5	27	56
Roy Campanella	20		1	32	53
Carl Furillo	24		3	26	53
		1956			
Duke Snider	33		2	43	78
Gil Hodges	29		4	32	65
Carl Furillo	30		0	21	51
		1957			
Duke Snider	25		7	40	72
Gil Hodges	28		7	27	62
		1959			
Charlie Neal	30		11	19	60
Wally Moon	26		11	19	56
		1962			
Tommy Davis	27		9	27	63
Frank Howard	25		6	31	62
		1966			
Jim Lefebvre	23		3	24	50
		1970			
Wes Parker	47		4	10	61
		1971			
Willie Davis	33		10	10	53
		1973			
Willie Davis	29		9	16	54
Joe Ferguson	26		0	25	51

50 Extra Base Hits in One Season (Continued)

Player	2B	Date	3B	HR	Total
		1974			
Steve Garvey	32		3	21	56
Jimmy Wynn	17		4	32	53
		1975			
Steve Garvey	38		6	18	62
Ron Cey	29		2	25	56
		1976			
Steve Garvey	37		4	13	54
		1977			
Reggie Smith	27		4	32	63
Steve Garvey	25		3	33	61
Dusty Baker	26		1	30	57
Ron Cey	22		3	30	55
		1978			
Steve Garvey	36		9	21	66
Reggie Smith	27		2	29	58
Ron Cey	32		0	23	55
		1979			
Steve Garvey	32		1	28	61
Davey Lopes	20		6	28	54
Dusty Baker	29		1	23	53
		1980			
Dusty Baker	26		4	29	59
Steve Garvey	27		1	26	54
Ron Cey	25		0	28	53
		1982			
Pedro Guerrero	27		5	32	64
Steve Garvey	35		1	16	52
		1983			
Pedro Guerrero	28		6	32	66

Players With 200-or-More Extra Base Hits

Player	2B	3B	HR	Total
Duke Snider	343	82	389	814
Zach Wheat	464	171	131	766
Gil Hodges	294	48	361	703
Willie Davis	321	110	154	585
Steve Garvey	333	35	211	579
Carl Furillo	324	56	192	572
Pee Wee Reese	330	80	126	536
Ron Cey	223	18	228	469
Jackie Robinson	273	54	137	464
Jim Gilliam	304	71	65	440
Roy Campanella	178	18	242	438
Babe Herman	232	66	112	410
Dixie Walker	274	56	67	397
Bill Russell	264	55	46	365
Dolph Camilli	151	55	139	345
Dusty Baker	169	12	144	325
Johnny Frederick	200	35	85	320

Players With 200-or-More Extra Base Hits (Continued)

Player	2B	3B	HR	Total
Tom Daly	190	76	44	310
Davey Lopes	165	39	99	303
Mike Griffin	210	64	28	302
John Roseboro	162	44	92	298
Wes Parker	194	32	64	290
Hy Myers	155	97	29	281
Ron Fairly	168	22	90	280
Jimmy Sheckard	162	78	36	276
Jimmy Johnston	181	73	20	274
Jake Daubert	138	87	33	258
John Hummel	127	82	29	238
Del Bissonette	117	50	66	233
Maury Wills	150	56	17	223
Steve Yeager	108	15	96	219
Jim Lefebvre	126	18	74	218
Frank Howard	80	14	123	217
Tommy Davis	109	22	86	217
George Pinckney	146	48	20	214
Harry Lumley	109	66	38	213
Cookie Lavagetto	143	28	35	206
Pete Reiser	135	35	34	204
Augie Galan	146	24	33	203
Jack Fournier	85	35	82	202

Extra Base Hits by Position (Season)

	Modern, Brooklyn		2B 3B HR Total
1B	Dolph Camilli	1941	29- 6-34—69
2B	Jackie Robinson	1949	38-12-16—66
SS	Glenn Wright	1930	28-12-22—62
3B	Jimmy Johnston	1921	41-14- 5—60
OF	Babe Herman	1930	48-11-35—94
OF	Duke Snider	1954	39-10-40—89
OF	Johnny Frederick	1929	52- 6-24—82
C	Roy Campanella	1953	26- 3-41—70

Los Angeles

2B	Steve Garvey	1978	36- 9-21—66
2B	Charlie Neal	1959	30-11-19—60
SS	Bill Russell	1978	32- 4- 3—39
3B	Pedro Guerrero	1983	28-6-32—66
OF	Pedro Guerrero	1982	27- 5-32—64
OF	Tommy Davis	1962	27- 9-27—63
OF	Reggie Smith	1977	27- 4-32—63
C	Joe Ferguson	1973	26- 0-25—51

19th Century

1B	Dan Brouthers	1892	30-20- 5—55
2B	Bil McClellan	1886	33- 9- 1—43
	Tom Daly	1893	21-14- 8—43

Extra Base Hits by Position (Season) (Continued)

			2B	3B	HR	Total
SS	Tommy Corcoran	1894	21-	20-	5—	46
3B	Bill Shindle	1897	32-	6-	3-	41
OF	Oyster Burns	1894	32-	14-	5—	51
OF	Mike Griffin	1895	38-	7-	4—	49
OF	Darby O'Brien	1889	30-	11-	5—	46
C	John Grim	1895	17-	5-	0—	22

All-Time

			2B	3B	HR	Total
1B	Dolph Camilli	1941	29-	6-	34—	69
2B	Jackie Robinson	1949	38-	12-	16—	66
SS	Glenn Wright	1930	28-	12-	22—	62
3B	Pedro Guerrero	1983	28-	6-	32—	66
OF	Babe Herman	1930	48-	11-	35 —	94
OF	Duke Snider	1954	39-	10-	40—	89
OF	Johnny Frederick	1929	52-	6-	25—	82
C	Johnny Campanella	1953	26-	3-	41—	70

Speedster Willie Davis had 585 extra base hits during his Dodger career.

LEADERS IN RUNS SCORED

Year-by-Year Leaders in Runs Scored

Year	Player	Total	Year	Player	Total
1884	Oscar Walker	59	1928	Del Bissonette	90
1885	Bill McClellan	85	1929	Johnny Frederick	127
1886	Bill McClellan	131	1930	Babe Herman	143
1887	George Pinckney	133	1931	Babe Herman	93
1888*	George Pinckney	134	1932	Lefty O'Doul	120
1889	Darby O'Brien	146	1933	Joe Stripp	69
1890*	Hub Collins	148	1934	Buzz Boyle	88
1891	Mike Griffin	106	1935	Lonny Frey	88
1892	Dan Brouthers	121	1936	Buddy Hassett	79
1893	Tom Daly	94	1937	Buddy Hassett	71
1894	Tom Daly	135	1938	Dolph Camilli	106
1895	Mike Griffin	140	1939	Dolph Camilli	105
1896	Mike Griffin	101	1940	Dolph Camilli	92
1897	Mike Griffin	136	1941*	Pete Reiser	117
1898	Fielder Jones	89	1942	Dolph Camilli	89
1899*	Willie Keeler	140		Pete Reiser	89
1900	Fielder Jones	108	1943*	Arky Vaughan	112
1901	Willie Keeler	124	1944	Augie Galan	96
1902	Willie Keeler	84	1945*	Eddie Stanky	128
	Jimmy Sheckard	84	1946	Eddie Stanky	98
1903	Sammy Strang	101	1947	Jackie Robinson	125
1904	Harry Lumley	79	1948	Jackie Robinson	108
1905	Emil Batch	64	1949*	Pee Wee Reese	132
1906	Harry Lumley	72	1950	Duke Snider	109
1907	Doc Casey	55	1951	Gil Hodges	118
1908	Tim Jordan	58	1952	Jackie Robinson	104
1909	Al Burch	80	1953*	Duke Snider	132
1910	Zach Wheat	78	1954*	Duke Snider	120
1911	Jake Daubert	89	1955*	Duke Snider	126
1912	Jake Daubert	81	1956	Duke Snider	112
1913	Jake Daubert	76	1957	Gil Hodges	94
1914	Jake Daubert	89	1958	Charlie Neal	87
1915	Ollie O'Mara	77	1959	Charlie Neal	103
1916	Zach Wheat	76	1960	Jim Gilliam	96
1917	Casey Stengel	69	1961	Maury Wills	105
1918	Ivy Olson	63	1962	Maury Wills	130
1919	Ivy Olson	73	1963	Maury Wills	83
1920	Zach Wheat	89	1964	Willie Davis	91
1921	Jimmy Johnston	104	1965	Maury Wills	92
1922	Jimmy Johnston	110	1966	Willie Davis	74
1923	Jimmy Johnston	111	1967	Willie Davis	65
1924	Andy High	98	1968	Willie Davis	86
1925	Zach Wheat	125	1969	Wes Parker	76
1926	Zach Wheat	68	1970	Willie Davis	92
1927	Jay Partridge	72		Billy Grabarkewitz	92
			1971	Willie Davis	84
			1972	Willie Davis	81

*Led League

Year-by-Year Leaders in Runs Scored (Continued)

Year	Player	Total	Year	Player	Total
1973	Joe Ferguson	84	1978	Davey Lopes	93
1974	Jimmy Wynn	104	1979	Davey Lopes	109
1975	Davey Lopes	108	1980	Ron Cey	81
1976	Steve Garvey	85	1981	Steve Garvey	63
1977	Reggie Smith	104	1982	Steve Sax	88
			1983	Steve Sax	94

*Led League

Steve Sax led the Dodgers in runs scored in both 1982 and 1983.

100-or-More Runs Scored in a Season

1886
Bill McClellan	131
George Pinckney	119

1887
George Pinckney	133
Jim McTamany	123
Bill McClellan	109

1888
George Pinckney	134
Darby O'Brien	105

1889
Darby O'Brien	146
Hub Collins	139
Dave Foutz	118
Oyster Burns	105
George Pinckney	103

1890
Hub Collins	148
George Pinckney	115
Dave Foutz	106
Oyster Burns	102

1891
Mike Griffin	106

1892
Dan Brouthers	121
Monte Ward	109
Mike Griffin	103

1894
Tom Daly	135
George Treadway	124
Tommy Corcoran	123
Mike Griffin	123
Oyster Burns	109

1895
Mike Griffin	140

1896
Mike Griffin	101

1897
Mike Griffin	136
Fielder Jones	134

1899
Willie Keeler	140
Joe Kelley	108

1900
Fielder Jones	108
Willie Keeler	106

1901
Willie Keeler	124
Jimmy Sheckard	116

1903
Sammy Strang	101

1921
Jimmy Johnston	104

1922
Jimmy Johnston	110

1923
Jimmy Johnston	111

1925
Zach Wheat	125

1929
Johnny Frederick	127
Babe Herman	105

1930
Babe Herman	143
Johnny Frederick	120
Del Bissonette	102

1932
Lefty O'Doul	120

1938
Dolph Camilli	106

1939
Dolph Camilli	105

1941
Pete Reiser	117
Joe Medwick	100

1943
Arky Vaughan	112

1945
Eddie Stanky	128
Goody Rosen	126
Augie Galan	114
Dixie Walker	102

100-or-More Runs Scored in a Season (Continued)

1947			1955		
Jackie Robinson	125		Duke Snider		126
			Jim Gilliam		110
1948					
Jackie Robinson	108		**1956**		
			Duke Snider		112
1949			Jim Gilliam		102
Pee Wee Reese	132				
Jackie Robinson	122		**1959**		
Duke Snider	100		Charlie Neal		103
1950			**1961**		
Duke Snider	109		Maury Wills		105
1951			**1962**		
Gil Hodges	118		Maury Wills		130
Jackie Robinson	106		Tommy Davis		120
			Willie Davis		103
1952					
Jackie Robinson	104		**1974**		
			Jimmy Wynn		104
1953					
Duke Snider	132		**1975**		
Jim Gilliam	125		Davey Lopes		108
Jackie Robinson	109				
Pee Wee Reese	108		**1977**		
Roy Campanella	103		Reggie Smith		104
Gil Hodges	101				
			1979		
1954			Davey Lopes		109
Duke Snider	120				
Jim Gilliam	107				
Gil Hodges	106				

Career Leaders in Runs Scored

Player	Total	Player	Total
Pee Wee Reese	1,338	Jimmy Johnston	727
Zach Wheat	1,255	Ron Cey	715
Duke Snider	1,199	Bill Russell	684
Jim Gilliam	1,163	Dixie Walker	666
Gil Hodges	1,088	Jake Daubert	648
Willie Davis	1,004	Roy Campanella	627
Jackie Robinson	947	Dave Foutz	580
Carl Furillo	895	Jimmy Sheckard	564
Mike Griffin	882	Dusty Baker	549
Maury Wills	876	Wes Parker	548
Steve Garvey	852	Babe Herman	540
Tom Daly	787	Dolph Camilli	540
George Pinckney	761	Wally Gilbert	534
Davey Lopes	759	Hy Myers	512
Bill Russell	731	Johnny Frederick	498

Career Leaders in Runs Scored (Continued)

Player	Total	Player	Total
Ron Fairly	491	George Cutshaw	350
Fielder Jones	488	Bill Buckner	347
Ivy Olson	486	Joe Stripp	345
Darby O'Brien	480	Billy Cox	334
Willie Keeler	469	John Anderson	332
Germany Smith	467	Tommy Griffith	331
John Roseboro	441	Steve Yeager	327
Willie Crawford	437	Jack Fournier	322
John Hummel	412	Reggie Smith	314
Pete Reiser	400	Jim Lefebvre	313
Cookie Lavagetto	398	Casey Stengel	311
Bill Shindle	394	Frenchy Bordagaray	307
Tommy Davis	392	Harry Lumley	300
Hub Collins	390	Frank Howard	293
Bill Dahlen	382	Al Lopez	289
Charlie Neal	374	Danny Taylor	284
Augie Galan	373	Joe Kelley	275
Wally Moon	373	Goody Rosen	271
Del Bissonette	359	Pedro Guerrero	257
Candy LaChance	356	Billy Herman	253
Eddie Stanky	355	Joe Medwick	251

Five-or-More Runs in a Game

Date	Player	Total
June 21, 1901	Willie Keeler	5
September 23, 1901	Tom Daly	5
April 24, 1902	Willie Keeler	5
June 10, 1922	Jimmy Johnston	5
May 18, 1929	Johnny Frederick	5
May 21, 1949	Pee Wee Reese	5
June 20, 1949	Bruce Edwards	5
August 31, 1950	Gil Hodges	5
May 26, 1970	Billy Grabarkewitz	5
August 28, 1977	Steve Garvey	5

Runs Scored by Position (Season)

Modern, Brooklyn

1B	Jackie Robinson	1947	125
2B	Eddie Stanky	1945	128
SS	Pee Wee Reese	1949	132
3B	Jimmy Johnston	1921	104
OF	Babe Herman	1930	143
OF	Duke Snider	1953	132
OF	Johnny Frederick	1929	127
C	Roy Campanella	1953	103

Los Angeles

1B	Steve Garvey	1974	95
2B	Davey Lopes	1979	109
SS	Maury Wills	1962	130
3B	Jim Gilliam	1960	96
OF	Tommy Davis	1962	120
OF	Jimmy Wynn	1974	104
OF	Reggie Smith	1977	104
C	Joe Ferguson	1973	84

19th Century

1B	Dan Brouthers	1892	121
2B	Hub Collins	1890	148
SS	Tommy Corcoran	1894	123
3B	George Pinckney	1888	134
OF	Darby O'Brien	1889	146
OF	Mike Griffin	1895	140
OF	Willie Keeler	1899	140
C	Tom Daly	1890	55

All-Time

1B	Jackie Robinson	1947	125
2B	Hub Collins	1890	148
SS	Pee Wee Reese	1949	132
3B	George Pinckney	1888	134
OF	Darby O'Brien	1889	146
OF	Babe Herman	1930	143
OF	Mike Griffin	1895	140
	Willie Keeler	1899	140
C	Roy Campanella	1953	103

RBI RECORDS
All-Time RBI Leaders

Player	Total	Player	Total
Duke Snider	1,271	George Cutshaw	360
Gil Hodges	1,254	Steve Yeager	360
Zach Wheat	1,223	John Anderson	353
Carl Furillo	1,058	Tommy Griffith	340
Steve Garvey	992	Willie Crawford	335
Pee Wee Reese	885	Wally Moon	330
Roy Campanella	856	Joe Ferguson	325
Willie Davis	849	Darby O'Brien	321
Ron Cey	842	Augie Galan	316
Jackie Robinson	734	Charlie Neal	312
Dixie Walker	725	Harry Lumley	305
Oyster Burns	614	Reggie Smith	301
Tom Daly	611	Pete Reiser	298
Babe Herman	594	Ivy Olson	297
Dusty Baker	586	Joe Medwick	293
Bill Russell	577	Casey Stengel	292
Dolph Camilli	572	Pedro Guerrero	292
Jim Gilliam	558	Babe Phelps	290
Dave Foutz	548	George Pinckney	288
Mike Griffin	544	Joe Stripp	284
Ron Fairly	541	Al Lopez	274
Hy Myers	496	Joe Kelley	249
John Roseboro	471	Luis Olmo	246
Wes Parker	470	Billy Cox	245
Tommy Davis	465	Glenn Wright	242
Jimmy Sheckard	420	Sam Leslie	241
Jake Daubert	415	Billy Herman	234
Jim Lefebvre	404	Otto Miller	231
Jack Fournier	396	Hank DeBerry	229
Cookie Lavagetto	395	Manny Mota	226
Del Bissonette	391	Rube Bressler	225
John Hummel	390	Willie Keeler	221
Jimmy Johnston	390	Danny Taylor	219
Davey Lopes	385	Harvey Hendrick	219
Frank Howard	382	Rick Monday	219
Candy LaChance	379	Bruce Edwards	208
Johnny Frederick	377	Hack Wilson	204
Maury Wills	374	Gene Hermanski	200
Bill Shindle	372	Reggie Smith	200
Bill Dahlen	365		

100-or-More RBI's, Season

1889	
Dave Foutz	113
Oyster Burns	100

1890	
Oyster Burns	128

1892	
Dan Brouthers	124

1894	
Oyster Burns	109
George Treadway	102

1895	
Candy LaChance	108

1897	
Bill Shindle	105

1901	
Jimmy Sheckard	104

1922	
Zach Wheat	112

1923	
Jack Fournier	102

1924	
Jack Fournier	116

1925	
Jack Fournier	130
Zach Wheat	103

1928	
Del Bissonette	106

1929	
Babe Herman	113

1930	
Babe Herman	130
Glenn Wright	126
Del Bissonette	113

1932	
Hack Wilson	123

1934	
Sam Leslie	102

1938	
Dolph Camilli	10C

1939	
Dolph Camilli	104

1941	
Dolph Camilli	120

1942	
Dolph Camilli	109

1943	
Billy Herman	100

1945	
Dixie Walker	124
Luis Olmo	110

1946	
Dixie Walker	116

1949	
Jackie Robinson	124
Gil Hodges	15
Carl Furillo	106

1950	
Gil Hodges	113
Duke Snider	107
Carl Furillo	106

1951	
Roy Campanella	108
Gil Hodges	103
Duke Snider	101

1952	
Gil Hodges	102

1953	
Roy Campanella	142
Duke Snider	126
Gil Hodges	122

1954	
Gil Hodges	130
Duke Snider	130

1955	
Duke Snider	136
Roy Campanella	107
Gil Hodges	102

100-or-More RBI's, Season (Continued)

1956			1977		
Duke Snider	101		Steve Garvey	115	
1962			Ron Cey	110	
Tommy Davis	153		1978		
Frank Howard	119		Steve Garvey	113	
1970			1979		
Wes Parker	111		Steve Garvey	110	
1974			1980		
Steve Garvey	111		Steve Garvey	106	
Jimmy Wynn	108		1982		
1975			Pedro Guerrero	100	
Ron Cey	101		1983		
			Pedro Guerrero	103	

9 RBI's in One Game

GIL HODGES
August 31, 1950
Dodgers 19, Braves 3
At Ebbets Field, Brooklyn

Second Inning—Homer	2 on
Third Inning—Homer	1 on
Sixth Inning—Homer	1 on
Eighth Inning—Homer	1 on
	9 RBI's

8 RBI's in One Game

GIL HODGES
June 12, 1949
Dodgers 20, Reds 7
At Ebbets Field, Brooklyn

Fifth Inning—Single	1 on
Homer	2 on
Seventh Inning—Homer	3 on
	8 RBI's

RON CEY
July 31, 1974
Dodgers 15, Padres 4
At San Diego Stadium

Third Inning—Single	3 on
Eighth Inning—Homer	2 on
Ninth Inning—Homer	2 on
	8 RBI's

5 RBI's in One Inning

DUSTY BAKER

September 13, 1977
Dodgers 18, Padres 4
At Dodger Stadium, Los Angeles
During 10-run Second Inning

First at-bat—Double	2 on
Second at-bat—Homer	2 on
	5 RBI's

RBI Leaders

And All Dodgers with 100-or-More RBI's

Year	Player	Total	Year	Player	Total
	(Note: 1884-1887 not available)				
1888	Dave Foutz	99	1918	Zach Wheat	51
1889	Dave Foutz	113	1919*	Hy Myers	73
	Oyster Burns	100	1920	Hy Myers	80
1890*	Oyster Burns	128	1921	Zach Wheat	85
1891	Oyster Burns	83	1922	Zach Wheat	112
1892*	Dan Brouthers	124	1923	Jack Fournier	102
1893	Tom Daly	70	1924	Jack Fournier	116
1894	Oyster Burns	109	1925	Jack Fournier	130
	George Treadway	102		Zach Wheat	103
1895	Candy LaChance	108	1926	Babe Herman	81
1896	Tommy Corcoran	73	1927	Babe Herman	73
1897	Bill Shindle	105	1928	Del Bissonette	106
1898	Fielder Jones	69	1929	Babe Herman	113
1899	Joe Kelley	93	1930	Babe Herman	130
1900	Joe Kelley	91		Glenn Wright	126
1901	Jimmy Sheckard	104		Del Bissonette	113
1902	Bill Dahlen	74	1931	Babe Herman	97
1903	Jack Doyle	91	1932	Hack Wilson	123
1904	Harry Lumley	78	1933	Tony Cuccinello	65
1905	Emil Batch	49	1934	Sam Leslie	102
1906	Tim Jordan	78	1935	Sam Leslie	93
1907	Harry Lumley	66	1936	Buddy Hassett	82
1908	Tim Jordan	60	1937	Heinie Manush	73
1909	John Hummel	52	1938	Dolph Camilli	100
1910	John Hummel	74	1939	Dolph Camilli	104
1911	Zach Wheat	76	1940	Dolph Camilli	96
1912	Jake Daubert	66	1941*	Dolph Camilli	120
1913	George Cutshaw	80	1942	Dolph Camilli	109
1914	Zach Wheat	89	1943	Billy Herman	100
1915	Zach Wheat	66	1944	Augie Galan	93
1916	Zach Wheat	73	1945*	Dixie Walker	124
1917	Casey Stengel	73		Luis Olmo	110

*Led League

And All Dodgers with 100-or-More RBI's (Continued)

Year	Player	Total	Year	Player	Total
1946	Dixie Walker	116	1961	Wally Moon	88
1947	Dixie Walker	94	1962*	Tommy Davis	153
1948	Jackie Robinson	85		Frank Howard	119
1949	Jackie Robinson	124	1963	Tommy Davis	88
	Gil Hodges	115	1964	Tommy Davis	86
	Carl Furillo	106	1965	Ron Fairly	70
1950	Gil Hodges	113	1966	Jim Lefebvre	74
	Duke Snider	107	1967	Ron Fairly	55
	Carl Furillo	106	1968	Tom Haller	53
1951	Roy Campanella	108	1969	Andy Kosco	74
	Gil Hodges	103	1970	Wes Parker	111
	Duke Snider	101	1971	Richie Allen	90
1952	Gil Hodges	102	1972	Willie Davis	79
1953*	Roy Campanella	142	1973	Joe Ferguson	88
	Duke Snider	126	1974	Steve Garvey	111
	Gil Hodges	122		Jimmy Wynn	108
1954	Gil Hodges	130	1975	Ron Cey	101
	Duke Snider	130	1976	Ron Cey	80
1955*	Duke Snider	136		Steve Garvey	80
	Roy Campanella	107	1977	Steve Garvey	115
	Gil Hodges	102		Ron Cey	110
1956	Duke Snider	101	1978	Steve Garvey	113
1957	Gil Hodges	98	1979	Steve Garvey	110
1958	Carl Furillo	83	1980	Steve Garvey	106
1959	Duke Snider	88	1981	Steve Garvey	65
1960	Norm Larker	78	1982	Pedro Guerrero	100
			1983	Pedro Guerrero	103

*Led League

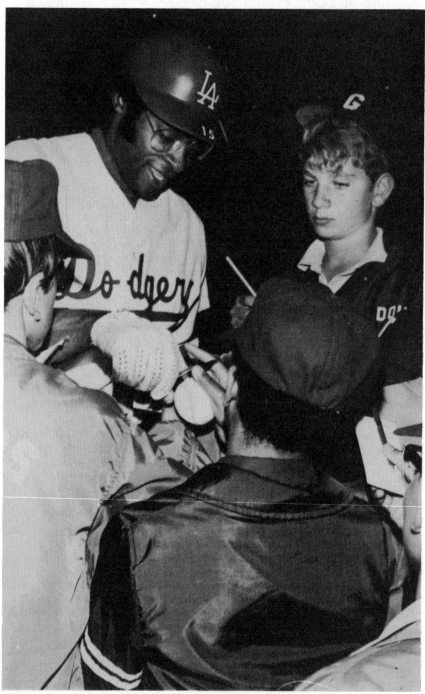

Richie Allen led the Dodgers with 90 RBI's in 1971.

Miscellaneous RBI Records

Miscellaneous RBI Records

Most RBI's, Lifetime	1271	Duke Snider
	992	Steve Garvey (Los Angeles)
Most RBI's, Season	153	Tommy Davis, 1962
	142	Roy Campanella, 1953 (Brooklyn)
Most RBI's, Two Consecutive Seasons	246	Jack Fournier, 1924 (116), 1925 (130)
	241	Tommy Davis, 1962 (153), 1963 (88) (Los Angeles)
Most RBI's, Game	9	Gil Hodges, August 31, 1950
	8	Ron Cey, July 31, 1974 (Los Angeles)
Most RBI's, Inning	5	Dusty Baker, September 13, 1977
Most Years, 100 RBI's	7	Gil Hodges, 1949-50-51-52-53-54-55
	5	Steve Garvey, 1974-77-78-79-80
Most RBI's, Right-Handed Batter	153	Tommy Davis, 1962
Most RBI's, Left-Handed Batter	130	Jack Fournier, 1925
		Babe Herman, 1930
Most RBI's, Month	41	Frank Howard, August, 1962

RBI's by Position (Season)

Modern, Brooklyn

1B	Jack Fournier	1925	130
	Gil Hodges	1954	130
2B	Jackie Robinson	1949	124
SS	Glenn Wright	1930	126
3B	Cookie Lavegetto	1939	87
OF	Duke Snider	1955	136
OF	Babe Herman	1930	130
OF	Dixie Walker	1945	124
C	Roy Campanella	1953	142

RBI's by Position (Season) (Continued)

Los Angeles

1B	Steve Garvey	1977	115
2B	Charlie Neal	1959	83
SS	Bill Russell	1974-76	65
3B	Ron Cey	1977	110
OF	Tommy Davis	1962	153
OF	Frank Howard	1962	119
OF	Jimmy Wynn	1974	108
C	Joe Ferguson	1973	88

19th Century

1B	Dan Brouthers	1892	124
2B	Tom Daly	1899	88
SS	Tommy Corcoran	1894	92
3B	Bill Shindle	1897	105
OF	Oyster Burns	1890	128
OF	George Treadway	1894	102
OF	Dave Foutz	1888	99
C	Joe Visner	1889	68

All-Time

1B	Jack Fournier	1925	130
	Gil Hodges	1954	130
2B	Jackie Robinson	1949	124
SS	Glenn Wright	1930	126
3B	Ron Cey	1977	110
OF	Tommy Davis	1962	153
OF	Duke Snider	1955	136
OF	Babe Herman	1930	130
C	Roy Campanella	1953	142

SLUGGING

Year-by-Year Leaders in Slugging Average

Year	Player	Total	Year	Player	Total
1884	Oscar Walker	.359	1896	John Anderson	.453
1885	Bill Phillips	.422	1897	John Anderson	.455
1886	Jim McTamany	.371	1898	Jimmy Sheckard	.406
1887	Adonis Terry	.392	1899	Willie Keeler	.454
1888	Dave Foutz	.375		Joe Kelley	.454
1889	Oyster Burns	.423	1901*	Jimmy Sheckard	.536
1890	Oyster Burns	.468	1902	Willie Keeler	.396
1891	Oyster Burns	.417	1903	Jimmy Sheckard	.476
1892	Dan Brouthers	.480	1904	Harry Lumley	.428
1893	Tom Daly	.445	1905	Harry Lumley	.412
1894	George Treadway	.518	1906*	Harry Lumley	.477
1895	Mike Griffin	.458	1907	Harry Lumley	.425

*Led League

Year-by-Year Leaders in Slugging Average (Continued)

Year	Player	Total	Year	Player	Total
1908	Tim Jordan	.371	1945	Luis Olmo	.462
1909	Tim Jordan	.379	1946	Dixie Walker	.448
1910	Zach Wheat	.403	1947	Carl Furillo	.437
1911	Zach Wheat	.412	1948	Gene Hermanski	.493
1912	Zach Wheat	.450	1949	Jackie Robinson	.528
1913	Red Smith	.441	1950	Duke Snider	.553
1914	Zach Wheat	.452	1951	Roy Campanella	.590
1915	Jake Daubert	.381	1952	Gil Hodges	.500
1916*	Zach Wheat	.461	1953*	Duke Snider	.627
1917	Zach Wheat	.423	1954	Duke Snider	.647
1918	Jake Daubert	.429	1955	Duke Snider	.628
1919*	Hy Myers	.436	1956*	Duke Snider	.598
1920	Zach Wheat	.463	1957	Duke Snider	.587
1921	Zach Wheat	.484	1958	Duke Snider	.505
1922	Zach Wheat	.503	1959	Duke Snider	.535
1923	Jack Fournier	.588	1960	Frank Howard	.464
1924	Zach Wheat	.549	1961	Wally Moon	.505
1925	Jack Fournier	.569	1962	Frank Howard	.560
1926	Babe Herman	.500	1963	Frank Howard	.518
1927	Babe Herman	.481	1964	Frank Howard	.432
1928	Del Bissonette	.543	1965	Lou Johnson	.391
1929	Babe Herman	.612	1966	Ron Fairly	.464
1930	Babe Herman	.678	1967	Al Ferrara	.467
1931	Babe Herman	.525	1968	Len Gabrielson	.428
1932	Lefty O'Doul	.555	1969	Willie Davis	.456
1933	Danny Taylor	.469	1970	Tom Haller	.465
1934	Len Koenecke	.509	1971	Richie Allen	.468
1935	Lonny Frey	.437	1972	Frank Robinson	.442
1936	Babe Phelps	.498	1973	Joe Ferguson	.470
1937	Babe Phelps	.469	1974	Jimmy Wynn	.497
1938	Dolph Camilli	.485	1975	Steve Garvey	.476
1939	Dolph Camilli	.524	1976	Ron Cey	.462
1940	Dolph Camilli	.529	1977	Reggie Smith	.576
1941*	Pete Reiser	.558	1978	Reggie Smith	.559
1942	Dolph Camilli	.471	1979	Ron Cey	.499
1943	Billy Herman	.417	1980	Reggie Smith	.508
1944	Dixie Walker	.529	1981	Ron Cey	.474
			1982	Pedro Guerrero	.536
			1983	Pedro Guerrero	.565

*Led League

(Note: Slugging averages based on at least 300 at bats.)

.500 Sluggers in One Season

1894
George Treadway	.518
Oyster Burns	.507

1901
Jimmy Sheckard	.536

1922
Zach Wheat	.503

1923
Jack Fournier	.588
Zach Wheat	.510

1924
Zach Wheat	.549
Jack Fournier	.536

1925
Jack Fournier	.569
Zach Wheat	.541

1926
Babe Herman	.500

1928
Del Bissonette	.543
Babe Herman	.514

1929
Babe Herman	.612
Harvey Hendrick	.560
Johnny Frederick	.545

1930
Babe Herman	.678
Glenn Wright	.543
Johnny Frederick	.524

1931
Babe Herman	.525

1932
Lefty O'Doul	.555
Hack Wilson	.538
Johnny Frederick	.508

1934
Len Koenecke	.509

1939
Dolph Camilli	.524

1940
Dolph Camilli	.529

1941
Pete Reiser	.558
Dolph Camilli	.556
Joe Medwick	.517

1944
Dixie Walker	.529

1949
Jackie Robinson	.528
Carl Furillo	.506

1950
Duke Snider	.553
Roy Campanella	.551
Gil Hodges	.508
Jackie Robinson	.500

1951
Roy Campanella	.590
Gil Hodges	.527
Jackie Robinson	.527

1952
Gil Hodges	.500

1953
Duke Snider	.627
Roy Campanella	.611
Carl Furillo	.580
Gil Hodges	.550
Jackie Robinson	.502

1954
Duke Snider	.647
Gil Hodges	.579
Jackie Robinson	.505

1955
Duke Snider	.628
Roy Campanella	.583
Carl Furillo	.520
Gil Hodges	.500

1956
Duke Snider	.598
Gil Hodges	.507

1957
Duke Snider	.587
Gil Hodges	.511

.500 Sluggers in One Season (Continued)

1958		1977	
Duke Snider	.505	Reggie Smith	.576
		Dusty Baker	.512
1959			
Duke Snider	.535	1978	
Gil Hodges	.513	Reggie Smith	.559
1961		1980	
Wally Moon	.505	Reggie Smith	.508
		Dusty Baker	.503
1962			
Frank Howard	.560	1982	
Tommy Davis	.535	Pedro Guerrero	.536
1963		1983	
Frank Howard	.518	Pedro Guerrero	.565

Slugging by Position (Season)

Modern, Brooklyn

1B	Jack Fournier	1923	.588
2B	Jackie Robinson	1949	.528
SS	Glenn Wright	1930	.543
3B	Jimmy Johnston	1921	.460
OF	Babe Herman	1930	.678
OF	Duke Snider	1954	.647
OF	Pete Reiser	1941	.558
C	Roy Campanella	1953	.611

Los Angeles

1B	Gil Hodges	1959	.513
2B	Charlie Neal	1959	.464
	Davey Lopes	1979	.464
SS	Maury Wills	1962	.373
3B	Pedro Guerrero	1983	.565
OF	Reggie Smith	1977	.576
OF	Frank Howard	1962	.560
OF	Pedro Guerrero	1982	.536
C	Joe Ferguson	1973	.470

19th Century

1B	Candy LaChance	1894	.494
2B	Tom Daly	1894	.476
SS	Tommy Corcoran	1894	.432
3B	George Pinckney	1890	.431
OF	George Treadway	1894	.518
OF	Oyster Burns	1894	.507
OF	Mike Griffin	1894	.499
C	Tom Kinslow	1892	.443

Slugging by Position (Season) (Continued)

All-Time

1B	Jack Fournier	1923	.588
2B	Jackie Robinson	1949	.528
SS	Glenn Wright	1930	.543
3B	Pedro Guerrero	1983	.565
OF	Babe Herman	1930	.678
OF	Duke Snider	1954	.647
OF	Reggie Smith	1977	.576
C	Roy Campanella	1953	.611

.400 Lifetime Sluggers (500-game minimum)

Player	Years	Average
Babe Herman	(1926-1931; 1945)	.557
Duke Snider	(1947-1962)	.553
Jack Fournier	(1923-1926)	.551
Reggie Smith	(1976-1981)	.527
Pedro Guerrero	(1978-1983)	.512
Dolph Camilli	(1938-1943)	.511
Roy Campanella	(1948-1957)	.500
Frank Howard	(1958-1964)	.495
Del Bissonette	(1928-1931; 1933)	.486
Johnny Frederick	(1929-1934)	.477
Babe Phelps	(1935-1941)	.475
Jackie Robinson	(1947-1956)	.474
Steve Garvey	(1969-1982)	.467
Carl Furillo	(1946-1960)	.458
Zach Wheat	(1909-1926)	.452
Pete Reiser	(1940-1942; 1946-1948)	.447
Dixie Walker	(1939-1947)	.441
Tommy Davis	(1959-1966)	.441
Gene Hermanski	(1943; 1946-1951)	.440
Augie Galan	(1941-1946)	.438
Willie Keeler	(1893; 1899-1902)	.438
Dusty Baker	(1976-1983)	.437
Wally Moon	(1959-1965)	.435
Jimmy Sheckard	(1897-1898; 1900-1905)	.429
Candy LaChance	(1893-1898)	.420
Mike Griffin	(1891-1898)	.416
Willie Davis	(1960-1973)	.413
Willie Crawford	(1964-1975)	.413
Tom Daly	(1890-1896; 1898-1901)	.412
Tony Cuccinello	(1932-1935)	.410
Charlie Neal	(1956-1961)	.409
Harry Lumley	(1904-1910)	.408

TOTAL BASES

Year-by-Year Leaders in Total Bases

Year	Player	Total	Year	Player	Total
1884	John Cassidy	138	1930	Babe Herman	416
1885	Bill McClellan	167	1931	Babe Herman	320
1886	Bill Phillips	216	1932	Lefty O'Doul	330
1887	Bill Phillips	204	1933	Johnny Frederick	228
1888	Dave Foutz	211	1934	Sam Leslie	249
1889	Darby O'Brien	237	1935	Lonny Frey	225
1890	Dave Foutz	223	1936	Buddy Hassett	257
1891	Mike Griffin	202	1937	Buddy Hassett	215
1892*	Dan Brouthers	282	1938	Dolph Camilli	247
1893	Tom Daly	209	1939	Dolph Camilli	296
1894	Oyster Burns	262	1940	Dolph Camilli	271
1895	Candy LaChance	246	1941*	Pete Reiser	299
1896	Mike Griffin	212	1942	Dolph Camilli	247
1897	John Anderson	224	1943	Arky Vaughan	252
1898	Fielder Jones	217	1944	Dixie Walker	283
1899	Willie Keeler	269	1945	Goody Rosen	279
1900	Willie Keeler	253	1946	Dixie Walker	258
1901	Jimmy Sheckard	299	1947	Jackie Robinson	252
1902	Willie Keeler	220	1948	Jackie Robinson	260
1903	Jimmy Sheckard	245	1949	Jackie Robinson	313
1904	Harry Lumley	247	1950*	Duke Snider	343
1905	Harry Lumley	208	1951	Gil Hodges	307
1906	Harry Lumley	231	1952	Duke Snider	264
1907	Harry Lumley	193	1953*	Duke Snider	370
1908	Tim Jordan	191	1954*	Duke Snider	378
1909	Al Burch	198	1955	Duke Snider	338
1910	Zach Wheat	244	1956	Duke Snider	324
1911	Jake Daubert	224	1957	Duke Snider	298
1912	Jake Daubert	232	1958	Charlie Neal	207
1913	Red Smith	238	1959	Charlie Neal	286
1914	Zach Wheat	241	1960	Wally Moon	212
1915	Jake Daubert	207	1961	Wally Moon	234
1916*	Zach Wheat	262	1962	Tommy Davis	356
1917	Casey Stengel	206	1963	Tommy Davis	254
1918	Jake Daubert	170	1964	Willie Davis	253
1919*	Hy Myers	223	1965	Maury Wills	214
1920	Zach Wheat	270	1966	Willie Davis	253
1921	Jimmy Johnston	287	1967	Willie Davis	209
1922	Zach Wheat	302	1968	Willie Davis	226
1923	Jack Fournier	303	1969	Willie Davis	227
1924	Zach Wheat	311	1970	Wes Parker	281
1925	Zach Wheat	333	1971	Willie Davis	281
1926	Babe Herman	248	1972	Willie Davis	271
1927	Jay Partridge	199	1973	Willie Davis	266
1928	Del Bissonette	319	1974	Steve Garvey	301
1929	Babe Herman	348	1975	Steve Garvey	314
			1976	Steve Garvey	284
*Led League			1977	Steve Garvey	322

Year-by-Year Leaders in Total Bases

Year	Player	Total
1978	Steve Garvey	319
1979	Steve Garvey	322
1980	Steve Garvey	307
1981	Dusty Baker	178
1982	Pedro Guerrero	308
1983	Pedro Guerrero	310

300 Total Bases in a Season

1922
Zach Wheat 302

1923
Jack Fournier 303

1924
Zach Wheat 311
Jack Fournier 302

1925
Zach Wheat 333
Jack Fournier 310

1928
Del Bissonette 319

1929
Babe Herman 348
Johnny Frederick 342

1930
Babe Herman 416
Johnny Frederick 323

1931
Babe Herman 320

1932
Lefty O'Doul 330

1949
Jackie Robinson 313

1950
Duke Snider 343

1951
Gil Hodges 307

1953
Duke Snider 370
Roy Campanella 317

1954
Duke Snider 378
Gil Hodges 335

1955
Duke Snider 338

1956
Duke Snider 324

1962
Tommy Davis 356

1974
Steve Garvey 301

1975
Steve Garvey 314

1977
Steve Garvey 322

1978
Steve Garvey 319

1979
Steve Garvey 322

1980
Steve Garvey 307

1982
Pedro Guerrero 308

1983
Pedro Guerrero 310

1,000-or-More Total Bases (Lifetime)

Player	Years	Total
Zach Wheat	(1909-1926)	4003
Duke Snider	(1946-1962)	3669
Gil Hodges	(1943; 1947-1961)	3357
Willie Davis	(1960-1973)	3094
Steve Garvey	(1969-1982)	3056
Pee Wee Reese	(1940-1942; 1946-1958)	3038
Carl Furillo	(1946-1960)	2922
Jim Gilliam	(1953-1966)	2530
Ron Cey	(1971-1982)	2321
Jackie Robinson	(1947-1956)	2310
Bill Russell	(1969-1983)	2295
Roy Campanella	(1948-1957)	2101
Maury Wills	(1959-1966; 1969-1972)	2045
Dixie Walker	(1939-1947)	1982
Jimmy Johnston	(1916-1925)	1827
Jake Daubert	(1910-1918)	1798
Babe Herman	(1926-1931; 1945)	1793
Dusty Baker	(1976-1983)	1769
Davey Lopes	(1972-1981)	1744
Hy Myers	(1909; 1911; 1914-1922)	1689
Tom Daly	(1890-1896; 1898-1901)	1655
Mike Griffin	(1891-1898)	1588
Wes Parker	(1964-1972)	1560
Dolph Camilli	(1938-1943)	1530
John Roseboro	(1957-1967)	1517
Ron Fairly	(1958-1969)	1492
Johnny Frederick	(1929-1934)	1479
Jim Gilliam	(1953-1966)	1405
Jimmy Sheckard	(1897-1898; 1900-1905)	1403
Ivy Olson	(1915-1924)	1369
John Hummel	(1905-1915)	1351
Tommy Davis	(1959-1966)	1323
George Pinckney	(1885-1891)	1314
Willie Crawford	(1964-1975)	1153
Steve Yeager	(1972-1983)	1145
Jim Lefebvre	(1965-1972)	1140
Del Bissonette	(1928-1931; 1933)	1114
Bill Buckner	(1969-1976)	1100
Harry Lumley	(1904-1910)	1083
George Cutshaw	(1912-1917)	1082
Cookie Lavagetto	(1937-1941; 1946-1947)	1067
Frank Howard	(1958-1964)	1044
Willie Keeler	(1893; 1899-1902)	1034
Jack Fournier	(1923-1926)	1030
Charlie Neal	(1956-1961)	1020
Tommy Griffith	(1919-1925)	1015

700 to 1,000 Total Bases, Lifetime

Player	Years	Total
Wally Moon	(1959-1965)	988
Joe Stripp	(1932-1937)	986
Pete Reiser	(1940-1942; 1946-1948)	973
Germany Smith	(1885-1890; 1897)	969
Tommy Corcoran	(1892-1896)	960
Fielder Jones	(1896-1900)	951
Billy Cox	(1948-1954)	941
Casey Stengel	(1912-1917)	933
Candy LaChance	(1893-1898)	933
Augie Galan	(1941-1946)	933
Reggie Smith	(1976-1981)	917
Pedro Guerrero	(1978-1983)	900
Bill Shindle	(1894-1898)	885
Darby O'Brien	(1888-1892)	878
Joe Ferguson	(1970-1976; 1978-1981)	876
Otto Miller	(1910-1922)	873
Al Lopez	(1928; 1930-1935)	870
Bill Dahlen	(1899-1903; 1910-1911)	865
Babe Phelps	(1935-1941)	849
John Anderson	(1894-1899)	825
Tony Cuccinello	(1932-1935)	807
Joe Medwick	(1940-1943; 1946)	803
Manny Mota	(1969-1980)	751
Frenchy Bordagaray	(1935-1936; 1942-1945)	718
Billy Herman	(1941-1943; 1946)	706

Total Bases by Position (Season)

Modern, Brooklyn

1B	Gil Hodges	1954	335
2B	Jackie Robinson	1949	313
SS	Glenn Wright	1930	289
3B	Jimmy Johnston	1921	287
OF	Babe Herman	1930	416
OF	Duke Snider	1954	378
OF	Zach Wheat	1925	333
C	Roy Campanella	1953	317

Los Angeles

1B	Steve Garvey	1979	322
2B	Charlie Neal	1959	286
SS	Maury Wills	1962	259
3B	Pedro Guerrero	1983	310
OF	Tommy Davis	1962	356
OF	Pedro Guerrero	1982	308
OF	Willie Davis	1971	281
	Reggie Smith	1977	281
C	Joe Ferguson	1973	229

19th Century

1B	Dan Brouthers	1892	282
2B	Tom Daly	1894	234
SS	Tommy Corcoran	1894	249
3B	George Pinckney	1890	209
OF	Willie Keeler	1899	269
OF	Oyster Burns	1894	262
OF	George Treadway	1894	248
C	John Grim	1895	119

All-Time

1B	Gil Hodges	1954	335
2B	Jackie Robinsoin	1949	313
SS	Glenn Wright	1930	289
3B	Pedro Guerrero	1983	310
OF	Babe Herman	1930	416
OF	Duke Snider	1954	378
OF	Tommy Davis	1962	356
C	Roy Campanella	1953	317

The jubilant Dodgers surround Rick Monday whose two-out, ninth inning home run off pitcher Steve Rodgers beat the Expos 2-1 and won the 1981 National League pennant for the Dodgers.

MISCELLANEOUS BATTING RECORDS

Cycle Hitters

Date	Player	Opponent
August 1, 1890	Oyster Burns	Pittsburgh (2nd game)
May 25, 1922	Jimmy Johnston	Philadelphia (1st game)
May 18, 1931	Babe Herman	Cincinnati
July 24, 1931	Babe Herman	Pittsburgh
September 2, 1944	Dixie Walker	New York
August 29, 1948	Jackie Robinson	St. Louis (1st game)
June 25, 1949	Gil Hodges	Pittsburgh
May 7, 1970	Wes Parker	New York Mets

Six Hits in a Game

Date	Player	AB	R	H	2B	3B	HR
	American Association						
July 30, 1884	Oscar Walker	6	2	6	1	1	0
June 25, 1885	George Pinckney	6	5	6	0	0	0
Aug. 8, 1889	Darby O'Brien	6	1	6	3	0	0
	National League						
Aug. 9, 1915	George Cutshaw	6	2	6	0	0	0
June 29, 1923	Jack Fournier	6	1	6	2	0	1
June 23, 1929	Hank DeBerry	7	0	6	0	0	0 (14 innings)
May 30, 1931	Wally Gilbert	7	3	6	1	0	0 (2nd game)
Sept. 23, 1939	Cookie Lavagetto	6	4	6	1	1	0 (1st game)
May 24, 1973	Willie Davis	9	1	6	0	0	0

Five Long Hits in a Game

Date	Player	2B	3B	HR	Total
Aug. 28, 1977	Steve Garvey	3	0	2	5

Four Long Hits in a Game

Date	Player	2B	3B	HR	Total
	American Association				
April 20, 1888	Mickey Hughes	2	2	0	4
Aug. 20, 1889	Darby O'Brien	2	2	0	4
	National League				
Aug. 22, 1892	Monte Ward	2	1	1	4
Aug. 20, 1894	George Treadway	2	1	1	4
Oct. 15, 1898	Jimmy Sheckard	3	0	1	4
June 26, 1901	Tom Daly	3	1	0	4
June 5, 1929	Babe Herman	2	2	0	4
Aug. 4, 1932	Lefty O'Doul	1	0	3	4

Four Long Hits in a Game (Continued)

Aug. 16, 1933	Johnny Frederick	3	1	0	4
Aug. 4, 1935	Sam Leslie	3	0	1	4
Aug. 21, 1937	Johnny Cooney	3	1	0	4
June 2, 1942	Pete Reiser	3	0	1	4
June 25, 1949	Gil Hodges	1	1	2	4
Aug. 31, 1950	Gil Hodges	0	0	4	4
June 1, 1954	Duke Snider	1	0	3	4
June 17, 1954	Jackie Robinson	2	0	2	4
Aug. 20, 1974	Davey Lopes	1	0	3	4

Consecutive Games Hitting Streaks

Player	Year	Games
Willie Davis	1969	31
Zach Wheat	1916	29
Joe Medwick	1942	27
Duke Snider	1953	27
Wee Willie Keeler	1902	26
Zach Wheat	1918	26
Harvey Hendrick	1929	25
Buzz Boyle	1934	25
Willie Davis	1971	25
Zach Wheat	1924	24
Hy Myers	1915	23
Duke Snider	1950	22
Pee Wee Reese	1951	22
Jackie Robinson	1947	21
Steve Garvey	1978	21
Jimmy Johnston	1921	20
Zach Wheat	1923	20
Johnny Frederick	1933	20
Tommy Davis	1960	20
Tommy Davis	1964	20
Maury Wills	1965	20
Steve Garvey	1978	20

4

STEALS AND LONG GAMES, STREAKS, SERVICE

STOLEN BASE LEADERS

Year-by-Year Stolen Base Leaders

(Data prior to 1887 not available. Before 1898 a player was credited with a stolen base if he advanced from first to third on a single.)

Year	Player	Total	Year	Player	Total
1887	Bill McClellan	70	1909	Al Burch	38
1888	Darby O'Brien	55	1910	Bill Davidson	27
1889	Darby O'Brien	91	1911	Bob Coulson	32
1890	Hub Collins	85		Jake Daubert	32
1891	Mike Griffin	65	1912	Jake Daubert	29
1892*	Monte Ward	88	1913	George Cutshaw	39
1893	Dave Foutz	39	1914	George Cutshaw	34
1894	Tom Daly	51	1915	George Cutshaw	28
1895	Candy LaChance	37	1916	George Cutshaw	27
1896	John Anderson	37	1917	George Cutshaw	22
1897	Fielder Jones	48	1918	Jimmy Johnston	22
1898	Fielder Jones	36	1919	Ivy Olson	26
1899	Willie Keeler	45	1920	Jimmy Johnston	19
1900	Willie Keeler	41	1921	Jimmy Johnston	28
1901	Jimmy Sheckard	42	1922	Jimmy Johnston	18
1902	Bill Dahlen	29	1923	Jimmy Johnston	16
1903*	Jimmy Sheckard	67	1924	Jack Fournier	7
1904	Charlie Babb	34	1925	Milt Stock	8
1905	Doc Gessler	26	1926	Bill Marriott	12
1906	Billy Maloney	38	1927	Max Carey	32
1907	Billy Maloney	25	1928	Max Carey	18
1908	Harry Pattee	24	1929	Babe Herman	21
			1930	Babe Herman	18
*Led League			1931	Babe Herman	17

Year-by-Year Stolen Base Leaders (Continued)

Year	Player	Total	Year	Player	Total
1932	Joe Stripp	14	1956	Jim Gilliam	21
1933	Jake Flowers	13	1957	Jim Gilliam	26
1934	Danny Taylor	12	1958	Jim Gilliam	18
1935	Frenchy Bordagaray	18	1959	Jim Gilliam	23
1936	Frenchy Bordagaray	12	1960*	Maury Wills	50
1937	Buddy Hassett	13	1961*	Maury Wills	35
	Cookie Lavagetto	13	1962*	Maury Wills	104
1938	Ernie Koy	15	1963*	Maury Wills	40
	Cookie Lavagetto	15	1964*	Maury Wills	53
1939	Cookie Lavagetto	14	1965*	Maury Wills	94
1940	Pee Wee Reese	15	1966	Maury Wills	38
1941	Pee Wee Reese	10	1967	Willie Davis	20
1942*	Pete Reiser	20	1968	Willie Davis	36
1943*	Arky Vaughan	20	1969	Maury Wills	25
1944	Luis Olmo	10	1970	Willie Davis	38
1945	Luis Olmo	15	1971	Willie Davis	20
1946*	Pete Reiser	34	1972	Willie Davis	20
1947*	Jackie Robinson	29	1973	Davey Lopes	36
1948	Pee Wee Reese	25	1974	Davey Lopes	59
1949*	Jackie Robinson	37	1975*	Davey Lopes	77
1950	Pee Wee Reese	17	1976*	Davey Lopes	63
1951	Jackie Robinson	25	1977	Davey Lopes	47
1952*	Pee Wee Reese	30	1978	Davey Lopes	45
1953	Pee Wee Reese	22	1979	Davey Lopes	44
1954	Jim Gilliam	8	1980	Rudy Law	40
	Don Hoak	8	1981	Davey Lopes	20
	Pee Wee Reese	8	1982	Steve Sax	49
1955	Jim Gilliam	15	1983	Steve Sax	56

*Led League

300-or-More Stolen Bases, Lifetime

Player	Years	Total
Maury Wills	(1959-1966; 1969-1972)	490
Davey Lopes	(1972-1981)	418
Willie Davis	(1960-1973)	335

200-or-More Stolen Bases, Lifetime

Player	Years	Total
Tom Daly	(1890-1896; 1898-1901)	298
Darby O'Brien	(1888-1892)	272
Mike Griffin	(1891-1898)	264
George Pinckney	(1885-1891)	248
Dave Foutz	(1888-1896)	241
Pee Wee Reese	(1940-1942; 1946-1958)	232
Jimmy Sheckard	(1897-1898; 1900-1905)	214

Davey Lopes, shown taking batting practice, is second on the all-time list of stolen bases for the Dodgers with 418. Lopes led the Dodgers in stolen bases eight different seasons.

Zach Wheat	(1909-1926)	203
Jim Gilliam	(1953-1966)	203

150-or-More Stolen Bases, Lifetime

Player	Years	Total
Jackie Robinson	(1947-1956)	197
Jake Daubert	(1910-1918)	187
George Cutshaw	(1912-1917)	166
Jimmy Johnston	(1916-1925)	164
Fielder Jones	(1896-1900)	153
Bill Russell	(1969-1983)	152

100-or-More Stolen Bases, Lifetime

Player	Years	Total
Bill Dahlen	(1899-1903; 1910-1911)	146
Monte Ward	(1891-1892)	145
Willie Keeler	(1893; 1899-1902)	128
Candy LaChance	(1893-1898)	123
John Anderson	(1894-1899)	122
Tommy Corcoran	(1892-1896)	119
John Hummel	(1905-1915)	114
Germany Smith	(1885-1890; 1897)	113
Harry Lumley	(1904-1910)	110
Steve Sax	(1981-1983)	110
Hy Myers	(1909; 1911; 1914-1922)	101

90-or-More Stolen Bases, Lifetime

Player	Years	Total
Duke Snider	(1947-1962)	99
Bill Buckner	(1969-1976)	93

80-or-More Stolen Bases, Lifetime

Player	Years	Total
Ivy Olson	(1915-1924)	88
Bill Shindle	(1894-1898)	86

70-or-More Stolen Bases, Lifetime

Player	Years	Total
Ken Landreaux	(1981-1983)	79
Adonis Terry	(1884-1891)	78
Pete Reiser	(1940-1942; 1946-1948)	78
Casey Stengel	(1912-1917)	77
Steve Garvey	(1969-1982)	77
Joe Kelley	(1899-1901)	77
Billy Maloney	(1906-1908)	77
Al Burch	(1907-1911)	74
Dusty Baker	(1976-1983)	73

60-or-More Stolen Bases, Lifetime

Player	Years	Total
Babe Herman	(1926-1931; 1945)	69
Jim McTamany	(1885-1887)	66
Doc Casey	(1899-1900; 1906-1907)	65
Tommy Davis	(1959-1966)	65
Gil Hodges	(1943; 1947-1961)	63
Sammy Strang	(1903-1904)	62
Harvey Hendrick	(1927-1931)	61
Red Smith	(1911-1914)	60

50-or-More Stolen Bases, Lifetime

Player	Years	Total
John Roseboro	(1957-1967)	59
Cookie Lavagetto	(1937-1941; 1946-1947)	56
Phil Lewis	(1905-1908)	55
Lew Ritter	(1902-1908)	55
Bob Clark	(1886-1890)	54
Pedro Guerrero	(1978-1983)	54
Doc Gessler	(1903-1906)	51
Max Carey	(1926-1929)	50

20-or-More Stolen Bases, Season

Year	Player	Total	Year	Player	Total
1887	Bill McClellan	70		Darby O'Brien	38
	Jim McTamany	66		Adonis Terry	32
	George Pinckney	59		Germany Smith	24
	Ed Greer	34		Oyster Burns	21
	Ed Swartwood	29		Tom Daly	20
	Adonis Terry	27	1891	Mike Griffin	65
	Germany Smith	26		Monte Ward	57
	Jimmy Peoples	22		Dave Foutz	48
1888	Darby O'Brien	55		George Pinckney	44
	George Pinckney	51		Hub Collins	32
	Dave Foutz	35		Darby O'Brien	31
	Paul Radford	33		Oyster Burns	21
	Germany Smith	27	1892	Monte Ward	88
	Bob Caruthers	23		Darby O'Brien	57
1889	Darby O'Brien	91		Mike Griffin	49
	Hub Collins	65		Tommy Corcoran	39
	George Pinckney	47		Tom Daly	34
	Dave Foutz	43		Oyster Burns	33
	Germany Smith	35		Dan Brouthers	31
	Oyster Burns	32		Bill Joyce	23
	Pop Corkhill	22	1893	Dave Foutz	39
1890	Hub Collins	85		Tom Daly	32
	George Pinckney	47		Mike Griffin	30
	Dave Foutz	42			

20-or-More Stolen Bases, Season (Continued)

Year	Player	Total	Year	Player	Total
1894	Tom Daly	51	1905	Doc Gessler	26
	Mike Griffin	39		Jimmy Sheckard	23
	Tommy Corcoran	33		Harry Lumley	22
	Oyster Burns	30		Emil Batch	21
	George Treadway	27	1906	Billy Maloney	38
	Candy LaChance	20		Harry Lumley	35
1895	Candy LaChance	37		Doc Casey	22
	Tom Daly	28	1907	Billy Maloney	25
	Mike Griffin	27	1908	Harry Pattee	24
	John Anderson	24		John Hummel	20
1896	John Anderson	37	1909	Al Burch	38
	Bill Shindle	24	1910	Bill Davidson	27
	Mike Griffin	23		Jake Daubert	23
	Tom McCarthy	22		John Hummel	21
1897	Fielder Jones	48	1911	Bob Coulson	32
	John Anderson	29		Jake Daubert	32
	Candy LaChance	26		Zach Wheat	21
	Bill Shindle	23	1912	Jake Daubert	29
1898	Fielder Jones	36		Herbie Moran	28
	Candy LaChance	23		Red Smith	22
1899	Willie Keeler	45	1913	George Cutshaw	39
	Tom Daly	43		Jake Daubert	25
	Joe Kelley	31		Red Smith	22
	Bill Dahlen	29		Herbie Moran	21
	John Anderson	25	1914	George Cutshaw	34
1900	Willie Keeler	41		Jake Daubert	25
	Fielder Jones	33		Zach Wheat	20
	Bill Dahlen	31	1915	George Cutshaw	28
	Hughie Jennings	31		Zach Wheat	21
	Jimmy Sheckard	30	1916	George Cutshaw	27
	Tom Daly	27		Jimmy Johnston	22
	Joe Kelley	26		Jake Daubert	21
1901	Jimmy Sheckard	42	1917	George Cutshaw	22
	Tom Daly	31	1918	Jimmy Johnston	22
	Willie Keeler	31		Ivy Olson	21
	Bill Dahlen	23	1919	Ivy Olson	26
	Joe Kelley	20	1921	Jimmy Johnston	28
1902	Bill Dahlen	29	1927	Max Carey	32
	Jimmy Sheckard	25		Harvey Hendrick	29
	Cozy Dolan	24	1929	Babe Herman	21
	Willie Keeler	23	1942	Pete Reiser	20
1903	Jimmy Sheckard	67	1943	Arky Vaughan	20
	Sammy Strang	46	1946	Pete Reiser	34
	Bill Dahlen	34	1947	Jackie Robinson	29
	Jack Doyle	34	1948	Pee Wee Reese	25
	John Dobbs	23		Jackie Robinson	22
1904	Charlie Babb	34	1949	Jackie Robinson	37
	Harry Lumley	30		Pee Wee Reese	26
	Dude McCormick	22	1951	Jackie Robinson	25
	Jimmy Sheckard	21		Pee Wee Reese	20

20-or-More Stolen Bases, Season (Continued)

Year	Player	Total	Year	Player	Total
1952	Pee Wee Reese	30	1970	Willie Davis	38
	Jackie Robinson	24		Maury Wills	28
1953	Pee Wee Reese	22	1971	Willie Davis	20
	Jim Gilliam	21	1972	Willie Davis	20
1956	Jim Gilliam	21	1973	Davey Lopes	36
1957	Jim Gilliam	26	1974	Davey Lopes	59
1959	Jim Gilliam	23		Bill Buckner	31
1960	Maury Wills	50	1975	Davey Lopes	77
1961	Maury Wills	35	1976	Davey Lopes	63
1962	Maury Wills	104		Bill Buckner	28
	Willie Davis	32	1977	Davey Lopes	47
1963	Maury Wills	40	1978	Davey Lopes	45
	Willie Davis	25		Bill North	27
1964	Maury Wills	53	1979	Davey Lopes	44
	Willie Davis	42	1980	Rudy Law	40
1965	Maury Wills	94		Davey Lopes	23
	Willie Davis	25	1981	Davey Lopes	20
1966	Maury Wills	38	1982	Steve Sax	49
	Willie Davis	21		Ken Landreaux	31
1967	Willie Davis	20		Pedro Guerrero	22
1968	Willie Davis	36	1983	Steve Sax	56
1969	Maury Wills	25		Ken Landreaux	30
	Willie Davis	24		Pedro Guerrero	23

Stolen Bases by Position (Season)

Modern, Brooklyn

1B	Jake Daubert	1911	32
2B	George Cutshaw	1913	39
SS	Bill Dahlen	1903	34
	Charlie Babb	1904	34
3B	Sammy Strang	1903	46
OF	Jimmy Sheckard	1903	67
OF	Willie Keeler	1900	41
OF	Billy Maloney	1906	38
	Al Burch	1909	38
C	Lew Ritter	1904	17

Los Angeles

1B	Steve Garvey	1976	19
2B	Davey Lopes	1975	77
SS	Maury Wills	1962	104
3B	Jim Gilliam	1959	23
	Pedro Guerrero	1983	23
OF	Willie Davis	1964	42
OF	Rudy Law	1980	40
OF	Bill Buckner	1974	31
	Ken Landreaux	1982	31
C	John Roseboro	1962	12

Stolen Bases by Position (Season) (Continued)

19th Century

1B	Dave Foutz	1891	48
2B	Monte Ward	1892	88
SS	Tommy Corcoran	1892	39
3B	George Pinckney	1887	59
OF	Darby O'Brien	1889	91
OF	Jim McTamany	1887	66
OF	Mike Griffin	1891	65
C	Jimmy Peoples	1887	22

All-Time

1B	Dave Foutz	1891	48
2B	Monte Ward	1892	88
SS	Maury Wills	1962	104
3B	George Pinckney	1887	59
OF	Darby O'Brien	1889	91
OF	Jimmy Sheckard	1903	67
OF	Jim McTamany	1887	66
C	Jimmy Peoples	1887	22

EXTRA INNING GAMES

Extra Inning Longest Games

Innings	Date	Score
26*	May 1, 1920	Dodgers 1, Boston 1
23	June 27, 1939	Dodgers 2, Boston 2
22	August 22, 1917	Dodgers 6, Pittsburgh 5
21	August 17-18, 1982	Dodgers 2, Chicago 1
20	April 30, 1919	Dodgers 9, Philadelphia 9
	July 5, 1940	Dodgers 6, Boston 2
19	June 17, 1915	Chicago 4, Dodgers 3
	May 3, 1920	Boston 2, Dodgers 1
	May 17, 1939	Dodgers 9, Chicago 9
	September 11, 1946	Dodgers 0, Cincinnati 0
	August 8, 1971 (n)	Cincinnati 2, Dodgers 1
	May 24, 1973 (n)	New York Mets 7, Dodgers 3
18	August 17, 1902	Dodgers 7, St. Louis 7
	July 29, 1914	Dodgers 4, St. Louis 3
	June 1, 1919	Philadelphia 10, Dodgers 9

Team Streaks

Most Consecutive Wins

Year	Total	Home	Away
1924	15	3	12
1947	13	2	11
1953	13	7	6

Los Angeles

1962	13	8	5
1965	13	7	6

Most Consecutive Losses

1944	16	0	16
1937	14	0	14

Los Angeles

1961	10	4	6

Team Player Longevity

Player	Years as Dodger	Total
Zach Wheat	1909-1926	18
Pee Wee Reese	1940-1942; 1946-1958	16
Duke Snider	1947-1962	16
Carl Furillo	1946-1960	15
Gil Hodges	1947-1961	15
Bill Russell	1969-1983	15
Don Drysdale	1956-1969	14
Willie Davis	1960-1973	14
Jim Gilliam	1953-1966	14
Don Sutton	1966-1979	14
Johnny Podres	1953-1955; 1957-1966	13
Steve Garvey	1970-1982	13
Jim Brewer	1964-1975	12
Carl Erskine	1948-1959	12
Sandy Koufax	1955-1966	12
Dazzy Vance	1922-1932; 1935	12
Steve Yeager	1972-1983	12

5

PITCHING RECORDS

WIN-LOSS RECORDS

Leading Pitchers, 1884 to Date
(Highest Won-Lost Percentage, 15 or More Decisions)

Year	Pitcher	W	L	Pct.
1884	Sam Kimber	17	20	.459
1885	Henry Porter	33	21	.611
1886	Henry Porter	27	19	.587
1887	Steve Toole	14	10	.583
1888	Bob Caruthers	29	15	.659
1889*	Bob Caruthers	40	11	.784
1890*	Tom Lovett	30	11	.732
1891	Bob Caruthers	18	14	.563
1892	George Haddock	29	13	.690
1893	Ed Stein	19	15	.559
1894	Ed Stein	27	14	.659
1895	Brickyard Kennedy	18	13	.581
1896	Dan Daub	12	11	.522
1897	Jack Dunn	14	9	.609
1898	Jack Dunn	16	21	.432
	Brickyard Kennedy	16	21	.432
1899*	Jim Hughes	28	6	.824
1900*	Iron Man McGinnity	29	9	.763
1901	Frank Kitson	19	11	.633
1902	Frank Kitson	19	12	.613
1903	Henry Schmidt	22	13	.629
1904	Oscar Jones	17	25	.405
1905	Doc Scanlan	15	11	.577
1906	Doc Scanlan	18	13	.581
1907	Jim Pastorius	16	12	.571
1908	Nap Rucker	17	19	.472
1909	Doc Scanlan	8	7	.533
1910	Cy Barger	15	15	.500
1911	Nap Rucker	22	18	.550
1912	Nap Rucker	18	21	.462

*Led League

183

Leading Pitchers, 1884 to Date (Continued)

Year	Pitcher	W	L	Pct.
1913	Nap Rucker	14	15	.483
1914	Jeff Pfeffer	23	12	.657
1915	Sherry Smith	14	8	.636
1916	Jeff Pfeffer	25	11	.694
1917	Rube Marquard	19	12	.613
1918	Burleigh Grimes	19	9	.679
1919	Jeff Pfeffer	17	13	.567
1920*	Burleigh Grimes	23	11	.676
1921	Burleigh Grimes	22	13	.629
1922	Dutch Ruether	21	12	.636
1923	Dazzy Vance	18	15	.545
1924	Dazzy Vance	28	6	.824
1925	Dazzy Vance	22	9	.710
1926	Jesse Petty	17	17	.500
1927	Bill Doak	11	8	.579
1928	Dazzy Vance	22	10	.688
1929	Johnny Morrison	13	7	.650
1930	Ray Phelps	14	7	.667
1931	Watty Clark	14	10	.583
1932	Watty Clark	20	12	.625
1933	Van Lingle Mungo	16	15	.516
1934	Dutch Leonard	14	11	.560
1935	Watty Clark	13	8	.619
1936	Fred Frankhouse	13	10	.565
1937	Luke Hamlin	11	13	.458
1938	Vito Tamulis	12	6	.667
1939	Luke Hamlin	20	13	.606
1940*	Freddie Fitzsimmons	16	2	.889
1941	Kirby Higbe	22	9	.710
1942*	Larry French	15	4	.789
1943	Whit Wyatt	14	5	.737
1944	Curt Davis	10	11	.476
1945	Tom Seats	10	7	.588
1946	Hugh Casey	11	5	.688
	Hank Behrman	11	5	.688
1947	Joe Hatten	17	8	.680
1948	Ralph Branca	14	9	.609
1949	Ralph Branca	13	5	.722
1950	Don Newcombe	19	11	.633
	Preacher Roe	19	11	.633
1951**	Preacher Roe	22	3	.880
1952	Joe Black	15	4	.789
1953*	Carl Erskine	20	6	.769
1954	Bill Loes	13	5	.722
1955*	Don Newcombe	20	5	.800
1956*	Don Newcombe	27	7	.794
1957	Don Drysdale	17	9	.654
1958	Stan Williams	9	7	.563

*Led League

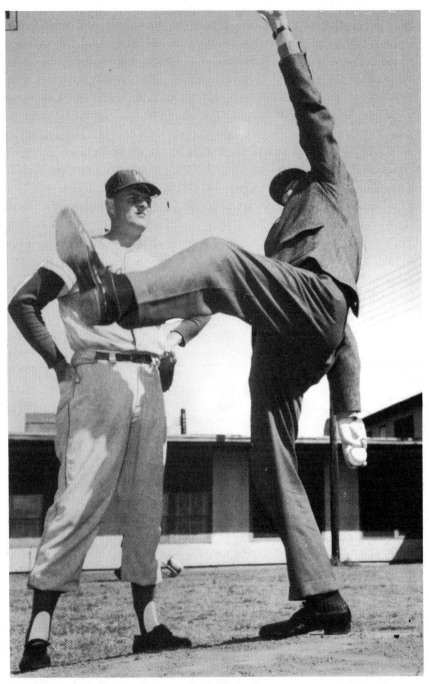

In 1968, the great Dazzy Vance at age 77 provides a few pointers to Don Drysdale.

Leading Pitchers, 1884 to Date (Continued)

Year	Pitcher	W	L	Pct.
1959	Roger Craig	11	5	.688
1960	Larry Sherry	14	10	.583
	Stan Williams	14	10	.583
1961*	Johnny Podres	18	5	.783
1962	Don Drysdale	25	9	.735
1963*	Ron Perranoski	16	3	.842
1964*	Sandy Koufax	19	5	.792
1965*	Sandy Koufax	26	8	.765
1966****	Phil Regan	14	1	.933
1967	Bill Singer	12	8	.600
1968	Don Drysdale	14	12	.538
1969	Bill Singer	20	12	.625
1970	Don Sutton	15	13	.536
1971	Al Downing	20	9	.690
1972	Tommy John	11	5	.688
1973*	Tommy John	16	7	.696
1974*	Tommy John	13	3	.813
1975	Burt Hooton	18	7	.720
1976*	Rick Rhoden	12	3	.800
1977	Tommy John	20	7	.741
1978	Burt Hooton	19	10	.655
1979	Rick Sutcliffe	17	10	.630
1980	Jerry Reuss	18	6	.750
1981***	Jerry Reuss	10	4	.714
1982	Jerry Reuss	18	11	.621
1983	Fernando Valenzuela	15	10	.600

*Led League
**National League Record, 20-game winner
***Season only 110 games due to players' strike.
****Highest in league

Most Victories by Pitcher, Season

Year	Pitcher	Record
1884	Adonis Terry	20-35
1885	Henry Porter	33-21
1886	Henry Porter	27-19
1887	Adonis Terry	16-16
1888	Bob Caruthers	29-15
1889	Bob Caruthers	40-11
1890	Tom Lovett	30-11
1891	Tom Lovett	23-19
1892	George Haddock	29-13
1893	Brickyard Kennedy	26-20
1894	Ed Stein	27-14
1895	Brickyard Kennedy	18-13
1896	Brickyard Kennedy	15-20
1897	Brickyard Kennedy	19-22

Most Victories by Pitcher, Season (Continued)

Year	Pitcher	Record
1898	Jack Dunn	16-21
	Brickyard Kennedy	16-21
1899	Jim Hughes	28-6
1900	Iron Man McGinnity	29-9
1901	Wild Bill Donovan	25-15
1902	Frank Kitson	19-12
1903	Henry Schmidt	22-13
1904	Oscar Jones	17-25
1905	Doc Scanlan	15-11
1906	Doc Scanlan	18-13
1907	Jim Pastorius	16-12
1908	Nap Rucker	17-19
1909	George Bell	16-15
1910	Nap Rucker	17-18
1911	Nap Rucker	22-18
1912	Nap Rucker	18-21
1913	Pat Ragan	15-18
1914	Jeff Pfeffer	23-12
1915	Jeff Pfeffer	19-14
1916	Jeff Pfeffer	25-11
1917	Rube Marquard	19-12
1918	Burleigh Grimes	19-9
1919	Jeff Pfeffer	17-13
1920	Burleigh Grimes	23-11
1921	Burleigh Grimes	22-13
1922	Dutch Ruether	21-12
1923	Burleigh Grimes	21-18
1924	Dazzy Vance	28-6
1925	Dazzy Vance	22-9
1926	Jesse Petty	17-17
1927	Dazzy Vance	16-15
1928	Dazzy Vance	22-10
1929	Watty Clark	16-19
1930	Dazzy Vance	17-15
1931	Watty Clark	14-10
1932	Watty Clark	20-12
1933	Van Lingle Mungo	16-15
1934	Van Lingle Mungo	18-16
1935	Van Lingle Mungo	16-10
1936	Van Lingle Mungo	18-19
1937	Luke Hamlin	11-13
	Max Butcher	11-15
1938	Vito Tamulis	12-6
	Luke Hamlin	12-15
1939	Luke Hamlin	20-13
1940	Freddie Fitzsimmons	16-2
1941	Kirby Higbe	22-9
	Whit Wyatt	22-10
1942	Whit Wyatt	19-7
1943	Whit Wyatt	14-5

Most Victories by Pitcher, Season (Continued)

Year	Pitcher	Record
1944	Curt Davis	10-11
1945	Hal Gregg	18-13
1946	Kirby Higbe	17-8
1947	Ralph Branca	21-12
1948	Rex Barney	15-13
1949	Don Newcombe	17-8
1950	Don Newcombe	19-11
	Preacher Roe	19-11
1951	Preacher Roe	22-3
1952	Joe Black	15-4
1953	Carl Erskine	20-6
1954	Carl Erskine	18-15
1955	Don Newcombe	20-5
1956	Don Newcombe	27-7
1957	Don Drysdale	17-9
1958	Johnny Podres	13-15
1959	Don Drysdale	17-13
1960	Don Drysdale	15-14
1961	Johnny Podres	18-5
	Sandy Koufax	18-13
1962	Don Drysdale	25-9
1963	Sandy Koufax	25-5
1964	Sandy Koufax	19-5
1965	Sandy Koufax	26-8
1966	Sandy Koufax	27-9
1967	Claude Osteen	17-17
1968	Don Drysdale	14-12
1969	Bill Singer	20-12
	Claude Osteen	20-15
1970	Claude Osteen	16-14
1971	Al Downing	20-9
1972	Claude Osteen	20-11
1973	Don Sutton	18-10
1974	Andy Messersmith	20-6
1975	Andy Messersmith	19-14
1976	Don Sutton	21-10
1977	Tommy John	20-7
1978	Burt Hooton	19-10
1979	Rick Sutcliffe	17-10
1980	Jerry Reuss	18-6
1981	Fernando Valenzuela	13-7
1982	Fernando Valenzuela	19-13
1983	Fernando Valenzuela	15-10
	Bob Welch	15-12

Fernando Valenzuela led the Dodgers in victories in 1981, 1982 and 1983.

20-Game Winners

Year	Pitcher	Record
1884	Adonis Terry	20-35
1885	Henry Porter	33-21
1886	Henry Porter	27-19
1888	Bob Caruthers	29-15
	Mickey Hughes	25-13
1889	Bob Caruthers	40-11
	Adonis Terry	22-15
1890	Tom Lovett	30-11
	Adonis Terry	26-16
	Bob Caruthers	23-11
1891	Tom Lovett	23-19
1892	George Haddock	29-13
	Ed Stein	27-16
1893	Brickyard Kennedy	26-20
1894	Ed Stein	27-14
	Brickyard Kennedy	22-19
1899	Jim Hughes	28-6
	Jack Dunn	23-13
	Brickyard Kennedy	22-8
1900	Iron Man McGinnity	29-9
	Brickyard Kennedy	20-13
1901	Wild Bill Donovan	25-15
1903	Henry Schmidt	22-13
	Oscar Jones	20-16
1911	Nap Rucker	22-18
1914	Jeff Pfeffer	23-12
1916	Jeff Pfeffer	25-11
1920	Burleigh Grimes	23-11
1921	Burleigh Grimes	22-13
1922	Dutch Ruether	21-12
1923	Burleigh Grimes	21-18
1924	Dazzy Vance	28-6
	Burleigh Grimes	22-13
1925	Dazzy Vance	22-9
1928	Dazzy Vance	22-10
1932	Watty Clark	20-12
1939	Luke Hamlin	20-13
1941	Kirby Higbe	22-9
	Whit Wyatt	22-10
1947	Ralph Branca	21-12
1951	Preacher Roe	22-3
	Don Newcombe	20-9
1953	Carl Erskine	20-6
1955	Don Newcombe	20-5
1956	Don Newcombe	27-7
1962	Don Drysdale	25-9
1963	Sandy Koufax	25-5
1965	Sandy Koufax	26-8
	Don Drysdale	23-12
1966	Sandy Koufax	27-9

20-Game Winners Continued)

Year	Pitcher	Record
1969	Bill Singer	20-12
	Claude Osteen	20-15
1971	Al Downing	20-9
1972	Claude Osteen	20-11
1974	Andy Messersmith	20-6
1976	Don Sutton	21-10
1977	Tommy John	20-7

100-or-More Wins, Pitcher

Pitcher	Year	Record
Don Sutton	1966-1980	230-175
Don Drysdale	1956-1969	209-166
Dazzy Vance	1922-1932; 1935	190-131
Brickyard Kennedy	1892-1901	176-148
Sandy Koufax	1955-1966	165-87
Burleigh Grimes	1918-1926	158-121
Claude Osteen	1965-1973	147-126
Johnny Podres	1953-1955; 1957-1966	136-104
Nap Rucker	1907-1916	135-136
Adonis Terry	1884-1891	127-139
Don Newcombe	1949-1951; 1954-1958	123-66
Carl Erskine	1948-1959	122-78
Jeff Pfeffer	1913-1921	113-80
Bob Caruthers	1888-1891	110-51
Burt Hooton	1975-1983	109-78
Watty Clark	1927-1937	106-88
Van Lingle Mungo	1931-1941	102-99

80 to 99 Wins

Preacher Roe	1948-1954	93-37
Ed Stein	1892-1896; 1898	91-66
Tommy John	1972-1978	87-42
Whit Wyatt	1939-1944	80-45
Ralph Branca	1944-1953; 1956	80-58
Doug Rau	1972-1980	80-58

Winningest Pitchers by Decades

1880's

Adonis Terry	95-107	.470
Henry Porter	75-64	.540
Bob Caruthers	69-26	.726
John Harkins	39-50	.438
Mickey Hughes	34-21	.618
Steve Toole	20-16	.556
Tom Lovett	17-10	.630
Sam Kimber	17-20	.459
Dave Foutz	15-7	.682
Hardie Henderson	15-12	.556

1890's

Brickyard Kennedy	151-132	.534
Ed Stein	91-66	.580
Tom Lovett	56-35	.615
Jack Dunn	53-43	.552
Dan Daub	43-50	.462
Bob Caruthers	41-25	.621
George Haddock	37-22	.627
Adonis Terry	32-32	.500
Harley Payne	29-33	.468
Jay Hughes	28-6	.824

1900's

Doc Scanlan	54-46	.540
Frank Kitson	53-36	.596
Nap Rucker	46-42	.523
Harry McIntire	46-98	.319
Oscar Jones	45-56	.446
Wild Bill Donovan	43-32	.573
Jay Hughes	32-23	.582
Jim Pastorius	30-55	.353
Iron Man McGinnity	29-9	.763
George Bell	28-47	.373

1910's

Jeff Pfeffer	96-66	.593
Nap Rucker	89-94	.486
Sherry Smith	47-42	.528
Rube Marquard	46-41	.529
Jack Coombs	41-43	.488
Larry Cheney	38-42	.475
Pat Ragan	36-54	.400
Burleigh Grimes	29-20	.592
Leon Cadore	28-25	.528
Cy Barger	27-39	.409

Don Sutton is the all-time leader in pitching victories for the Dodgers with 230.

Winningest Pitchers by Decades (Continued)

1920's

Dazzy Vance	147-105	.583
Burleigh Grimes	129-101	.560
Dutch Ruether	54-52	.509
Jesse Petty	54-59	.478
Leon Cadore	40-44	.476
Watty Clark	35-30	.538
Doug McWeeney	33-45	.423
Bill Doak	25-21	.543
Sherry Smith	22-28	.440
Rube Ehrhardt	21-32	.396

1930's

Van Lingle Mungo	98-98	.500
Watty Clark	71-60	.542
Luke Hamlin	43-41	.512
Dazzy Vance	43-41	.512
Hollis Thurston	33-29	.532
Ray Benge	33-38	.465
Fred Frankhouse	26-28	.481
Ray Phelps	25-21	.543
Max Butcher	22-25	.468
Fred Fitzsimmons	22-25	.468

1940's

Curt Davis	74-65	.532
Whit Wyatt	72-42	.632
Kirby Higbe	70-38	.648
Ralph Branca	56-30	.651
Joe Hatten	56-37	.602
Hugh Casey	55-31	.640
Hal Gregg	37-41	.474
Rex Barney	35-31	.530
Vic Lombardi	35-32	.522
Preacher Roe	27-14	.659
Ed Head	27-23	.540

1950's

Carl Erskine	108-74	.593
Don Newcombe	106-58	.646
Clem Labine	70-53	.569
Johnny Podres	68-54	.557
Preacher Roe	56-23	.709
Don Drysdale	51-40	.560
Billy Loes	50-26	.658
Roger Craig	36-29	.554
Russ Meyer	32-13	.711
Sandy Koufax	28-27	.509

Don Newcombe, shown above in 1982, won 106 games for the Dodgers in the 50's.

Winningest Pitchers by Decades (Continued)

1960's

Don Drysdale	158-126	.556
Sandy Koufax	137-60	.695
Claude Osteen	81-79	.506
Johnny Podres	68-50	.576
Ron Perranoski	52-41	.559
Don Sutton	51-60	.459
Bill Singer	45-38	.542
Stan Williams	43-34	.558
Bob Miller	29-33	.468
Jim Brewer	27-20	.574
Larry Sherry	27-23	.540

1970's

Don Sutton	166-110	.601
Doug Rau	80-58	.580
Burt Hooton	71-49	.592
Tommy John	76-42	.644
Claude Osteen	66-47	.584
Andy Messersmith	53-30	.639
Al Downing	46-37	.554
Charlie Hough	46-41	.529
Rick Rhoden	42-24	.636
Jim Brewer	34-31	.523

1980-3

Jerry Ruess	58-32	.644
Bob Welch	54-37	.593
Fernando Valenzuela	49-30	.620
Burt Hooton	38-29	.567
Steve Howe	23-24	.489
Dave Stewart	18-13	.581
Tom Niedenfuer	14-8	.636
Don Sutton	13-5	.722
Alejandro Pena	13-12	.520
Bob Castillo	10-10	.500

Winning Streaks by Pitchers

Pitcher	Year	Total
Dazzy Vance	1924	15
Phil Regan	1966	13
Bob Caruthers	1889	12
Burt Hooton	1975	12
Tom Lovett	1890	11
Don Drysdale	1962	11
Sandy Koufax	1964	11
Sandy Koufax	1965	11

Winning Streaks (Continued)

Iron Man McGinnity	1900	10
Burleigh Grimes	1918	10
Dazzy Vance	1923	10
Bill Doak	1924	10
Larry French	1942	10
Whit Wyatt (twice)	1943	10
Preacher Roe (twice)	1951	10
Preacher Roe	1953	10
Don Newcombe	1955	10

Losing Streaks

Jim Pastorius	1908	14
Mal Eason	1905	12

ERA

Lowest Earned Run Average By Pitcher, Season

(Minimum 150 Innings)

Year	Pitcher	ERA
1884	Adonis Terry	3.49
1885	Henry Porter	2.78
1886	Adonis Terry	3.09
1887	Adonis Terry	4.02
1888	Adonis Terry	2.03
1889	Bob Caruthers	3.13
1890	Tom Lovett	2.78
1891	Bob Caruthers	3.12
1892	Ed Stein	2.84
1893	Brickyard Kennedy	3.72
1894	Ed Stein	4.54
1895	Dan Daub	4.29
1896	Harley Payne	3.39
1897	Brickyard Kennedy	3.91
1898	Brickyard Kennedy	3.37
1899	Jay Hughes	2.68
1900	Iron Man McGinnity	2.90
1901	Wild Bill Donovan	2.77
1902	Doc Newton	2.42
1903	Oscar Jones	2.94
1904	Ned Garvin	1.68
1905	Doc Scanlan	2.92
1906	Elmer Stricklett	2.72
1907	Nap Rucker	2.06
1908	Kaiser Wilhelm	1.87

Lowest Earned Run Average By Pitcher, Season (Continued)

1909	Nap Rucker	2.24
1910	Nap Rucker	2.58
1911	Nap Rucker	2.71
1912	Nap Rucker	2.21
1913	Frank Allen	2.83
1914	Jeff Pfeffer	1.97
1915	Jeff Pfeffer	2.10
1916	Rube Marquard	1.58
1917	Jeff Pfeffer	2.23
1918	Burleigh Grimes	2.14
1919	Sherry Smith	2.24
1920	Burleigh Grimes	2.22
1921	Burleigh Grimes	2.83
1922	Dutch Ruether	3.53
1923	Dazzy Vance	3.50
1924*	Dazzy Vance	2.16
1925	Dazzy Vance	3.53
1926	Jesse Petty	2.84
1927	Dazzy Vance	2.70
1928*	Dazzy Vance	2.09
1929	Watty Clark	3.74
1930*	Dazzy Vance	2.61
1931	Watty Clark	3.20
1932	Watty Clark	3.49
1933	Van Lingle Mungo	2.72
1934	Dutch Leonard	3.28
1935	Watty Clark	3.30
1936	Van Lingle Mungo	3.35
1937	Van Lingle Mungo	2.91
1938	Freddie Fitzsimmons	3.02
1939	Hugh Casey	2.93
1940	Luke Hamlin	3.06
1941	Whit Wyatt	2.34
1942	Curt Davis	2.36
1943	Whit Wyatt	2.49
1944	Curt Davis	3.34
1945	Curt Davis	3.25
1946	Joe Hatten	2.84
1947	Ralph Branca	2.67
1948	Preacher Roe	2.63
1949	Preacher Roe	2.79
1950	Preacher Roe	3.30
1951	Preacher Roe	3.04
1952	Billy Loes	2.69
1953	Carl Erskine	3.54
1954	Russ Meyer	3.99
1955	Don Newcombe	3.20
1956	Sal Maglie	2.87
1957	Johnny Podres	2.66

*Led League

Lowest Earned Run Average By Pitcher, Season (Continued)

Year	Pitcher	ERA
1958	Johnny Podres	3.72
1959	Roger Craig	2.06
1960	Don Drysdale	2.84
1961	Sandy Koufax	3.52
1962*	Sandy Koufax	2.54
1963*	Sandy Koufax	1.88
1964*	Sandy Koufax	1.74
1965*	Sandy Koufax	2.04
1966*	Sandy Koufax	1.73
1967	Bill Singer	2.64
1968	Don Drysdale	2.15
1969	Bill Singer	2.34
1970	Claude Osteen	3.82
1971	Don Sutton	2.55
1972	Don Sutton	2.08
1973	Don Sutton	2.42
1974	Mike Marshall	2.42
1975	Andy Messersmith	2.29
1976	Doug Rau	2.57
1977	Burt Hooton	2.62
1978	Burt Hooton	2.71
1979	Burt Hooton	2.97
1980*	Don Sutton	2.21
1981	Jerry Reuss	2.29
1982	Fernando Valenzuela	2.87
1983	**Bob Welch**	**2.65**

NO-HITTERS

No-Hit Games

* October 4, 1884—Sam Kimber vs. Toledo, A.A., tied 0-0 (11 innings)

July 24, 1886—Adonis Terry vs. St. Louis, A.A., won 1-0

May 27,1888—Adonis Tery vs. Louisville, A.A., won 4-0

** June 22, 1891—Tom Lovett vs. New York, won 4-0

*** June 2, 1894—Ed Stein vs. Chicago, won 1-0 (6 innings)

July 20, 1906—Mal Eason vs. St. Louis, won 2-0

**** August 1, 1906—Harry McIntire vs. Pittsburgh, lost 1-0 (13 innings)

September 5, 1908—Nap Rucker vs. Boston, won 6-0 (2nd game)

September 13, 1925—Dazzy Vance vs. Philadelphia, won 10-1 (1st game)

***** August 27, 1937—Fred Frankhouse vs. Cincinnati, won 5-0 (7⅔ innings)

April 30, 1940—Tex Carlton vs. Cincinnati, won 3-0

April 23, 1946—Ed Head vs. Boston, won 5-0

September 9, 1948—Rex Barney vs. New York, won 2-0

****** June 19, 1952—Carl Erskine vs. Chicago, won 5-0

May 12, 1956—Carl Erskine vs. New York, won 3-0

September 25, 1956—Sal Maglie vs. Philadelphia, won 5-0

June 30, 1962—Sandy Koufax vs. New York Mets, won 5-0

May 11, 1963—Sandy Koufax vs. San Francisco, won 8-0

******* June 4, 1964—Sandy Koufax vs. Philadelphia, won 3-0

******** September 9, 1965—Sandy Koufax vs. Chicago, won 1-0

July 20, 1970—Bill Singer vs. Philadelphia, won 5-0

June 27, 1980—Jerry Reuss vs. San Francisco, won 8-0

* Called because of darkness.
** First Dodger-Giants no-hitter.
*** Called because of rain.
**** No-hitter for 10.2 innings; lost on 4 hits.
***** Called because of rain.
****** Interrupted 40 minutes by thunderstorm.
******* Set new Dodgers record **for career (3) no-hitters**.
******** Perfect game; National League record **for most (4) career no-hitters**.

No-Hit Games Pitched Against the Dodgers

July 31, 1891—Amos Rusie of New York, won 6-0

August 6, 1892—John Stivetts of Boston, won 11-0

August 21, 1898—Walt Thornton of Chicago, won 2-0

May 1, 1906—Johnny Lush of Philadelphia, won 6-0

* August 24, 1906—John Weimer of Cincinnati, won 1-0 (2nd game, 7 innings)

** September 24, 1906—Grant McGlynn of St. Louis, tied 1-1 (2nd game, 7 innings)

September 20, 1907—Nick Maddox of Pittsburgh, won 2-1

*** August 6, 1908—Johnny Lush of St. Louis, won 2-0 (6 innings)

**** April 15, 1909—Leon Ames of New York, lost 3-0 **(13 innings)**

April 15, 1915—Rube Marquard of New York, won 2-0

***** September 21, 1934—Paul Dean of St. Louis, won 3-0 (2nd game)

****** June 15, 1938—Johnny Vander Meer of Cincinnati, won 6-0

April 27, 1944—Jim Tobin of Boston, won 2-0

August 11, 1950—Vern Bickford of Boston, won 7-0

******* October 8, 1956—Don Larsen of New York Yankees, won 2-0 (World Series)

August 9, 1976—John Candelaria of Pittsburgh, won 2-0

******** September 26,1981—Nolan Ryan of Houston, won 5-0

* **Called so Dodgers could meet train schedule.**

** Game called.

*** Called because of rain.

**** No-hitter for 9.1 innings; lost on 7 hits.

***** Brother, Dizzy, pitched first game, a 3-hitter.

****** Second straight no-hitter, a **major-league** record.

******* Perfect game.

******** Fifth no-hitter, a career **and major-league** record.

PITCHER LONGEVITY

Most Complete Games, Season

Year	Pitcher	CG	Year	Pitcher	CG
1884	Adonis Terry	55	1927*	Dazzy Vance	25
1885	Henry Porter	53	1928	Dazzy Vance	24
1886	Henry Porter	48	1929	Watty Clark	19
1887	Henry Porter	38	1930	Dazzy Vance	20
1888	Bob Caruthers	42	1931	Watty Clark	16
1889	Bob Caruthers	46	1932	Watty Clark	19
1890	Tom Lovett	39	1933	Van Lingle Mungo	18
1891	Tom Lovett	39	1934	Van Lingle Mungo	22
1892	George Haddock	39	1935	Van Lingle Mungo	18
1893	Brickyard Kennedy	40	1936	Van Lingle Mungo	22
1894	Ed Stein	38	1937	Van Lingle Mungo	14
1895	Brickyard Kennedy	26	1938	Freddie Fitzsimmons	12
1896	Brickyard Kennedy	28	1939	Luke Hamlin	19
1897	Brickyard Kennedy	36	1940	Whit Wyatt	16
1898	Brickyard Kennedy	38	1941	Whit Wyatt	23
1899	Jay Hughes	30	1942	Whit Wyatt	16
1900	Iron Man McGinnity	32	1943	Whit Wyatt	13
1901	Wild Bill Donovan	36	1944	Curt Davis	12
1902	Wild Bill Donovan	30	1945	Hal Gregg	13
1903	Oscar Jones	31	1946	Joe Hatten	13
1904	Oscar Jones	38		Vic Lombardi	13
1905	Harry McIntire	29	1947	Ralph Branca	15
1906	Doc Scanlan	28	1948	Rex Barney	12
	Elmer Stricklett	28	1949	Don Newcombe	19
1907	Nap Rucker	26	1950	Don Newcombe	20
1908	Kaiser Wilhelm	33	1951	Preacher Roe	19
1909	George Bell	29	1952	Carl Erskine	10
1910*	Nap Rucker	27	1953	Carl Erskine	16
1911	Nap Rucker	23	1954	Carl Erskine	12
1912	Nap Rucker	23	1955	Don Newcombe	17
1913	Nap Rucker	16	1956	Don Newcombe	18
1914	Jeff Pfeffer	27	1957	Don Newcombe	12
1915	Jeff Pfeffer	26	1958	Johnny Podres	10
1916	Jeff Pfeffer	30	1959	Don Drysdale	15
1917	Jeff Pfeffer	24	1960	Don Drysdale	15
1918	Burleigh Grimes	19	1961	Sandy Koufax	15
	Rube Marquard	19	1962	Don Drysdale	19
1919	Jeff Pfeffer	26	1963	Sandy Koufax	20
1920	Burleigh Grimes	25	1964	Don Drysdale	21
1921*	Burleigh Grimes	30	1965*	Sandy Koufax	27
1922	Dutch Ruether	26	1966*	Sandy Koufax	27
1923*	Burleigh Grimes	33	1967	Claude Osteen	14
1924*	Burleigh Grimes	30	1968	Don Drysdale	12
	Dazzy Vance	30		Bill Singer	12
1925	Dazzy Vance	26	1969	Claude Osteen	16
1926	Jesse Petty	23		Bill Singer	16
			1970	Claude Osteen	11

*Led League

Most Complete Games, Season (Continued)

Year	Pitcher	CG
1971	Al Downing	12
	Don Sutton	12
1972	Don Sutton	18
1973	Don Sutton	14
1974	Andy Messersmith	13
1975	Andy Messersmith	19
1976	Don Sutton	15
1977	Tommy John	11
1978	Don Sutton	12
1979	Burt Hooton	12
1980	Jerry Reuss	10
1981	Fernando Valenzuela	11
1982	Fernando Valenzuela	18
1983	**Fernando Valenzuela**	9

Most Innings Pitched, Season

Year	Pitcher	IP	Year	Pitcher	IP
1884	Adonis Terry	485	1914	Jeff Pfeffer	315
1885	Henry Porter	482	1915	Jeff Pfeffer	292
1886	Henry Porter	424	1916	Jeff Pfeffer	329
1887	Henry Porter	340	1917	Jeff Pfeffer	266
1888	Bob Caruthers	392	1918	Burleigh Grimes	270
1889	Bob Caruthers	445	1919	Jeff Pfeffer	267
1890	Tom Lovett	372	1920	Burleigh Grimes	304
1891	Tom Lovett	366	1921	Burleigh Grimes	302
1892	George Haddock	381	1922	Dutch Ruether	267
1893	Brickyard Kennedy	383	1923*	Burleigh Grimes	327
1894	Brickyard Kennedy	361	1924*	Burleigh Grimes	311
1895	Brickyard Kennedy	280	1925	Dazzy Vance	265
1896	Brickyard Kennedy	306	1926	Jesse Petty	276
1897	Brickyard Kennedy	343	1927	Dazzy Vance	273
1898	Brickyard Kennedy	339	1928	Dazzy Vance	280
1899	Jack Dunn	299	1929*	Watty Clark	279
1900*	Iron Man McGinnity	347	1930	Dazzy Vance	259
1901	Wild Bill Donovan	351	1931	Watty Clark	233
1902	Wild Bill Donovan	298	1932	Watty Clark	273
1903	Oscar Jones	324	1933	Boom-Boom Beck	257
1904	Oscar Jones	377	1934*	Van Lingle Mungo	315
1905	Harry McIntire	309	1935	Van Lingle Mungo	214
1906	Elmer Stricklett	292	1936	Van Lingle Mungo	312
1907	Nap Rucker	275	1937	Max Butcher	192
1908	Nap Rucker	333	1938	Luke Hamlin	237
1909	Nap Rucker	309	1939	Luke Hamlin	270
1910*	Nap Rucker	320	1940	Whit Wyatt	239
1911	Nap Rucker	316	1941	Kirby Higbe	298
1912	Nap Rucker	298	1942	Kirby Higbe	222
1913	Pat Ragan	265	1943	Kirby Higbe	185

*Led League

Most Innings Pitched, Season (Continued)

Year	Pitcher	IP	Year	Pitcher	IP
1944	Hal Gregg	198	1962*	Don Drysdale	314
1945	Hal Gregg	254	1963	Don Drysdale	315
1946	Joe Hatten	222	1964*	Don Drysdale	321
1947	Ralph Branca	280	1965*	Sandy Koufax	336
1948	Rex Barney	247	1966*	Sandy Koufax	323
1949	Don Newcombe	244	1967	Claude Osteen	288
1950	Don Newcombe	267	1968	Bill Singer	256
1951	Don Newcombe	272	1969	Claude Osteen	321
1952	Carl Erskine	207	1970	Don Sutton	260
1953	Carl Erskine	247	1971	Don Sutton	265
1954	Carl Erskine	260	1972	Don Sutton	273
1955	Don Newcombe	234	1973	Don Sutton	256
1956	Don Newcombe	268	1974	Andy Messersmith	292
1957	Don Drysdale	221	1975*	Andy Messersmith	322
1958	Don Drysdale	212	1976	Don Sutton	268
1959	Don Drysdale	271	1977	Don Sutton	240
1960	Don Drysdale	269	1978	Don Sutton	238
1961	Sandy Koufax	256	1979	Rick Sutcliffe	242
			1980	Jerry Reuss	229
			1981*	Fernando Valenzuela	192
*Led League			1982	Fernando Valenzuela	285
			1983	**Fernando Valenzuela**	**257**

300-or-More Innings Pitched, Season

Year	Pitcher	IP	Year	Pitcher	IP
1884	Adonis Terry	485	1900	Iron Man McGinnity	347
	Sam Kimber	352	1901	Wild Bill Donovan	351
1885	Henry Porter	482	1903	Oscar Jones	324
1886	Henry Porter	424		Henry Schmidt	301
1887	Henry Porter	340	1904	Oscar Jones	377
	Adonis Terry	318		Jack Cronin	307
1888	Bob Caruthers	392	1905	Harry McIntire	309
	Mickey Hughes	363	1908	Nap Rucker	333
1889	Bob Caruthers	445		Kaiser Wilhelm	332
	Adonis Terry	326	1909	Nap Rucker	309
1890	Tom Lovett	372	1910	Nap Rucker	320
	Adonis Terry	370		George Bell	310
	Bob Caruthers	300	1911	Nap Rucker	316
1891	Tom Lovett	366	1914	Jeff Pfeffer	315
1892	George Haddock	381	1916	Jeff Pfeffer	329
	Ed Stein	377	1920	Burleigh Grimes	304
1893	Brickyard Kennedy	383	1921	Burleigh Grimes	302
1894	Brickyard Kennedy	361	1923	Burleigh Grimes	327
	Ed Stein	359	1924	Burleigh Grimes	311
1896	Brickyard Kennedy	306		Dazzy Vance	309
1897	Brickyard Kennedy	343	1934	Van Lingle Mungo	315
1898	Brickyard Kennedy	339	1936	Van Lingle Mungo	312
	Jack Dunn	323	1962	Don Drysdale	314

300-or-More Innings Pitched, Season (Continued)

Year	Pitcher	IP
1963	Don Drysdale	315
	Sandy Koufax	311
1964	Don Drysdale	321
1965	Sandy Koufax	336
	Don Drysdale	308
1966	Sandy Koufax	323
1969	Claude Osteen	321
	Bill Singer	316
1975	Andy Messersmith	322

2500-or-More Innings Pitched, Lifetime

Pitcher	IP
Don Sutton (1966-1980)	3728
Don Drysdale (1956-1969)	3432
Brickyard Kennedy (1892-1901)	2857
Dazzy Vance (1922-1932; 1935)	2758

2000-or-More Innings Pitched, Lifetime

Burleigh Grimes (1918-1926)	2426
Claude Osteen (1965-1973)	2397
Adonis Terry (1884-1891)	2385
Nap Rucker (1907-1916)	2375
Sandy Koufax (1955-1966)	2324
Johnny Podres (1953-1955; 1957-1966)	2030

1500-or-More Innings Pitched, Lifetime

Pitcher	IP
Burt Hooton (1975-1983)	1752
Jeff Pfeffer (1913-1921)	1748
Van Lingle Mungo (1931-1941)	1738
Carl Erskine (1948-1959)	1719
Don Newcombe (1949-1951; 1954-1958)	1662
Watty Clark (1927-1937)	1659

Andy Messersmith had several fine seasons for the Dodgers, including 1975 in which he pitched 322 innings.

1000-or-More Innings Pitched, Lifetime

Bob Caruthers (1888-1891)	1434
Ed Stein (1892-1896; 1898)	1403
Ralph Branca (1944-1953; 1956)	1325
Harry McInquire (1905-1909)	1301
Preacher Roe (1948-1954)	1279
Bill Singer (1964-1972)	1273
Leon Cadore (1915-1923)	1251
Doug Rau (1972-1980)	1251
Henry Porter (1885-1887)	1245
Doc Scanlan (1904-1907; 1909-1911)	1221
Tommy John (1972-1978)	1198
Sherry Smith (1915-1922)	1197
George Bell (1907-1911)	1086
Whit Wyatt (1939-1944)	1072
Tom Lovett (1889-1893)	1062
Luke Hamlin (1937-1941)	1011
Curt Davis (1940-1946)	1006

SHUTOUTS

Year-by-Year Leaders in Shutouts

Year	Pitcher	Shutouts
1884	Sam Kimber	3
	Adonis Terry	3
1885	Henry Porter	2
1886	Adonis Terry	5
1887	Henry Porter	1
	Adonis Terry	1
	Steve Toole	1
1888	Bob Caruthers	4
1889*	Bob Caruthers	7
1890	Tom Lovett	4
1891	Tom Lovett	3
1892	Ed Stein	6
1893	Brickyard Kennedy	2
1894	Ed Stein	2
1895	Brickyard Kennedy	2
1896	Harley Payne	2
1897	Brickyard Kennedy	2
1898	NO SHUTOUTS	—
1899	Jay Hughes	3
1900	Harry Howell	2
	Brickyard Kennedy	2
	Frank Kitson	2
1901	Frank Kitson	5
1902	Doc Newton	4
	Wild Bill Donovan	4

Year-by-Year Leaders in Shutouts (Continued)

Year	Pitcher	Shutouts
1903	Henry Schmidt	5
1904	Jack Cronin	4
1905	Mal Eason	3
1906	Don Scanlan	6
1907	Jim Pastorius	4
	Nap Rucker	4
	Elmer Stricklett	4
1908	Nap Rucker	6
	Kaiser Wilhelm	6
1909	George Bell	6
	Nap Rucker	6
1910	Nap Rucker	6
1911	Nap Rucker	5
1912*	Nap Rucker	6
1913	Nap Rucker	4
1914	Raleigh Aitchison	3
	Jeff Pfeffer	3
	Ed Reulbach	3
1915	Jeff Pfeffer	6
1916	Jeff Pfeffer	6
1917	Jeff Pfeffer	3
1918	Burleigh Grimes	7
1919	Jeff Pfeffer	4
1920	Burleigh Grimes	5
1921*	Clarence Mitchell	3
1922*	Dazzy Vance	5
1923	Dazzy Vance	3
1924	Dazzy Vance	3
1925*	Dazzy Vance	4
1926	Jesse Barnes	1
	Burleigh Grimes	1
	Doug McWeeney	1
	Jesse Petty	1
	Dazzy Vance	1
1927	Jim Elliott	2
	Jesse Petty	2
	Dazzy Vance	2
1928*	Doug McWeeney	4
	Dazzy Vance	4
1929	Watty Clark	3
1930*	Dazzy Vance	4
1931	Watty Clark	3
1932	Watty Clark	2
	Hollis Thurston	2
1933	Boom-Boom Beck	3
	Van Lingle Mungo	3
1934	Van Lingle Mungo	3
1935*	Van Lingle Mungo	4

*Led League

Van Lingle Mungo led the Dodgers in shutouts pitched for four consecutive years, 1933-1936.

Year-by-Year Leaders in Shutouts (Continued)

Year	Pitcher	Shutouts
1936	Van Lingle Mungo	2
1937	Max Butcher	1
	Fred Frankhouse	1
	Luke Hamlin	1
	Waite Hoyt	1
	George Jeffcoat	1
1938	Freddie Fitzsimmons	3
1939	Luke Hamlin	2
	Tot Pressnell	2
	Whit Wyatt	2
1940*	Whit Wyatt	5
1941*	Whit Wyatt	7
1942	Curt Davis	5
1943	Ed Head	3
	Whit Wyatt	3
1944	Curt Davis	1
	Ed Head	1
	Art Herring	1
	Rube Melton	1
1945	Hal Gregg	2
	Art Herring	2
	Tom Seats	2
1946	Kirby Higbe	3
1947	Ralph Branca	4
1948	Rex Barney	4
1949*	Don Newcombe	5
1950	Don Newcombe	4
1951	Ralph Branca	3
	Don Newcombe	3
1952	Carl Erskine	4
	Billy Loes	4
1953	Carl Erskine	4
1954	Carl Erskine	2
	Russ Meyer	2
	Johnny Podres	2
	Karl Spooner	2
1955	Carl Erskine	2
	Sandy Koufax	2
	Johnny Podres	2
1956	Don Newcombe	5
1957*	Johnny Podres	6
1958	Johnny Podres	2
	Stan Williams	2
1959*	Roger Craig	4
	Don Drysdale	4
1960	Don Drysdale	5
1961	Don Drysdale	3

*Led League

Year-by-Year Leaders in Shutouts (Continued)

Year	Pitcher	Shutouts
1962	Don Drysdale	2
	Sandy Koufax	2
1963*	Sandy Koufax	11
1964*	Sandy Koufax	7
1965	Sandy Koufax	8
1966*	Sandy Koufax	5
1967	Claude Osteen	5
1968	Don Drysdale	8
1969	Claude Osteen	7
1970	Claude Osteen	4
	Don Sutton	4
1971*	Al Downing	5
1972*	Don Sutton	9
1973	Andy Messersmith	3
	Claude Osteen	3
	Don Sutton	3
1974	Don Sutton	5
1975*	Andy Messersmith	7
1976	Burt Hooton	4
	Don Sutton	4
1977	Tommy John	3
	Don Sutton	3
1978	Burt Hooton	3
	Rick Rhoden	3
	Bob Welch	3
1979	Burt Hooton	1
	Doug Rau	1
	Jerry Reuss	1
	Rick Sutcliffe	1
	Don Sutton	1
1980*	Jerry Reuss	6
1981*	Fernando Valenzuela	8
1982	Jerry Reuss	4
	Fernando Valenzuela	4
1983	**Fernando Valenzuela**	**4**

*Led League

Five-or-More Shutouts, Season

Year	Pitcher	Total
1886	Adonis Terry	5
1889	Bob Caruthers	7
1901	Frank Kitson	5
1903	Henry Schmidt	5
1906	Doc Scanlan	6
	Elmer Stricklett	5
1908	Nap Rucker	6
	Kaiser Wilhelm	6

Five-or-More Shutouts, Season (Continued)

Year	Pitcher	Total
1909	George Bell	6
	Nap Rucker	6
1910	Nap Rucker	6
1911	Nap Rucker	5
1912	Nap Rucker	6
1915	Jeff Peffer	6
1916	Jeff Pfeffer	6
	Larry Cheney	5
1918	Burleigh Grimes	7
1920	Burleigh Grimes	5
1922	Dazzy Vance	5
1940	Whit Wyatt	5
1941	Whit Wyatt	7
	Curt Davis	5
1942	Curt Davis	5
1949	Don Newcombe	5
1956	Don Newcombe	5
1957	Johnny Podres	6
1960	Don Drysdale	5
1963	Sandy Koufax	11
	Johnny Podres	5
1964	Sandy Koufax	7
	Don Drysdale	5
1965	Sandy Koufax	8
	Don Drysdale	7
1966	Sandy Koufax	5
1967	Claude Osteen	5
1968	Don Drysdale	8
	Bill Singer	6
1969	Claude Osteen	7
1971	Al Downing	5
1972	Don Sutton	9
1975	Andy Messersmith	7
1980	Jerry Reuss	6
1981	Fernando Valenzuela	8

Pitchers With 15-or-More Shutouts

Pitcher	Total
Don Sutton (1966-1980)	52
Don Drysdale (1956-1969)	49
Sandy Koufax (1955-1966)	40
Nap Rucker (1907-1916)	38
Claude Osteen (1965-1973)	34
Dazzy Vance (1922-32; 1935)	30
Jeff Pfeffer (1913-1921)	25
Johnny Podres (1953-1955; 1957-1966)	23
Don Newcombe (1949-1951; 1954-1958)	22
Burt Hooton (1975-1983)	22

Pitchers With 15-or-More Shutouts (Continued)

Pitcher	Total
Burleigh Grimes (1918-1926)	20
Bill Singer (1964-1972)	18
George Bell (1907-1911)	17
Whit Wyatt (1939-1944)	17
Van Lingle Mungo (1931-1941)	16
Fernando Valenzuela (1980-1983)	**16**
Adonis Terry (1884-1891)	15
Bob Caruthers (1888-1891)	15
Doc Scanlan (1904-1907; 1909-1911)	15

Shutout Records

Most Career Shutouts—52, Don Sutton (1966-1980)

Most Shutouts, Season (50-Foot pitching distance)—
7, Bob Caruthers, 1889

Most Shutouts, Season (60-Foot pitching distance)—
11, Sandy Koufax, 1963

Most Shutouts, Season (Brooklyn)—7, Burleigh Grimes, 1918
7, Whit Wyatt,1941

Most Consecutive Shutouts-6, Don Drysdale, 1968

Most Shutouts, Month—5, Don Drysdale, May, 1968

Most Shutouts, Rookie Season—5, Henry Schmidt, 1903
5, Don Newcombe, 1949

Most Consecutive Shutout Innings—58, ⅔, Don Drysdale,
May 14-June 4, 1968

STRIKEOUTS

Most Strikeouts by Pitcher, Season

Year	Pitcher	Strikeouts
1884	Adonis Terry	233
1885	Henry Porter	197
1886	Henry Porter	163
1887	Adonis Terry	138
1888	Mickey Hughes	159
1889	Adonis Terry	186
1890	Adonis Terry	185
1891	Tom Lovett	129
1892	Ed Stein	190
1893	Brickyard Kennedy	107
1894	Brickyard Kennedy	107
1895	Ed Stein	55
1896	Brickyard Kennedy	76
1897	Harley Payne	86

Most Strikeouts by Pitcher, Season (Continued)

Year	Pitcher	Strikeouts
1898	Brickyard Kennedy	73
1899	Doc McJames	105
1900	Iron Man McGinnity	93
1901	Wild Bill Donovan	226
1902	Wild Bill Donovan	170
1903	Ned Garvin	154
1904	Jack Cronin	110
1905	Harry McIntire	135
	Doc Scanlan	135
1906	Harry McIntire	121
1907	Nap Rucker	131
1908	Nap Rucker	199
1909	Nap Rucker	201
1910	Nap Rucker	147
1911	Nap Rucker	190
1912	Nap Rucker	151
1913	Nap Rucker	111
1914	Jeff Pfeffer	135
1915	Wheezer Dell	94
1916	Larry Cheney	166
1917	Rube Marquard	117
1918	Burleigh Grimes	113
1919	Leon Cadore	94
1920	Burleigh Grimes	131
1921*	Burleigh Grimes	136
1922*	Dazzy Vance	134
1923*	Dazzy Vance	197
1924*	Dazzy Vance	262
1925*	Dazzy Vance	221
1926*	Dazzy Vance	140
1927*	Dazzy Vance	184
1928*	Dazzy Vance	200
1929	Watty Clark	140
1930	Dazzy Vance	173
1931	Dazzy Vance	150
1932	Van Lingle Mungo	107
1933	Van Lingle Mungo	110
1934	Van Lingle Mungo	184
1935	Van Lingle Mungo	143
1936*	Van Lingle Mungo	238
1937	Van Lingle Mungo	122
1938	Luke Hamlin	97
1939	Luke Hamlin	88
1940	Whit Wyatt	124
1941	Whit Wyatt	176
1942	Kirby Higbe	115
1943	Kirby Higbe	108
1944	Hal Gregg	92
1945	Hal Gregg	139

*Led League

Most Strikeouts by Pitcher, Season (Continued)

Year	Pitcher	Strikeouts
1946	Kirby Higbe	134
1947	Ralph Branca	148
1948	Rex Barney	138
1949	Don Newcombe	149
1950	Erv Palica	131
1951	Don Newcombe	164
1952	Carl Erskine	131
1953	Carl Erskine	187
1954	Carl Erskine	166
1955	Don Newcombe	143
1956	Don Newcombe	139
1957	Don Drysdale	148
1958	Johnny Podres	143
1959*	Don Drysdale	242
1960*	Don Drysdale	246
1961*	Sandy Koufax	269
1962*	Don Drysdale	232
1963*	Sandy Koufax	306
1964	Don Drysdale	237
1965*	Sandy Koufax	382
1966*	Sandy Koufax	317
1967	Don Drysdale	196
1968	Bill Singer	227
1969	Bill Singer	247
1970	Don Sutton	201
1971	Don Sutton	194
1972	Don Sutton	207
1973	Don Sutton	200
1974	Andy Messersmith	221
1975	Andy Messersmith	213
1976	Don Sutton	161
1977	Burt Hooton	153
1978	Don Sutton	154
1979	Don Sutton	146
1980	Bob Welch	141
1981*	Fernando Valenzuela	180
1982	Fernando Valenzuela	199
1983	**Fernando Velenzuela**	**189**

*Led League

Joe Black was an instant winner with the Dodgers. In his rookie season he was 15-4, a record good enough to garner rookie-of-the-year honors. He never quite regained the effectiveness of his first year in Brooklyn and was traded to the Cincinnati Reds in 1955.

200-or-More Strikeouts by Pitcher, Season

Year	Pitcher	Strikeouts
1884	Adonis Terry	233
1901	Wild Bill Donovan	226
1909	Nap Rucker	201
1924	Dazzy Vance	262
1925	Dazzy Vance	221
1928	Dazzy Vance	200
1936	Van Lingle Mungo	238
1959	Don Drysdale	242
1960	Don Drysdale	246
1961	Sandy Koufax	269
	Stan Williams	205
1962	Don Drysdale	232
	Sandy Koufax	216
1963	Sandy Koufax	306
	Don Drysdale	251
1964	Don Drysdale	237
	Sandy Koufax	223
1965	Sandy Koufax	382
	Don Drysdale	210
1966	Sandy Koufax	317
	Don Sutton	209
1968	Bill Singer	227
1969	Bill Singer	247
	Don Sutton	217
1970	Don Sutton	201
1972	Don Sutton	207
1973	Don Sutton	200
1974	Andy Messersmith	213

100-or-More Strikeouts by Pitcher, Season

Year	Pitcher	Strikeouts
1884	Adonis Terry	233
	Sam Kimber	119
1885	Henry Porter	197
	John Harkins	141
1886	Henry Porter	163
	Adonis Terry	162
	John Harkins	118
1887	Adonis Terry	138
1888	Mickey Hughes	159
	Bob Caruthers	140
	Adonis Terry	138
1889	Adonis Terry	186
	Bob Caruthers	118
1890	Adonis Terry	185
	Tom Lovett	124
1891	Tom Lovett	129

100-or-More Strikeouts by Pitcher, Season (Continued)

Year	Pitcher	Strikeouts
1892	Ed Stein	190
	George Haddock	153
	Brickyard Kennedy	108
1893	Brickyard Kennedy	107
1894	Brickyard Kennedy	107
1899	Doc McJames	105
1901	Wild Bill Donovan	226
	Frank Kitson	127
1902	Wild Bill Donovan	170
	Frank Kitson	107
	Doc Newton	107
1903	Ned Garvin	154
1904	Jack Cronin	110
1905	Harry McIntire	135
	Doc Scanlan	135
1906	Harry McIntire	121
	Doc Scanlan	120
1907	Nap Rucker	131
1908	Nap Rucker	199
	Harry McIntire	108
1909	Nap Rucker	201
1910	Nap Rucker	147
	Doc Scanlan	103
	George Bell	102
1911	Nap Rucker	190
1912	Nap Rucker	151
	Pat Ragan	101
1913	Nap Rucker	111
	Pat Ragan	109
1914	Jeff Pfeffer	135
	Ed Reulbach	119
	Pat Ragan	106
1916	Larry Cheney	166
	Jeff Pfeffer	128
	Rube Marquard	107
1917	Rube Marquard	117
	Leon Cadore	115
	Jeff Pfeffer	115
	Larry Cheney	102
1918	Burleigh Grimes	118
1920	Burleigh Grimes	131
	Al Mamaux	101
1921	Burleigh Grimes	136
1922	Dazzy Vance	134
1923	Dazzy Vance	197
	Burleigh Grimes	119
1924	Dazzy Vance	262
	Burleigh Grimes	135
1925	Dazzy Vance	221

100-or-More Strikeouts by Pitcher, Season (Continued)

Year	Pitcher	Strikeouts
1926	Dazzy Vance	140
	Jesse Petty	101
1927	Dazzy Vance	184
	Jesse Petty	101
1928	Dazzy Vance	200
1929	Watty Clark	140
	Dazzy Vance	126
1930	Dazzy Vance	173
1931	Dazzy Vance	150
1932	Van Lingle Mungo	107
	Dazzy Vance	103
1933	Van Lingle Mungo	110
1934	Van Lingle Mungo	184
1935	Van Lingle Mungo	143
1936	Van Lingle Mungo	238
	Ed Brandt	104
1937	Van Lingle Mungo	122
1940	Whit Wyatt	124
1941	Whit Wyatt	176
	Kirby Higbe	121
1942	Kirby Higbe	115
	Whit Wyatt	104
1943	Kirby Higbe	108
1945	Hal Gregg	139
1946	Kirby Higbe	134
1947	Ralph Branca	148
1948	Rex Barney	138
	Ralph Branca	122
1949	Don Newcombe	149
	Ralph Branca	109
	Preacher Roe	109
1950	Erv Palica	131
	Don Newcombe	130
	Preacher Roe	125
	Ralph Branca	100
1951	Don Newcombe	164
	Ralph Branca	118
	Preacher Roe	113
1952	Carl Erskine	131
	Ben Wade	118
	Billy Loes	115
1953	Carl Erskine	187
	Russ Meyer	106
1954	Carl Erskine	166
1955	Don Newcombe	143
	Johnny Podres	114
1956	Don Newcombe	139
	Roger Craig	109
	Sal Maglie	108

100-or-More Strikeouts by Pitcher, Season (Continued)

Year	Pitcher	Strikeouts
1957	Don Drysdale	148
	Sandy Koufax	122
	Johnny Podres	109
1958	Johnny Podres	143
	Don Drysdale	131
	Sandy Koufax	131
1959	Don Drysdale	242
	Sandy Koufax	173
	Johnny Podres	145
	Danny McDevitt	106
1960	Don Drysdale	246
	Sandy Koufax	197
	Stan Williams	175
	Johnny Podres	159
	Larry Sherry	114
1961	Sandy Koufax	269
	Stan Williams	205
	Don Drysdale	182
	Johnny Podres	124
1962	Don Drysdale	232
	Sandy Koufax	216
	Johnny Podres	178
	Stan Willliams	108
1963	Sandy Koufax	306
	Don Drysdale	251
	Johnny Podres	134
	Bob Miller	125
1964	Don Drysdale	237
	Sandy Koufax	223
	Phil Ortega	107
1965	Sandy Koufax	382
	Don Drysdale	210
	Claude Osteen	162
1966	Sandy Koufax	317
	Don Sutton	209
	Don Drysdale	177
	Claude Osteen	137
1967	Don Drysdale	196
	Bill Singer	169
	Don Sutton	169
	Claude Osteen	152
1968	Bill Singer	227
	Don Sutton	162
	Don Drysdale	155
	Claude Osteen	119
1969	Bill Singer	247
	Don Sutton	217
	Claude Osteen	183
1970	Don Sutton	201
	Claude Osteen	114

100-or-More Strikeouts by Pitcher, Season (Continued)

Year	Pitcher	Strikeouts
1971	Don Sutton	194
	Bill Singer	144
	Al Downing	136
	Claude Osteen	109
1972	Don Sutton	207
	Al Downing	117
	Tommy John	117
	Bill Singer	101
	Claude Osteen	100
1973	Don Sutton	200
	Andy Messersmith	177
	Al Downing	124
	Tommy John	116
1974	Andy Messersmith	221
	Don Sutton	179
	Mike Marshall	143
	Doug Rau	126
1975	Andy Messersmith	213
	Don Sutton	175
	Doug Rau	151
	Burt Hooton	148
1976	Don Sutton	161
	Burt Hooton	116
1977	Burt Hooton	153
	Don Sutton	150
	Doug Rau	126
	Tommy John	123
	Rick Rhoden	122
	Charlie Hough	105
1978	Don Sutton	154
	Tommy John	124
	Burt Hooton	104
1979	Don Sutton	146
	Burt Hooton	129
	Rick Sutcliffe	117
1980	Bob Welch	141
	Don Sutton	128
	Burt Hooton	118
	Jerry Reuss	111
1981	Fernando Valenzuela	180
1982	Fernando Valenzuela	199
	Bob Welch	176
	Jerry Reuss	138
1983	Fernando Valenzuela	189
	Bob Welch	156
	Jerry Reuss	143
	Alejandro Pena	120

Reliever Mike Marshall had several fine seasons with the Dodgers, particularly 1974 when he appeared in a major league record-setting 108 games.

500-or-More Strikeouts by Pitcher, Lifetime

Year	Pitcher	Total
Don Sutton	(1966-1980)	2652
Don Drysdale	(1956-1969)	2486
Sandy Koufax	(1955-1966)	2396
Dazzy Vance	(1922-1932; 1935)	1918
Johnny Podres	(1953-1955; 1957-1966)	1331
Nap Rucker	(1907-1916)	1217
Adonis Terrry	(1884-1891)	1203
Claude Osteen	(1965-1973)	1162
Van Lingle Mungo	(1931-1941)	1031
Bill Singer	(1964-1972)	989
Carl Erskin	(1948-1959)	981
Burt Hooton	(1975-1983)	980
Burleigh Grimes	(1918-1926)	952
Don Newcombe	(1949-1951; 1954-1958)	913
Ralph Branca	(1944-1953; 1956)	757
Brickyard Kennedy	(1892-1901)	749
Doug Rau	(1972-1980)	694
Bob Welch	(1978-1983)	691
Jim Brewer	(1964-1975)	672
Stan Williams	(1958-1962)	657
Jeff Pfeffer	(1913-1921)	656
Tommy John	(1972-1978)	649
Preacher Roe	(1948-1954)	632
Watty Clark	(1927-1937)	620
Andy Messersmith	(1973-1975; 1979)	611
Fernando Valenzuela	(1980-1983)	584
Doc Scanlan	(1904-1907; 1909-1911)	574
Whit Wyatt	(1939-1944)	540
Charlie Hough	(1970-1980)	536
Al Downing	(1971-1977)	532
Jerry Reuss	(1980-1983)	526

Most Strikeouts in a Game by Pitcher

Total	Pitcher	Date and Opponent
18	Sandy Koufax	August 31, 1959 vs. San Francisco
18	Sandy Koufax	April 24, 1962 vs. Chicago
17	Dazzy Vance	July 20, 1925 vs. St. Louis (10 inn.)
16	Nap Rucker	July 24, 1909 vs. Pittsburgh
16	Sandy Koufax	June 22, 1959 vs. Philadlphia
16	Sandy Koufax	May 26, 1962 vs. Philadelphia
16	Sandy Koufax	July 27, 1966 vs. Philadelphia (11 inn.)
15	Dazzy Vance	May 2, 1922 vs.New York
15	Dazzy Vance	August 1, 1924 vs. St. Louis
15	Dazzy Vance	September 26, 1926 vs. Chicago
15	Dazzy Vance	June 17, 1927 vs. Chicago
15	Van Lingle Mungo	September 29, 1935 vs. Philadelphia
15	Karl Spooner	September 26, 1953 vs. New York
15	Sandy Koufax	September 20, 1961 vs. Chicago (13 inn.)
15	Sandy Koufax	October 2, 1963 vs. New York Yankees (World Series)
14	Carl Erskine	October 2, 1965 vs. New York Yankees (World Series)
14	Don Drysdale	April 12, 1960 vs. Chicago

Strikeout Records

Most Strikeouts, Lifetime—2,652, Don Sutton (1966-1980)

Most Strikeouts, Season (50-Foot Pitching Distance)—233, Adonis Terry (1884)

Most Strikeouts, Season (60-Foot Pitching Distance)—382, Sandy Koufax (1965)

Most Strikeouts, Season (Brooklyn)—262, Dazzy Vance (1924)

Most Strikeouts, Nine Inning Game
—18, Sandy Koufax, August 31, 1959
—18, Sandy Koufax, April 24, 1962

Most Times, 200 Strikeouts Per Season—6, Don Drysdale (1956-1969); and Sandy Koufax (1955-1966)

Most Times, 100 Strikeouts Per Season—15, Don Sutton (1966-1980)

Most Games, 10-or-More Strikeouts—98, Sandy Koufax (1955-1966)

Most Strikeouts, Rookie Season—209, Don Sutton (1966)

Most Consecutive Strikeouts, Game—8, Johnny Podres, July 2, 1962 (1st-G)

Most Strikeouts, Inning—4, Pete Richert, April 12, 1962; Don Drysdale, April 17, 1965.

Highest Strikeout Ratio (Per Nine Innings)—9.27, Sandy Koufax (1955-1966)

FEATURES

THE DODGERS IN WORLD SERIES PLAY

Don Larsen's perfect game in 1956. Cookie Lavagetto's ninth-inning double in 1947 that ruined Bill Bevens' bid for a no-hitter. Bill Wambganss' unassisted triple play in 1920. Mickey Owen's dropped third strike in 1941. Reggie Jackson's three homers in one game in 1977.

All dramatic incidents in the World Series—and they all involved the Dodgers.

With the lone exception of the New York Yankees, no team in baseball has played in as many of the fall classics as the Dodgers—17 from their first appearance in 1916 against the Boston Red Sox through 1981 and the Yankees.

And perhaps no team, including the Yankees, has had quite as many still-talked-about fanciful moments. Most, in fact, were against the Yankees.

Let's take a quick review of down through the years.

In 1916, the second game, Babe Ruth of Boston and Sherry Smith of the Dodgers hooked up in the longest game ever, 14 innings, before the Red Sox won 2-1. Ruth twirled 13 consecutive scoreless innings after a Dodger homer.

The 1920 Series, against Cleveland, featured second baseman Wambsganss' triple play that occurred in the fifth inning of the fifth game. He snagged a sharp line drive, stepped on second base to retire that runner, then chased down the Dodger running from first.

Having lost their first two World Series, the Dodgers had high hopes when they reappeared in 1941 after a 21-year hiatus. Owen's failure to hold on to a swinging third strike of a Hugh Casey sinking pitch that would have tied the Series at two games each settled that one.

The batter, Tommy Heinrich of the Yankees, got life, the New Yorkers scored four, and they won the game, 7-4. And the Series.

Brooklyn, however, was on the plus side of the 1947 dramatics which occurred in the fourth game when pinch-hitter Lavagetto laced his historic two-out hit that drove in two Dodgers, who'd walked, for a 3-2 victory and the ruination of Yankee Bevens' 10-walk no-hitter.

This, also, was the Series that Dodgers sub outfielder Al Gionfriddo robbed Joe DiMaggio of a homer when he flagged down his potential score-tying homer at the 415-foot mark.

But still the Dodgers lost. In fact, they were 0-7 in World Series action until 1955 when Johnny Podres hurled his 2-0 seventh-game gem that gave all Brooklyn a chance to quit hollering "wait 'til next year." That date: October 4, at Yankee Stadium.

But a year later the Dodgers reverted to form, the crusher being Larsen's 27-straight-outs performance in the fifth game, the only World Series "perfecto" ever pitched. That gave the Brooklyn Dodgers a 1-8 Series standing, hardly worthy of their fans' zeal.

With the move to Los Angeles came—seemingly—new World Series life. Behind reliever Larry Sherry's 1959 heroics they beat the Chicago White Sox in six games, three of them marked by 90,000-plus crowds at the L.A. Coliseum.

In 1963 the Dodgers even polished off the dreaded Yankees four games straight, unbelievably, behind the great pitching of Sandy Koufax (2-0), Don Drysdale, and Podres.

And they trimmed the Minnesota Twins in seven in 1965 to go three-up as a Los Angeles entry. All they lacked were a few of those extraordinary incidents that had colored their past!

The Dodgers got one such incident in the fifth inning of the second game in 1966, but as usual it occurred against them. Center fielder Willie Davis lost two flies in the sun at Dodger Stadium and compounded one with a throwing error—the only player ever to make three errors in one World Series inning.

Los Angeles dropped four straight that fall to Baltimore, which put the Dodgers into a tailspin as they then lost successively to Oakland in 1974 and to the Yankees again in 1977 and 1978, the latter two being Tommy Lasorda's first two Series as pilot.

New York's Jackson provided the dramatics in 1977 when he belted three first pitches out of Yankee Stadium in the sixth contest. In 1978 it was third baseman Graig Nettles' glove that turned the Series in the Yankees' favor after the Dodgers had won the first two games at home.

That, then, put the Los Angeles Dodgers at 3-4, a deficit rectified in 1981 as the Dodgers fought from behind after being down by two games to win over the Yankees four games to two.

Memorable moments were Fernando Valenzuela's gutty third-game pitching, the beaning of Dodger third baseman Ron Cey by Rich Gossage in the fifth contest at Dodger Stadium, and Pedro Guerrero's three hits and five RBI's that won the sixth and deciding game.

Despite their lukewarm 5-12 won-lost record, 3-8 vs. the Yanks, the Dodgers have managed to turn in some eye-catching statistics. Podres, with 4-1, has the best pitching mark, though Sherry posted a 2-0 record and he along with Sherry Smith and Koufax all have remarkable earned run averages of under one.

Burleigh Grimes (1920), Preacher Roe (1949), Podres (1955), Clem Labine (1956), Don Drysdale (1963), Claude Osteen (1965), and Koufax (1965 twice) have all pitched shutouts.

On October 2, 1953 Carl Erskine whiffed 14 Yanks for a one-game Series record that stood 10 years to the day when Koufax fanned 15—including the first five batters in the game.

On the batting ledger, Steve Garvey has a healthily-consistent .344 average, probably better than any Dodger considering his number of times at-bat, though there are others higher. Garvey, too, is the only Dodger who has twice (1974, 1981) hit safely in every game of a World Series.

Slugging honors, though, definitely go to Duke Snider who in his six World Series and 133 at-bats belted 11 homers, 8 doubles, and had 26 RBI's—all Dodger highs. Eight of the Duke's homers came in two Series—four each in 1952 and 1955.

Pee Wee Reese has the most hits, 46, and Jackie Robinson the most runs scored, 22.

During their 17 World Series, the Dodgers have played 100 games and have won 41 while losing 59. They are 28-21 on their grounds and 13-38 in foreign ball yards.

In Brooklyn they were 14-14 at home and 6-24 away while the Los Angeles numbers are 14-7, home, and 7-16 away, giving credence to the belief that Dodger Stadium, indeed, may be a special ally for its resident.

Ebbets Field , apparently, wasn't.

Celebrating the Dodgers'1955 World Series triumph over the N.Y. Yankees are (left to right) Clem Labine, Walter O'Malley, Coach Jake Pitter, Billy Herman and Rube Walker.

Line Scores of World Series Games

1916

First game—October 7, at Boston

						R	H	E
Dodgers*	000	100	004			5	10	4
Bost.	001	010	31x			6	8	1

Second game—October 9, at Boston

						R	H	E
Dodgers	100	000	000	000	00	1	6	2
Bost.	001	000	000	000	01	2	7	1

Third game—October 10, at Ebbets Field, Brooklyn

Bost.	000	002	100	3	7	1
Dodgers	001	120	00x	4	10	0

Fourth game—October 11, at Brooklyn

Bost.	030	110	100	6	10	1
Dodgers	200	000	000	2	5	4

Fifth game—October 12, at Boston

Dodgers	010	000	000	1	3	3
Bost.	012	010	00x	4	7	2

1920

First game—October 5, at Brooklyn

				R	H	E
Clev.	020	100	000	3	5	0
Dodgers	000	000	100	1	5	1

Second game—October 6, at Brooklyn

Clev.	000	000	000	0	7	1
Dodgers	101	010	00x	3	7	0

Third game—October 7, at Brooklyn

Clev.	000	100	000	1	3	1
Dodgers	200	000	00x	2	6	1

Fourth game—October 9, at Cleveland

Dodgers	000	100	000	1	5	1
Clev.	202	001	00x	5	12	2

Fifth game—October 10, at Cleveland

Dodgers	000	000	001	1	13	1
Clev.	400	310	00x	8	12	2

Sixth game—October 11, at Cleveland

Dodgers	000	000	000	0	3	0
Clev.	000	001	00x	1	7	3

Seventh game—October 12, at Cleveland

Dodgers	000	000	000	0	5	2
Clev.	000	110	10x	3	7	3

Line Scores of World Series Games (Continued)

1941

First game—October 1, at New York

				R	H	E
Dodgers	000	010	100	2	6	0
Yankees	010	101	00x	3	6	1

Second game—October 2, at New York

| Dodgers | 000 | 021 | 000 | 3 | 6 | 2 |
| Yankees | 011 | 000 | 000 | 2 | 9 | 1 |

Third game—October 4, at Brooklyn

| Yankees | 000 | 000 | 020 | 2 | 8 | 0 |
| Dodgers | 000 | 000 | 010 | 1 | 4 | 0 |

Fourth game—October 5, at Brooklyn

| Yankees | 100 | 200 | 004 | 7 | 12 | 0 |
| Dodgers | 000 | 220 | 000 | 4 | 9 | 1 |

Fifth game—October 6, at Brooklyn

| Yankees | 020 | 010 | 000 | 3 | 6 | 0 |
| Dodgers | 001 | 000 | 000 | 1 | 4 | 1 |

1947

First game—September 30, at New York

				R	H	E
Dodgers	100	001	100	3	6	0
Yankees	000	050	00x	5	4	0

Second game—October 1, at New York

| Dodgers | 001 | 100 | 001 | 3 | 9 | 2 |
| Yankees | 101 | 121 | 40x | 10 | 15 | 1 |

Third game—October 2, at Brooklyn

| Yankees | 002 | 221 | 100 | 8 | 13 | 0 |
| Dodgers | 061 | 200 | 00x | 9 | 13 | 1 |

Fourth game—October 3, at Brooklyn

| Yankees | 100 | 100 | 000 | 2 | 8 | 1 |
| Dodgers | 000 | 010 | 002 | 3 | 1 | 3 |

Fifth game—October 4, at Brooklyn

| Yankees | 000 | 110 | 000 | 2 | 5 | 0 |
| Dodgers | 000 | 001 | 000 | 1 | 4 | 1 |

Sixth game—October 5, at New York

| Dodgers | 202 | 004 | 000 | 8 | 12 | 1 |
| New York | 004 | 100 | 001 | 6 | 15 | 2 |

Seventh game—October 6, at New York

| Dodgers | 020 | 000 | 000 | 2 | 7 | 0 |
| Yankees | 010 | 201 | 10x | 5 | 7 | 0 |

Line Scores of World Series Games (Continued)

1949

First game—October 5, at New York

				R	H	E
Dodgers	000	000	000	0	2	0
Yankees	000	000	001	1	5	1

Second game—October 6, at New York

Dodgers	010	000	000	1	7	2
Yankees	000	000	000	0	6	1

Third game—October 7, at Brooklyn

Yankees	001	000	003	4	5	0
Dodgers	000	100	002	3	5	0

Fourth game—October 8, at Brooklyn

Yankees	000	330	000	6	10	0
Dodgers	000	004	000	4	9	1

Fifth game—October 9, at Brooklyn

Yankees	203	113	000	10	11	1
Dodgers	001	001	400	6	11	2

1952

First game—October 1, at Brooklyn

				R	H	E
Yankees	001	000	010	2	6	2
Dodgers	010	002	01x	4	6	0

Second game—October 2, at Brooklyn

Yankees	000	115	000	7	10	0
Dodgers	001	000	000	1	3	1

Third game—October 3, at New York

Dodgers	001	010	012	5	11	0
Yankees	010	000	011	3	6	2

Fourth game—October 4, at New York

Dodgers	000	000	000	0	4	1
Yankees	000	100	01x	2	4	1

Fifth game—October 5, at New York

Dodgers	010	030	100	01	6	10	0
Yankees	000	050	000	00	5	5	1

Sixth game—October 6, at Brooklyn

Yankees	000	000	210	3	9	0
Dodgers	000	001	010	2	8	1

Seventh game—October 7, at Brooklyn

Yankees	000	111	100	4	10	4
Dodgers	000	110	000	2	8	1

Line Scores of World Series Games (Continued)
1953

First game—September 30, at New York

				R	H	E
Dodgers	000	013	100	5	12	2
Yankees	400	010	13x	9	12	0

Second game—October 1, at New York

				R	H	E
Dodgers	000	200	000	2	9	1
Yankees	100	000	12x	4	5	0

Third game—October 2, at Brooklyn

				R	H	E
Yankees	000	010	010	2	6	0
Dodgers	000	011	01x	3	9	0

Fourth game—October 3, at Brooklyn

				R	H	E
Yankees	000	020	001	3	9	0
Dodgers	300	102	10x	7	12	0

Fifth game—October 4, at Brooklyn

				R	H	E
Yankees	105	000	311	11	11	1
Dodgers	010	010	041	7	14	1

Sixth game—October 5, at New York

				R	H	E
Dodger	000	001	002	3	8	3
Yankees	210	000	001	4	13	0

1955

First game—September 28, at New York

				R	H	E
Dodgers	021	000	020	5	10	0
Yankees	021	102	00x	6	9	1

Second game—September 29, at New York

				R	H	E
Dodgers	000	110	000	2	5	2
Yankees	000	400	00x	4	8	0

Third game—September 30, at Brooklyn

				R	H	E
Yankees	020	000	100	3	7	0
Dodgers	220	200	20x	8	11	1

Fourth game—October 1, at Brooklyn

				R	H	E
Yankees	110	102	000	5	9	0
Dodgers	001	330	10x	8	14	0

Fifth game—October 2, at Brooklyn

				R	H	E
Yankees	000	100	110	3	6	0
Dodgers	021	010	01x	5	9	2

Sixth game—October 3, at New York

				R	H	E
Dodgers	000	100	000	1	4	1
Yankees	500	000	00x	5	8	0

Seventh game—October 4, at New York

				R	H	E
Dodgers	000	101	000	2	5	0
Yankees	000	000	000	0	8	1

Line Scores of World Series Games (Continued)
1956

First game—October 3, at Brooklyn

				R	H	E
Yankees	200	100	000	3	9	1
Dodgers	023	100	00x	6	9	0

Second game—October 5, at Brooklyn

Yankees	150	100	001	8	12	2
Dodgers	061	220	02x	13	12	0

Third game—October 6, at New York

Dodgers	010	001	100	3	8	1
Yankees	010	003	01x	5	8	1

Fourth game—October 7, at New York

Dodgers	000	100	001	2	6	0
Yankees	100	201	20x	6	7	2

Fifth game—October 8, at New York

Dodgers	000	000	000	0	0	0
Yankees	000	101	00x	2	5	0

Sixth game—October 9, at Brooklyn

Yankees	000	000	000	0	0	7	0
Dodgers	000	000	000	1	1	4	0

Seventh game—October 10, at Brooklyn

Yankees	202	100	400	9	10	0
Dodgers	000	000	000	0	3	1

1959

First game—October 1, at Chicago

				R	H	E
Dodgers	000	000	000	0	8	3
White Sox	207	200	00x	11	11	0

Second game—October 2, at Chicago

Dodgers	000	010	300	4	9	1
White Sox	200	000	010	3	8	0

Third game—October 4, at Memorial Coliseum, Los Angeles

White Sox	000	000	010	1	12	0
Dodgers	000	000	21x	3	5	0

Fourth game—October 5, at Los Angeles

White Sox	000	000	400	4	10	3
Dodgers	004	000	01x	5	9	0

Fifth game—October 6, at Los Angeles

White Sox	000	100	000	1	5	0
Dodgers	000	000	000	0	9	0

Sixth game—October 8, at Chicago

Dodgers	002	600	001	9	13	0
White Sox	000	300	000	3	6	1

Line Scores of World Series Games (Continued)

1963

First game—October 2, at New York

				R	H	E
Dodgers	041	000	000	5	9	0
Yankees	000	000	020	2	6	0

Second game—October 3, at New York

Dodgers	200	100	010	4	10	1
Yankees	000	000	001	1	7	0

Third game—October 5, at Dodger Stadium, Los Angeles

Yankees	000	000	000	0	3	0
Dodgers	100	000	00x	1	4	1

Fourth game—October 6, at Los Angeles

Yankees	000	000	100	1	6	1
Dodgers	000	010	10x	2	2	1

1965

First game—October 6, at Minnesota

				R	H	E
Dodgers	010	000	001	2	10	1
Minn.	016	001	00x	8	10	0

Second game—October 7, at Minnesota

Dodgers	000	000	100	1	7	3
Minn.	000	002	12x	5	9	0

Third game—October 9, at Los Angeles

Minn.	000	000	000	0	5	0
Dodgers	000	211	00x	4	10	1

Fourth game—October 10, at Los Angeles

Minn.	000	101	000	2	5	2
Dodgers	110	103	01x	7	10	0

Fifth game—October 11, at Los Angeles

Minn.	000	000	000	0	4	1
Dodgers	202	100	20x	7	14	0

Sixth game—October 13, at Minnesota

Dodgers	000	000	100	1	6	1
Minn.	000	203	00x	5	6	1

Seventh game—October 14, at Minnesota

Dodgers	000	200	000	2	7	0
Minn.	000	000	000	0	3	1

Line Scores of World Series Games (Continued)

1966

First game—October 5, at Los Angeles

				R	H	E
Balt.	310	100	000	5	9	0
Dodgers	011	000	000	2	3	0

Second game—October 6, at Los Angeles

				R	H	E
Balt.	000	031	020	6	8	0
Dodgers	000	000	000	0	4	6

Third game—October 8, at Baltimore

				R	H	E
Dodgers	000	000	000	0	6	0
Balt.	000	010	00x	1	3	0

Fourth game—October 9, at Baltimore

				R	H	E
Dodgers	000	000	000	0	4	0
Balt.	000	100	00x	1	4	0

1974

First game—October 12, at Los Angeles

				R	H	E
Oak.	010	010	010	3	6	2
Dodgers	000	010	001	2	11	1

Second game—October 13, at Los Angeles

				R	H	E
Oak.	000	000	002	2	6	0
Dodgers	010	002	00x	3	6	1

Third game—October 15, at Oakland

				R	H	E
Dodgers	000	000	011	2	7	2
Oak.	002	100	00x	3	5	2

Fourth game-October 16, at Oakland

				R	H	E
Dodgers	000	200	000	2	7	1
Oak.	001	004	00x	5	7	0

Fifth game—October 17, at Oakland

				R	H	E
Dodgers	000	002	000	2	5	1
Oak.	110	000	10x	3	6	1

1977

First game—October 11, at New York

					R	H	E
Dodgers	200	000	001	000	3	6	0
Yankees	100	001	010	001	4	11	0

Second game—October 12 at New York

				R	H	E
Dodgers	212	000	001	6	9	0
Yankees	000	100	000	1	5	0

Line Scores of World Series Games (Continued)

Third game—October 14, at Los Angeles

Yankees	300	110	000	5	10	0
Dodgers	003	000	000	3	7	1

Fourth game—October 15, at Los Angeles

Yankees	030	001	000	4	7	0
Dodgers	002	000	000	2	4	0

Fifth game—October 16, at Los Angeles

Yankees	000	000	220	4	9	2
Dodgers	100	432	00x	10	13	0

Sixth game—October 18, at New York

Dodgers	201	000	001	4	9	0
Yankees	020	320	01x	8	8	1

1978

First game-October 10, at Los Angeles

				R	H	E
Yankees	000	000	320	5	9	1
Dodgers	030	310	31x	11	15	2

Second game—October 11, at Los Angeles

Yankees	002	000	100	3	11	0
Dodgers	000	103	00x	4	7	0

Third game—October13, at New York

Dodgers	001	000	000	1	8	0
Yankees	110	000	30x	5	10	1

Fourth game—October 14, at New York

Dodgers	000	030	000	0	3	6	1
Yankees	000	002	010	1	4	9	0

Fifth game—October 15, at New York

Dodgers	101	000	000	2	9	3
Yankees	004	300	41x	12	18	0

Sixth game—October 17, at Los Angeles

Yankees	030	002	200	7	11	0
Dodgers	101	000	000	2	7	1

1981

First game—October 20, at New York

				R	H	E
Dodgers	000	010	020	3	5	0
Yankees	301	100	00x	5	6	0

Second game—October 21, at New York

Dodgers	000	000	000	0	4	2
Yankees	000	010	02x	3	6	1

Line Scores of World Series Games (Continued)

Third game—October 23, at Los Angeles

Yankees	022	000	000	4	9	0
Dodgers	300	020	00x	5	11	1

Fourth game—October 24, at Los Angeles

Yankees	211	002	010	7	13	1
Dodgers	002	013	20x	8	14	2

Fifth game—October 25, at Los Angeles

Yankees	010	000	000	1	5	0
Dodgers	000	000	20x	2	4	3

Sixth game—October 28, at New York

Dodgers	000	134	010	9	13	1
Yankees	001	001	000	2	7	2

*During this time Dodgers were also called the Superbas, and Robins

World Series Batting Records

Player—Year	G	AB	R	H	2B	3B	HR	RBI	Pct.
Johnny Allen (1941)	3	0	0	0	0	0	0	0	.000
Sandy Amoros (1952-55-56)	12	31	4	5	0	0	1	4	.161
Rick Auerbach (1974)	1	0	0	0	0	0	0	0	.000
Dusty Baker (1977-78-81)	18	69	9	16	0	0	2	7	.232
Dan Bankhead (1947)	1	0	1	0	0	0	0	0	.000
Jack Banta (1949)	3	1	0	0	0	0	0	0	.000
Jim Barbieri (1966)	1	1	0	0	0	0	0	0	.000
Rex Barney (1947-49)	4	1	0	0	0	0	0	0	.000
Hank Behrman (1947)	5	0	0	0	0	0	0	0	.000
Wayne Berlardi (1953)	2	2	0	0	0	0	0	0	.000
Don Bessant (1955-56)	5	3	0	1	0	0	0	1	.333
Joe Black (1952-53)	4	6	0	0	0	0	0	0	.000
Bobby Bragan (1947)	1	1	0	1	1	0	0	1	1.000
Ralph Branca (1947-49)	4	7	0	0	0	0	0	0	.000
Jim Brewer (1965-66-74)	3	0	0	0	0	0	0	0	.000
Tommy Brown (1949)	2	2	0	0	0	0	0	0	.000
Bill Buckner (1974)	5	20	1	5	1	0	1	1	.250
Glenn Burke (1977)	3	5	0	1	0	0	0	0	.200
Leon Cadore (1920)	2	0	0	0	0	0	0	0	.000
Dolph Camilli (1941)	5	18	1	3	1	0	0	1	.167
Roy Campanella (1949-52-53-55-56)	32	114	14	27	5	0	4	12	.237
Hugh Casey (1941-47)	9	3	0	1	0	0	0	0	.333
Babo Castillo (1981)	1	0	0	0	0	0	0	0	.000
Larry Cheney (1916)	1	0	0	0	0	0	0	0	.000
Ron Cey (1974-77-78-81)	23	79	8	20	1	0	3	13	.253
Chuck Churn (1959)	1	0	0	0	0	0	0	0	.000

World Series Batting Records (Continued)

Player—Year	G	AB	R	H	2B	3B	HR	RBI	Pct.
Gino Cimoli (1956)	1	0	0	0	0	0	0	0	.000
Jack Combs (1916)	1	3	0	1	0	0	0	1	.333
Pete Coscarart (1941)	3	7	1	0	0	0	0	0	.000
Wes Covington (1966)	1	1	0	0	0	0	0	0	.000
Billy Cox (1949-52-53)	15	23	7	16	5	0	1	6	.302
Roger Craig (1955-56-59)	5	5	0	1	0	0	0	0	.200
Willie Crawford (1965-74)	5	8	1	3	0	0	1	0	.375
George Cutshaw (1916)	5	19	2	2	1	0	0	2	.105
Jake Daubert (1916)	4	17	1	3	0	1	0	0	.176
Vic Davalillo (1977-78)	5	6	0	2	0	0	0	1	.333
Curt Davis (1941)	1	2	0	0	0	0	0	0	.000
Tommy Davis (1963-66)	8	23	0	8	0	2	0	2	.348
Willie Davis (1963-65-66)	15	54	5	9	2	0	0	3	.167
Wheezer Dell (1916)	1	0	0	0	0	0	0	0	.000
Don Demeter (1959)	6	12	2	3	0	0	0	0	.250
Al Downing (1974)	1	1	0	0	0	0	0	0	.000
Don Drysdale (1956-59-63-65-66)	8	10	0	0	0	0	0	0	.000
Bruce Edwards (1947-49)	9	29	3	7	1	0	0	2	.241
Carl Erskine (1949-52-53-55-56)	11	12	1	1	0	0	0	0	.083
Chuck Essegian (1959)	4	3	2	2	0	0	2	2	.667
Ron Fairly (1959-63-65-66)	20	40	7	12	3	0	2	6	.300
Joe Ferguson (1974-78)	7	20	3	4	2	0	1	2	.200
Al Ferrara (1966)	1	1	0	1	0	0	0	0	1.000
Fred Fitzsimmons (1941)	1	2	0	0	0	0	0	0	.000
Terry Forster (1978-81)	5	0	0	0	0	0	0	0	.000
Herman Franks (1941)	1	1	0	0	0	0	0	0	.000
Larry French (1941)	2	0	0	0	0	0	0	0	.000
Carl Furillo (1947-49-52-53-55-56-59)	40	128	13	34	9	0	2	13	.266
Augie Galan (1941)	2	2	0	0	0	0	0	0	.000
Mike Garman (1977)	2	0	0	0	0	0	0	0	.000
Steve Garvey (1974-77-78-81)	23	93	11	32	3	1	1	4	.344
Gus Getz (1916)	1	1	0	0	0	0	0	0	.000
Jim Gilliam (1953-55-56-59-63-65-66)	39	147	15	31	5	0	2	12	.211
Al Gionfriddo (1947)	4	3	2	0	0	0	0	0	.000
Dave Goltz (1981)	2	0	0	0	0	0	0	0	.000
Ed Goodson (1977)	1	1	0	0	0	0	0	0	.000
Hal Gregg (1947)	3	3	2	0	0	0	0	0	.000
Tommy Griffith (1920)	7	21	1	4	2	0	0	3	.190
Burleigh Grimes (1920)	3	6	1	2	0	0	0	0	.333
Jerry Grote (1977-78)	3	1	0	0	0	0	0	0	.000
Pedro Guerrero (1981)	6	21	2	7	1	1	2	7	.333
Joe Hatten (1947-49)	6	3	1	1	0	0	0	0	.333
Billy Herman (1941)	4	8	0	1	0	0	0	0	.125
Gene Hermanski (1947-49)	11	32	5	7	0	2	0	3	.219
Kirby Higbe (1941)	1	1	0	1	0	0	0	0	1.000
Don Hoak (1955)	3	3	0	1	0	0	0	0	.333

World Series Batting Records (Continued)

Player—Year	G	AB	R	H	2B	3B	HR	RBI	Pct.
Gil Hodges									
(1947-49-52-53-55-56-59)	39	131	15	35	2	1	5	21	.267
Tommy Holmes (1952)	1	1	0	0	0	0	0	0	.000
Burt Hooton (1977-78-81)	6	9	1	0	0	0	0	0	.000
Charlie Hough (1974-77-78)	5	0	0	0	0	0	0	0	.000
Frank Howard (1963)	3	10	2	3	1	0	1	1	.300
Steve Howe (1981)	3	2	0	0	0	0	0	0	.000
Jim Hughes (1953)	1	1	0	0	0	0	0	0	.000
Randy Jackson (1956)	3	3	0	0	0	0	0	0	.000
Tommy John (1977-78)	3	2	0	0	0	0	0	0	.000
Lou Johnson (1965-66)	11	42	4	12	3	0	2	4	.286
Jimmy Johnston (1916-20)	7	24	3	6	0	1	0	0	.250
Jay Johnstone (1981)	3	3	1	2	0	0	1	3	.667
Spider Jorgensen (1947-49)	11	31	2	6	4	0	0	3	.194
Von Joshua (1974)	4	4	0	0	0	0	0	0	.000
Frank Kellert (1955)	3	3	0	1	0	0	0	0	.333
John Kennedy (1965-66)	6	6	0	1	0	0	0	0	.167
Pete Kilduff (1920)	7	21	0	2	0	0	0	0	.095
Johnny Klippstein (1959)	1	0	0	0	0	0	0	0	.000
Ed Konetchy (1920)	7	23	0	4	0	1	0	2	.174
Sandy Koufax (1959-63-65-66)	8	19	0	1	0	0	0	1	.053
Ernie Krueger (1920)	4	6	0	1	0	0	0	0	.167
Clem Labine (1953-55-56-59)	10	10	0	1	1	0	0	0	.100
Lee Lacy (1974-77-78)	9	22	1	5	0	0	0	3	.227
Bill Lamar (1920)	3	3	0	0	0	0	0	0	.000
Rafael Landestoy (1977)	1	0	0	0	0	0	0	0	.000
Ken Landreaux (1981)	5	6	1	1	1	0	0	0	.167
Norm Larker (1959)	6	16	2	3	0	0	0	0	.188
Cookie Lavagetto (1941-47)	8	17	1	2	1	0	0	3	.176
Jim Lefebvre (1965-66)	7	22	3	6	0	0	1	1	.273
Ken Lehman (1952)	1	0	0	0	0	0	0	0	.000
Don LeJohn (1965)	1	1	0	0	0	0	0	0	.000
Billy Loes (1952-53-55)	4	7	0	3	0	0	0	0	.429
Vic Lombardi (1947)	3	3	0	0	0	0	0	0	.000
Davey Lopes (1974-77-78-81)	23	90	18	19	1	1	4	11	.211
Sal Maglie (1956)	2	5	0	0	0	0	0	0	.000
Al Mamaux (1920)	3	1	0	0	0	0	0	0	.000
Rube Marquard (1916-20)	4	4	0	0	0	0	0	0	.000
Mike Marshall (1974)	5	0	0	0	0	0	0	1	.000
Bill McCabe (1920)	1	0	0	0	0	0	0	0	.000
Mike McCormick (1949)	1	0	0	0	0	0	0	0	.000
Joe Medwick (1941)	5	17	1	4	1	0	0	0	.235
Fred Merkle (1916)	3	4	0	1	0	0	0	0	.250
Andy Messersmith (1974)	2	4	0	2	0	0	0	0	.500
Russ Meyer (1953-55)	2	3	0	0	0	0	0	0	.000
Chief Meyers (1916)	3	10	0	2	0	1	0	1	.200
Eddie Miksis (1947-49)	8	11	1	3	1	0	0	0	.275
Bob Miller (1965-66)	3	0	0	0	0	0	0	0	.000
Otto Miller (1916-20)	8	22	0	3	0	0	0	0	.136
Bob Milliken (1953)	1	0	0	0	0	0	0	0	.000

World Series Batting Records(Continued)

Player—Year	G	AB	R	H	2B	3B	HR	RBI	Pct.
Paul Minner (1949)	1	0	0	0	0	0	0	0	.000
Clarence Mitchell (1920)	1	3	0	1	0	0	0	0	.333
Dale Mitchell (1956)	4	4	0	0	0	0	0	0	.000
Joe Moeller (1966)	1	0	0	0	0	0	0	0	.000
Rick Monday (1977-78-81)	14	38	3	7	2	0	0	0	.184
Wally Moon (1959-65)	8	25	3	6	0	0	1	2	.240
Bobby Morgan (1952-53)	3	2	0	0	0	0	0	0	.000
Manny Mota (1977-78)	4	3	0	0	0	0	0	0	.000
Mike Mowrey (1916)	5	17	2	3	0	0	0	1	.176
Hy Myers (1916-20)	12	48	2	10	0	0	1	4	.208
Charlie Neal (1956-59)	7	31	4	10	2	0	2	6	.323
Bernie Neis (1920)	4	5	0	0	0	0	0	0	.000
Rocky Nelson (1952)	4	3	0	0	0	0	0	0	.000
Don Newcombe (1949-55-56)	5	8	0	0	0	0	0	0	.000
Tom Niedenfuer (1981)	2	0	0	0	0	0	0	0	.000
Billy North (1978)	4	8	2	1	1	0	0	2	.125
Johnny Oates (1977-78)	2	2	0	1	0	0	0	0	.500
Nate Oliver (1966)	1	0	0	0	0	0	0	0	.000
Luis Olmo (1949)	4	11	2	3	0	0	1	2	.273
Ivy Olsen (1916-20)	12	41	3	12	1	1	0	2	.293
Ollie O'Mara (1916)	1	1	0	0	0	0	0	0	.000
Claude Osteen (1965-66)	3	5	0	1	0	0	0	0	.200
Mickey Owen (1941)	5	12	1	2	0	1	0	2	.167
Tom Paciorek (1974)	3	2	1	1	1	0	0	0	.500
Andy Pafco (1952)	7	21	0	4	0	0	0	2	.190
Erv Palica (1949)	1	0	0	0	0	0	0	0	.000
Wes Parker (1965-66)	11	36	3	10	2	1	1	2	.278
Ron Perranoski (1963-65-66)	5	0	0	0	0	0	0	0	.000
Jeff Pfeffer (1916-20)	4	5	0	1	0	0	0	0	.200
Joe Pignatano (1959)	1	0	0	0	0	0	0	0	.000
Johnny Podres (1953-55-59-63)	7	16	2	5	1	0	0	1	.313
Doug Rau (1977-78)	3	0	0	0	0	0	0	0	.000
Lance Rautzhan (1977-78)	3	0	0	0	0	0	0	0	.000
Marv Rackley (1949)	2	5	0	0	0	0	0	0	.000
Howie Reed (1965)	2	0	0	0	0	0	0	0	.000
Pee Wee Reese (1941-47-49-52-53-55-56)	44	169	20	46	3	2	2	16	.272
Phil Regan (1966)	2	0	0	0	0	0	0	0	.000
Pete Reiser (1941-47)	10	28	2	6	1	1	1	3	.214
Rip Repulski (1959)	1	0	0	0	0	0	0	0	.000
Jerry Reuss (1981)	2	3	0	0	0	0	0	0	.000
Rick Rhoden (1977)	2	2	1	1	1	0	0	0	.500
Lew Riggs (1941)	3	8	0	2	0	0	0	1	.250
Jackie Robinson (1947-49-52-53-55-56)	38	137	22	32	7	1	2	12	.234
Preacher Roe (1949-52-53)	5	8	0	0	0	0	0	0	.000
Ed Roebuck (1955-56)	4	0	0	0	0	0	0	0	.000
John Roseboro (1959-63-65-66)	21	70	2	11	1	0	1	7	.157
Nap Rucker (1916)	1	0	0	0	0	0	0	0	.000

World Series Batting Records (Continued)

Player—Year	G	AB	R	H	2B	3B	HR	RBI	Pct.
Bill Russell (1974-77-78-81)	23	95	5	25	2	2	0	8	.263
Johnny Rutherford (1952)	1	0	0	0	0	0	0	0	.000
Steve Sax (1981)	2	1	0	0	0	0	0	0	.000
Ray Schmandt (1920)	1	1	0	0	0	0	0	0	.000
Mike Scioscia (1981)	3	4	1	1	1	0	0	0	.250
Jack Sheehan (1920)	3	11	0	2	0	0	0	0	.182
Larry Sherry (1959)	4	4	0	2	0	0	0	0	.500
George Shuba (1952-53-55)	7	12	1	4	1	0	1	2	.333
Bill Skowron (1963)	4	13	2	5	0	0	1	3	.385
Reggie Smith (1977-78-81)	14	49	10	12	1	0	4	10	.245
Sherry Smith (1916-20)	3	11	0	1	1	0	0	0	.091
Duke Snider (1949-52-53-55-56-59)	36	133	21	38	8	0	11	26	.286
Elias Sosa (1977)	2	0	0	0	0	0	0	0	.000
Karl Spooner (1955)	2	0	0	0	0	0	0	0	.000
Eddie Stanky (1947)	7	25	4	6	1	0	0	2	.240
Casey Stengel (1916)	4	11	2	4	0	0	0	0	.364
Dave Stewart (1981)	2	0	0	0	0	0	0	0	.000
Dick Stuart (1966)	2	2	0	0	0	0	0	0	.000
Don Sutton (1974-77-78)	6	9	0	0	0	0	0	0	.000
Harry Taylor (1947)	1	0	0	0	0	0	0	0	.000
Derrel Thomas (1981)	5	7	2	0	0	0	0	0	.000
Don Thompson (1953)	2	0	0	0	0	0	0	0	.000
Dick Tracewski (1963-65)	10	30	1	4	0	0	0	0	.235
Fernando Valenzuela (1981)	1	3	0	0	0	0	0	0	.000
Arky Vaughan (1947)	3	2	0	1	1	0	0	0	.500
Ben Wade (1953)	2	0	0	0	0	0	0	0	.000
Dixie Walker (1941-47)	12	45	4	10	3	0	1	4	.222
Rube Walker (1956)	2	2	0	0	0	0	0	0	.000
Jimmy Wasdell (1941)	3	5	0	1	1	0	0	2	.200
Bob Welch (1978-81)	4	0	0	0	0	0	0	0	.000
Zach Wheat (1916-20)	12	46	4	13	2	1	0	3	.283
Dick Whitman (1949)	1	1	0	0	0	0	0	0	.000
Dick Williams (1953)	3	2	0	1	0	0	0	0	.500
Stan Williams (1959)	1	0	0	0	0	0	0	0	.000
Maury Wills (1959-63-65-66)	21	78	6	19	3	0	0	4	.282
Whit Wyatt (1941)	2	6	1	1	1	0	0	0	.167
Jimmy Wynn (1974)	5	16	1	3	1	0	1	2	.188
Stever Yeager (1974-77-78-81)	21	57	6	17	4	0	4	10	.298
Don Zimmer (1955-59)	5	10	0	2	0	0	0	2	.200
Totals		3223	325	753	113	20	78	307	.234

World Series Pitching Records

Pitcher—Years	G	IP	CG	SH	H	R	ER	BB	SO	W	L	ERA
Johnny Allen (1941)	3	3.2	0	0	1	0	0	3	0	0	0	0.00
Jack Banta (1949)	3	5.2	0	0	5	2	2	1	4	0	0	3.18
Rex Barney (1947-49)	4	9.1	0	0	7	7	7	16	5	0	2	6.75
Hank Behrman (1947)	5	6.1	0	0	9	5	5	5	3	0	0	7.11
Don Bessent (1955-56)	5	13.1	0	0	11	2	2	4	6	1	0	1.35
Joe Black (1952-53)	4	22.1	1	0	16	7	7	8	11	1	2	2.82
Ralph Branca (1947-49)	4	1.7	0	0	16	12	12	9	14	1	2	6.35
Jim Brewer (1965-66-74)	3	3.1	0	0	3	1	1	0	3	0	0	2.70
Leon Cadore (1920)	2	2	0	0	4	2	2	1	1	0	1	9.00
Hugh Casey(1941-47)	9	15.2	0	0	14	7	3	3	4	2	2	1.72
Babo Castillo (1981)	1	1	0	0	0	1	1	5	0	0	0	9.00
Larry Cheney (1916)	1	3	0	0	4	2	1	1	5	0	0	3.00
Chuck Churn (1959)	1	.2	0	0	5	6	2	0	0	0	0	27.00
Jack Coombs (1916)	1	6.1	0	0	7	3	3	1	1	1	0	4.26
Roger Craig (1955-56-59)	5	21.1	0	0	29	19	19	13	16	1	2	6.49
Curt Davis (1941)	1	5.1	0	0	6	3	3	3	1	0	1	5.06
Wheezer Dell (1916)	1	1	0	0	1	0	0	0	0	0	0	0.00
Al Downing (1974)	1	3.2	0	0	4	3	1	4	3	0	1	2.45
Don Drysdale (1956-59-63-65-66)	7	39.2	3	1	36	17	13	12	36	3	3	2.95
Carl Erskine (1949-52-53-55-56)	11	41.2	2	0	36	27	27	24	31	2	2	5.83
Fred Fitzsimmons (1941)	1	7	0	0	11	0	0	3	1	0	0	0.00
Terry Forster (1978-81)	5	6	0	0	6	0	0	4	6	0	0	0.00
Larry French (1941)	2	1	0	0	0	0	0	0	0	0	0	0.00
Mike Garman (1977)	2	4	0	0	2	0	0	1	3	0	0	0.00
Dave Goltz (1981)	2	3.1	0	0	4	2	2	1	2	0	0	6.00
Hal Gregg (1947)	3	12.2	0	0	9	5	5	8	10	0	1	3.55
Burleigh Grimes (1920)	3	19.1	1	1	25	10	9	9	4	1	2	4.19
Joe Hatten (1947-49)	6	10.2	0	0	16	10	10	9	5	0	0	8.44
Kirby Higbe (1941)	1	3.2	0	0	6	3	3	2	1	0	0	7.36
Burt Hooton (1977-78-81)	6	31.2	1	0	29	15	13	14	18	3	3	3.66
Charlie Hough (1974-77-78)	5	12.1	0	0	13	6	6	3	14	0	0	4.38
Steve Howe (1981)	3	7	0	0	7	3	3	1	4	1	0	3.86
Jim Hughes (1953)	1	4	0	0	3	1	1	1	3	0	0	2.25
Tommy John (1977-78)	3	20.2	0	0	23	13	9	7	13	1	1	5.32
Johnny Klippstein (1959)	1	2	0	0	1	0	0	0	2	0	0	0.00
Sandy Koufax (1959-63-65-66)	8	57	4	2	36	10	6	11	61	4	3	0.95
Clem Labine (1953-55-56-59)	10	27.1	1	1	24	6	5	6	13	2	2	1.65
Ken Lehman (1952)	1	2	0	0	2	0	0	1	0	0	0	0.00
Billy Loes (1952-53-55)	4	22	0	0	26	13	12	8	18	1	2	4.91
Vic Lombardi (1947)	2	6.2	0	0	14	9	9	1	5	0	1	12.15
Sal Maglie (1956)	2	17	2	0	14	5	5	6	15	1	1	2.65
Al Mamaux (1920)	3	4	0	0	2	2	2	0	5	0	0	4.50
Rube Marquard (1916-20)	4	20	0	0	19	12	9	9	15	0	3	4.05
Mike Marshall (1974)	5	9	0	0	6	1	1	1	10	0	1	1.00
Andy Messersmith (1974)	2	14	0	0	11	8	7	7	12	0	2	4.50
Russ Meyer (1953-55)	2	10	0	0	12	4	3	6	9	0	0	6.23

World Series Pitching Records (Continued)

Pitcher—Years	G	IP	CG	SH	H	R	ER	BB	SO	W	L	ERA
Bob Miller (1965-66)	3	4.1	0	0	2	0	0	2	1	0	0	0.00
Bob Milliken (1953)	1	2	0	0	2	0	0	1	0	0	0	0.00
Paul Minner (1949)	1	1	0	0	1	0	0	0	0	0	0	0.00
Clarence Mitchell (1920)	1	4.2	0	0	3	1	0	3	1	0	0	0.00
Joe Moeller (1966)	1	2	0	0	1	1	1	1	0	0	0	4.50
Don Newcombe (1949-55-56)	5	22	1	0	29	21	21	8	19	0	4	8.59
Tom Niedenfuer (1981)	2	5	0	0	3	2	0	1	0	0	0	0.00
Claude Osteen (1965-66)	3	21	1	1	12	3	2	6	7	1	2	0.86
Erv Palica (1949)	1	2	0	0	1	0	0	1	1	0	0	0.00
Ron Perranoski (1965-66)	5	7.2	0	0	8	5	5	5	4	0	0	5.87
Jeff Pfeffer (1916-20)	4	13.2	0	0	11	6	3	6	6	0	1	2.63
Johnny Podres (1953-55-59-63)	6	38.1	2	1	29	14	9	13	18	4	1	2.11
Doug Rau (1977-78)	3	4.1	0	0	5	3	3	0	4	0	1	6.23
Lance Rautzhan (1977-78)	3	2.1	0	0	4	3	3	2	0	0	0	11.57
Howie Reed (1965)	2	3.1	0	0	2	3	3	2	4	0	0	8.10
Phil Regan (1966)	2	1.2	0	0	0	0	0	1	2	0	0	0.00
Jerry Reuss (1981)	2	11.2	1	0	10	5	5	3	8	1	1	3.75
Rick Rhoden (1977)	2	7	0	0	4	2	2	1	5	0	1	2.57
Preacher Roe (1949-52-53)	5	28.1	3	1	20	8	8	10	14	2	1	2.54
Ed Roebuck (1955-56)	4	6.1	0	0	2	1	1	0	5	0	0	1.42
Nap Rucker (1916)	1	2	0	0	1	0	0	0	3	0	0	0.00
Johnny Rutherford (1952)	1	1	0	0	1	1	1	1	1	0	0	9.00
Larry Sherry (1959)	4	12.2	0	0	8	1	1	2	5	2	0	0.71
Sherry Smith (1916-20)	3	30.1	3	0	17	4	3	9	5	1	2	0.89
Elias Sosa (1977)	2	2.1	0	0	3	3	3	1	1	0	0	11.57
Karl Spooner (1955)	2	3.1	0	0	4	5	5	3	6	0	1	13.50
Dave Stewart (1981)	2	1.2	0	0	1	0	0	2	1	0	0	0.00
Don Sutton (1974-77-78)	6	41	1	0	43	21	21	8	26	2	2	4.61
Harry Taylor (1947)	1	0	0	0	2	1	0	1	0	0	0	0.00
Fernando Valenzuela (1981)	1	9	1	0	9	4	4	7	6	1	0	4.00
Ben Wade (1953)	2	2.1	0	0	4	4	4	1	2	0	0	15.43
Bob Welch (1978-81)	4	4.1	0	0	7	5	5	3	6	0	1	10.38
Stan Williams (1959)	1	2	0	0	0	0	0	2	1	0	0	0.00
Whit Wyatt (1941)	2	18	2	0	15	5	5	10	14	1	1	2.50
Totals		875.1	30	8	797	396	349	348	569	41	59	3.59

THE DODGERS IN
THE PLAYOFFS

As masters of the heart-wrenching contest and narrow finish, the Dodgers have a playoffs record quite unlike any team in major league history.

Prior to the beginning of intra-league Championship Series playoffs in 1969, there had been only four playoffs of National League season-ending ties to determine a World Series representative and the Dodgers were involved in all four.

Perhaps baseball's most-dramatic-game-ever—when the New York Giants nipped the Brooklyn Dodgers 5-4 on Bobby Thomson's three-run, ninth-inning "shot heard 'round the world" in 1951—was one of these tie-breakers.

But the Dodgers lost two others, the first-ever playoffs to the St. Louis Cardinals in 1946—two games to zero—and the 1962 showdown to the hated Giants, now of San Francisco, two games to one in the first year of Dodger Stadium.

Their only post-season triumph came in 1959, their second season in Los Angeles, when they knocked off the Milwaukee Braves two straight games.

Since 1969, however, the Dodgers have had an almost perfect record, blemished only by their failure to trip Houston in a one-game 1980 playoff for the division crown and by 1983's loss to Philadelphia in the Championship Series.

In succession, in the Championship Series, the Dodgers have stopped Eastern Division representatives Pittsburgh (1974), Philadelphia (1977,1978), and Montreal (1981). And during that players' strike-interrupted 1981 season they beat Houston, after losing the first two games in the Texas city, in the only "Division Series."

Not surprisingly, the Dodgers' "Mr. Consistency," Steve Garvey has carried a hot bat, going 24-for-70 for .343 in his 17 Championship Series games. But Dusty Baker, with a .371 batting average, and Bill Russell with a .337 have been hot, too.

However, Garvey has seven homers (to Baker's three and Russell's none) and 14 runs-scored and 14 runs-batted-in. Baker's RBI total is 13.

Among the Dodger pitchers, both Burt Hooton and Tommy John are 2-0 in the Championship Series, while Don Sutton has a fine 3-1 record, two of his victories being 3-0 and 12-1 efforts over the Pirates in 1974. Contrarily, Jerry Reuss is 0-3.

Hooton's 1981 heroics, capturing the turnaround third game in the Division Series and then winning two more in the Championship Series plus Game Six of the World Series, earned him the sobriquet of the "Dodgers' Mr. October."

If the Dodgers had to pick a date NOT to compete in a playoffs game it would be October 3. For on that "jinx date" they've dropped the deciders of all three of their pre-1969 playoffs losses—8-4 to the Cards in 1946; 5-4 to the "Jints" in 1951; and again to the Giants in 1962 when another four-run ninth-inning rally beat them out, 6-4.

Happily, the 1959 playoff against the Braves was in late September and all the post-1969 Championship Series games have been after October 3.

In the Championship Series the Dodgers have had two extraordinarily-dramatic wins. They were down 5-3 with two outs in the ninth inning at Philadelphia in 1977 but rallied for a 6-5 victory on Vic Davalillo's drag bunt followed by a Manny Mota double, Davey Lopes' close-call infield single, and Bill Russell's bouncer through the middle after Lopes had gone to second on an errant pickoff attempt. It gave them a two-games-to-one series lead.

And in 1981, at Montreal, they were deadlocked 2-2 in the series and 1-1 in a Fernando Valenzuela-pitched game when Rick Monday smacked a ninth-inning home-run-decider that put Los Angeles in the World Series.

245

Line Scores of Playoff Games

1946

National League Tiebreaker

First game—October 1, at St. Louis

				R	H	E
Dodgers	001	000	100	2	8	0
Cardinals	102	000	003	4	12	1

Second game—October 3, at Brooklyn

Cardinals	020	030	120	8	13	0
Dodgers	100	000	003	4	6	0

1951

National League Tiebreaker

First game—October 1, at Brooklyn

Giants	000	200	010	3	6	1
Dodgers	010	000	000	1	5	1

Second game—October 2, at New York

Dodgers	200	013	202	10	13	2
Giants	000	000	000	0	6	5

Third game—October 3, at New York

Dodgers	100	000	030	4	8	0
Giants	000	000	104	5	8	0

1959

National League Tiebreaker

First game—September 28, at Milwaukee

				R	H	E
Dodgers	101	001	000	3	10	1
Braves	020	000	000	2	6	0

Second game—September 29, at Los Angeles

Braves	210	010	010	000	5	10	2
Dodgers	100	100	003	001	6	15	2

1962

National League Tiebreaker

First game—October 1, at San Francisco

Dodger	000	000	000	0	3	1
Giants	210	002	03x	8	10	0

Second game—October 2, at Los Angeles

Giants	010	004	020	7	13	1
Dodgers	000	007	001	8	7	2

Third game—October 3, at Los Angeles

Giants	002	000	004	6	13	3
Dodgers	000	102	100	4	8	4

Line Scores of Playoff Games (Continued)

1974

Championship Series
First game—October 5, at Pittsburgh

				R	H	E
Dodgers	010	000	002	3	9	2
Pitt.	000	000	000	0	4	0

Second game—October 6, at Pittsburgh

Dodgers	100	100	030	5	12	0
Pitt.	000	000	200	2	8	3

Third game—October 8, at Los Angeles

Pitt.	502	000	000	7	10	0
Dodgers	000	000	000	0	4	5

Fourth game—October 9, at Los Angeles

Pitt.	000	000	100	1	3	1
Dodgers	102	022	23x	12	12	0

1977

Championship Series
First game—Octber 4, at Los Angeles

				R	H	E
Phil.	200	021	002	7	9	0
Dodgers	000	010	400	5	9	2

Second game—October 5, at Los Angeles

Phil.	001	000	000	1	9	1
Dodgers	001	401	10x	7	9	1

Third game—October 7, at Philadelphia

Dodgers	020	100	003	6	12	2
Phil.	030	000	020	5	6	2

Fourth game—October 8, at Philadelphia

Dodgers	020	020	000	4	5	0
Phil.	000	100	000	1	7	0

1978

Championship Series
First game—October 4, at Philadelphia

				R	H	E
Dodgers	004	211	001	9	13	1
Phil.	010	030	001	5	12	1

Second game—October 5, at Philadelphia

Dodgers	000	120	100	4	8	0
Phil.	000	000	000	0	4	0

Third game—October 6, at Los Angeles

Phil.	040	003	101	9	11	1
Dodgers	012	000	010	4	8	2

Line Scores of Playoff Games (Continued)

Fourth game—October 7, at Los Angeles

Phil.	002	000	100	0	3	8	2
Dodgers	010	101	000	1	4	13	0

1980

West Division Playoff
Only game—October 6, at Los Angeles

Houst.	202	300	000	7	12	1
Dodgers	000	100	000	1	6	2

1981

Division Series
First game—October 6, at Houston

Dodgers	000	000	100	1	2	0
Houst.	000	001	002	3	8	0

Second game—October 7, at Houston

Dodgers	000	000	000	00	0	9	1
Houst.	000	000	000	01	1	9	0

Third game—October 9, at Los Angeles

Houst.	001	000	000	1	3	2
Dodgers	300	000	03x	6	10	0

Fourth game—October 10, at Los Angeles

Houst.	000	000	001	1	4	0
Dodgers	00	010	10x	2	4	0

Fifth game—October 11, at Los Angeles

Houst.	000	000	000	0	5	3
Dodgers	000	003	10x	4	7	2

Championship Series
First game—October 13, at Los Angeles

				R	H	E
Mont.	000	000	001	1	9	0
Dodgers	020	000	03x	5	8	0

Second game—October 14, at Los Angeles

Mont.	020	001	000	3	10	1
Dodgers	000	000	000	0	5	1

Third game—October 16, at Montreal

Dodgers	000	100	000	1	7	0
Mont.	000	004	00x	4	7	1

Fourth game—October 17, at Montreal

Dodgers	001	000	024	7	12	1
Mont.	000	100	000	1	5	1

Fifth game—October 19, at Montreal

Dodgers	000	010	001	2	6	0
Mont.	100	000	000	1	3	1

Line Scores of Playoff Games (Continued)

1983

Championship Series

First game—October 4, at Los Angeles

				R	H	E
Phil.	100	000	000	1	5	1
Dodgers	000	000	000	0	7	0

Second game—October 5, at Los Angeles

Phil.	010	000	000	1	7	2
Dodgers	100	020	01x	4	6	1

Third game—October 7, at Philadelphia

Dodgers	000	200	000	2	4	0
Phil.	021	120	10x	7	9	1

Fourth game—October 8, at Philadelphia

Dodgers	000	100	010	2	10	0
Phil.	300	022	00x	7	13	1

Championship And Division Series Batting Records

Players—Years	G	AB	R	H	2B	3B	HR	RBI	Pct.
Rick Auerbach (1974)	1	1	0	1	1	0	0	0	1.000
Dusty Baker (1977-78-81-83)	17	62	12	23	5	0	3	13	.371
1981 Div.	5	18	2	3	1	0	0	1	.167
Joe Beckwith (1983)	2	0	0	0	0	0	0	0	.000
Greg Brock (1983)	3	9	1	0	0	0	0	0	.000
Bill Buckner (1974)	4	18	0	3	1	0	0	0	.167
Glenn Burke (1977)	3	7	0	0	0	0	0	0	.000
Babo Castillo (1981)	1	0	0	0	0	0	0	0	.000
Ron Cey (1974-77-78-81)	17	63	11	19	6	0	3	11	.302
1981 Div.				Did Not Play					
Willie Crawford	2	4	1	1	0	0	0	1	.250
Vic Davalillo (1977)	1	1	1	1	0	0	0	0	1.000
Al Downing (1974)	1	1	0	0	0	0	0	0	.000
Joe Ferguson (1974-78)	6	15	3	3	0	0	0	2	.200
Jack Fimple (1983)	3	7	0	1	0	0	0	1	.143
Terry Forster (1978-81)	2	0	0	0	0	0	0	0	.000
1981 Div.	1	0	0	0	0	0	0	0	.000
Mike Garman (1977)	2	0	0	0	0	0	0	0	.000
Steve Garvey (1974-77-78-81)	17	70	14	24	2	1	7	14	.343
1981 Div.	5	19	4	7	0	1	2	4	.368
Ed Goodson (1977)	1	1	0	0	0	0	0	0	.000
Jerry Grote (1977-78)	2	0	0	0	0	0	0	0	.000
Pedro Guerrero (1981-83)	9	31	2	5	1	1	1	4	.161
1981 Div.	5	17	1	3	1	0	1	1	.176
Rick Honeycutt (1983)	2	0	0	0	0	0	0	0	.000
Burt Hooton (1977-78-81)	4	8	0	1	1	0	0	0	.125
1981 Div.	1	3	0	0	0	0	0	0	.000
Charlie Hough (1974-77-78)	3	0	0	0	0	0	0	0	.000
Steve Howe (1981)	2	0	0	0	0	0	0	0	.000
1981 Div.	2	0	0	0	0	0	0	0	.000
Tommy John (1977-78)	3	8	0	1	0	0	0	0	.125
Jay Johnstone (1981)	2	2	0	0	0	0	0	0	.000
1981 Div.	1	1	0	0	0	0	0	0	.000
Von Joshua (1974)	1	0	0	0	0	0	0	0	.000
Lee Lacy (1974-77-78)	4	3	1	1	0	0	0	0	.333
Rafael Landestoy (1983)	2	2	0	0	0	0	0	0	.000
Ken Landreaux (1981-83)	9	24	0	3	1	0	0	1	.125
1981 Div.	5	20	1	4	1	0	0	0	.200
Davey Lopes (1974-77-78-81)	17	68	9	20	1	2	2	11	.294
1981 Div.	5	20	1	4	1	0	0	0	.200
Candy Maldonado (1983)	2	2	0	0	0	0	0	0	.000
Mike Marshall (1974)	2	0	0	0	0	0	0	0	.000
Michael Marshall (1981-83)	4	15	1	2	1	0	1	2	.133
1981 Div.	1	1	0	0	0	0	0	0	.000
Andy Messersmith (1974)	1	3	0	0	0	0	0	0	.000
Ken McMillen (1974)	1	1	0	0	0	0	0	0	.000
Rick Monday (1977-78-81-83)	10	26	5	7	1	1	1	1	.269
1981 Div.	5	14	1	3	0	0	0	1	.214
Jose Morales (1983)	2	2	0	0	0	0	0	0	.000
Manny Mota (1974-77-78)	6	5	1	3	2	0	0	1	.600

Championship And Division Series Batting Records
(Continued)

Player—Years	G	AB	R	H	2B	3B	HR	RBI	Pct.
Tom Niedenfuer (1981-83)	3	0	0	0	0	0	0	0	.000
1981 Div.	1	0	0	0	0	0	0	0	.000
Billy North (1978)	4	8	0	0	0	0	0	0	.000
Tom Paciorek (1974)	1	1	0	1	0	0	0	0	1.000
Alejandro Pena (1981-83)	3	1	0	1	0	0	0	1	1.000
1981 Div.				Did Not Play					
Doug Rau (1974-77-78)	3	1	0	0	0	0	0	0	.000
Lance Rautzhan (1977-78)	2	0	0	0	0	0	0	0	.000
Jerry Reuss (1981-83)	3	5	0	0	0	0	0	0	.000
1981 Div.	2	8	0	0	0	0	0	0	.000
Rick Rhoden (1977-78)	2	1	0	0	0	0	0	0	.000
Bill Russell (1974-77-78-81-83)	21	83	8	28	2	1	0	8	.337
1981 Div.	5	16	1	4	1	0	0	2	.250
Steve Sax (1981-83)	5	16	0	4	0	0	0	0	.250
1981 Div.	1	0	0	0	0	0	0	0	.000
Mike Scioscia (1981)	5	15	1	2	0	0	1	1	.133
1981 Div.	4	13	0	2	0	0	0	1	.154
Reggie Smith (1977-78-81)	9	33	4	7	1	1	0	3	.212
1981 Div.	2	1	0	0	0	0	0	1	.000
Eddie Solomon (1974)	1	0	0	0	0	0	0	0	.000
Elias Sosa (1977)	2	1	0	0	0	0	0	0	.000
Dave Stewart (1981)				Did Not Play					
1981 Div.	2	0	0	0	0	0	0	0	.000
Don Sutton (1974-77-78)	4	12	0	2	0	0	0	1	.167
Derrel Thomas (1981-83)	6	10	2	5	1	0	0	0	.500
1981 Div.	4	2	1	0	0	0	0	0	.000
Fernando Valenzuela (1981-83)	3	8	0	0	0	0	0	0	.000
1981 Div.	2	4	0	0	0	0	0	0	.000
Bob Welch (1978-81-83)	5	2	0	0	0	0	0	0	.000
1981 Div.	1	0	0	0	0	0	0	0	.000
Jimmy Wynn (1974)	4	10	4	2	2	0	0	2	.200
Steve Yeager (1974-77-78-81-83)	13	43	5	8	1	0	1	4	.186
Pat Zachry	2	0	0	0	0	0	0	0	.000
Totals									
Championship Series		705	86	179	30	7	20	83	.254
Division Series		161	13	32	6	1	3	11	.199

Championship And Division Series Pitching Records

Pitcher—Years	G	IP	CG	SH	H	R	ER	BB	SO	W	L	ERA
Joe Beckwith (1983)	2	2.1	0	0	1	0	0	2	3	0	0	0.00
Babe Castillo (1981)	1	1	0	0	0	0	0	0	1	0	0	0.00
Al Downing (1974)	1	4	0	0	1	0	0	1	0	0	0	0.00
Terry Forster (1978-81)	2	1.1	0	0	1	0	0	0	3	1	0	0.00
1981 Div.	1	.1	0	0	0	0	0	0	0	0	0	0.00
Mike Garman (1977)	2	1.1	0	0	0	0	0	0	1	0	0	0.00
Rick Honeycutt (1983)	2	1.2	0	0	4	4	4	0	2	0	0	24.00
Burt Hooton (1977-78-81)	4	21	0	0	23	8	7	10	13	2	0	3.00
1981 Div.	1	7	0	0	3	1	1	3	2	1	0	1.29
Charlie Hough (1974-77-78)	3	6.1	0	0	7	4	4	0	6	0	0	5.68
Steve Howe (1981)	2	2	0	0	1	0	0	0	2	0	0	0.00
1981 Div.	2	2	0	0	1	0	0	0	2	0	0	0.00
Tommy John (1977-78)	3	22.2	2	1	15	5	1	7	15	2	0	0.40
Mike Marshall (1974)	2	3	0	0	0	0	0	0	1	0	0	0.00
Andy Messersmith (1974)	1	7	0	0	8	2	2	3	0	1	0	2.57
Tom Niedenfuer (1981-83)	3	3	0	0	2	0	0	1	3	0	0	0.00
1981 Div.	1	.1	0	0	1	0	0	1	1	0	0	0.00
Alejandro Pena (1981-83)	3	5	0	0	5	2	2	1	3	0	0	3.60
Doug Rau (1974-77-78)	3	6.2	0	0	8	7	5	3	2	0	1	6.75
Lance Rautzhan (1977-78)	2	1.2	0	0	3	1	1	2	0	1	0	5.40
Jerry Reuss (1981-83)	3	19	0	0	21	10	10	4	6	0	3	4.74
1981 Div.	2	18	1	1	10	0	0	5	7	1	0	0.00
Rick Rhoden (1977-78)	2	8.1	0	0	4	1	1	3	3	0	0	1.08
Eddie Solomon (1974)	1	2	0	0	2	0	0	1	1	0	0	0.00
Elias Sosa (1977)	2	2.2	0	0	5	4	3	0	0	0	1	10.13
Dave Stewart					Did Not Play							
1981 Div.	2	.2	0	0	4	3	3	0	1	0	2	27.00
Don Sutton (1974-77-78)	4	31.2	2	1	23	9	6	4	17	3	1	1.71
Fernando Valenzuela(1981-83)	3	23	0	0	17	5	5	9	15	2	1	1.96
1981 Div.	2	17	1	0	10	2	2	3	10	1	0	1.06
Bob Welch (1978-81-83)	5	7.1	0	0	4	4	3	2	7	1	1	3.86
1981 Div.	1	1	0	0	0	0	0	1	1	0	0	0.00
Pat Zachry (1983)	2	4	0	0	4	1	1	2	2	0	0	2.25
Totals:												
Championship Series		187	4	2	159	67	55	55	106	12	8	2.65
Division Series:		46.1	2	1	29	6	6	14	24	3	2	1.17

THE DODGERS ALL-STAR STORY

Steve Garvey has twice been the Most Valuable Player. Don Drysdale was starting pitcher a record-tying five times. And Walter Alston managed the National League nine times—also a record. These are just a few of Dodger exploits during the first 50 years of the All-Star Game.

Plus, the Dodgers are the only team to have hosted the star-studded contest in three different ball parks: Ebbets Field in Brooklyn, 1949. And in Los Angeles at the Coliseum, 1959, and Dodger Stadium, 1980.

Let's take a trip down through the seasons and recall some of those Dodger All-Star "moments."

In 1933, the year the game began, only one of the then Daffy Dodgers was picked—second baseman Tony Cuccinello who struck out as a pinch-hitter in the ninth inning.

The first Dodger starter in 1938 ironically later (1942) became the first Dodger to manage in the game, shortstop Leo Durocher. He made history with his sacrifice bunt that turned into a "home run" when American League fielders threw wildly as he raced around the bases.

When the ball finally rolled into the National League dugout, coach Casey Stengel tossed it into a bucket of ice water and commented, "This one is just too hot to handle."

Whit Wyatt, in 1941, became the first of a long line of Dodger starting All-Star pitchers that have included Ralph Branca, 1948; Drysdale, 1959 (two games), 1962, 1964, and 1968; Johnny Podres, 1962 (second game); Sandy Koufax, 1966; Andy Messersmith, 1974; Don Sutton, 1977; and Fernando Valenzuela, 1981.

Both Drysdale, in 1968, and Sutton, in 1977, had the distinction of not only starting the game but also being the winning pitcher. And Sutton who at famed Yankee Stadium fanned four while giving up only one hit and a walk in his three innings won MVP honors.

Dodger winning pitchers, all in "relief," have been Koufax in 1965; Drysdale, 1967; Claude Osteen, 1970; and Jerry Reuss, 1980. The three losing twirlers were Van Lingle Mungo, 1934, who gave up four hits and four earned runs in one inning as the first Dodger All-Star moundsman; Don Newcombe, 1949; and Drysdale, 1959, the second game.

Drysdale's All-Star records, besides the five starts, are for eight pitching appearances and 19⅓ innings during which he struck out 19, allowed nine hits and four runs, and compiled an earned run average of 1.40.

The 1949 game at Ebbets also turned into an historic occasion as for the first time black players appeared, three of them Dodgers: Jackie Robinson, Roy Campanella, and Newcombe. Larry Doby of the Cleveland Indians was the fourth.

Robinson, the first black to bat, doubled to left in the first inning, scored three runs in an 11-7 defeat, and went on to hit .333 in six All-Star games—including a homer in 1952.

A decade later, before a hometown crowd of 45,480 that included President Kennedy at Washington, D.C., another great Dodger black player, Maury Wills, stole the show.

That was the season (1962) of his then-record 104 thefts. Wills entered the All-Star Game in the sixth inning as a pinch-runner for Stan Musial, who'd singled. He promptly stole second and scored on Dick Groat's single.

Then in the eighth, Wills singled and further showed his basepath daring as he slid under a relayed throw to third on a short single to left field—scoring later on a sacrifice fly to wind up with two runs.

Catcher Mickey Owen at the Polo Grounds in 1942 hit the first Dodger All-Star Game home run in a 3-1 National League loss. But Dodgers Steve Garvey and Jimmy Wynn made it almost an art form when they socked back-to-back round-trippers in the second inning of the 1975 game at Milwaukee, a 6-3 NL victory.

This was the second of seven consecutive starts for first baseman Garvey, who first appeared as a 1974 write-in candidate and emerged as the MVP with two hits, one run scored, an RBI, and a sensational rally-killing stop in the field.

He became the first Dodger two-time MVP in 1978 when he singled home two runs, then later tripled and came home for a third during a 7-3 triumph at San Diego Stadium. Going into that contest, Garvey had become the first player ever to amass more than 4 million fans' votes.

Garvey's .409 All-Star average for 22 at-bats is by far the best for any Dodger with more than 10 trips to the plate. But Willie Davis went three-for-three including a homer in 1973 at Kansas City in his two games. And second baseman Billy Herman was .444 in nine plate appearances during three of the contests.

Duke Snider's three safeties in 1954 at Cleveland is the most Dodger hits in one All-Star Game. But the Duke was shut out in seven other trips during his five other games.

Two Dodgers standouts who, surprisingly, didn't do so well were Campanella, hitless in his first 13 at-bats before winding up 2-for-20. And Pee Wee Reese, hitless in his first seven games before finally connecting for a pair in his eighth in 1953 at Cincinnati.

Reese, Drysdale, and Garvey are the only Dodgers to appear in as many as eight All-Star classics.

The old saying is that no manager ever won without the great players. And both Walter Alston and Tommy Lasorda have ridden the NL's latter-years success to unbeaten All-Star Game heights.

As a Los Angeles Dodger Alston was 6-0 (he was 1-2 in Brooklyn), while Lasorda is 3-0 with triumphs in 1978, 1979, and 1982. Previously, both Burt Shotton (1950) and Chuck Dressen (1953) were 1-0, while Durocher (1942, 1948) with 0-2 is the only Dodgers' losing All-Star manager.

Shotton, in his lone showing, was responsible for some lively pre-game debate and a voting rule change. Since none of the three outfielders chosen by the fans in 1950 was a center fielder he wanted to start his own Dodger center fielder, Snider.

Baseball Commissioner A.B. (Happy) Chandler, after numerous fan and player complaints, instructed Shotton to play the outfield as originally picked. The controversy, however, brought about the change whereby fans vote by position instead of the outfielders as a group.

Dodgers All-Star Batting Averages

Player	G	AB	R	H	2B	3B	HR	RBI	Avg.
Dusty Baker	2	4	0	1	0	0	0	0	.250
Ralph Branca	1	1	0	0	0	0	0	0	.000
Jim Brewer	1	0	0	0	0	0	0	0	.000
Dolph Camilli	1	1	0	0	0	0	0	0	.000
Roy Campanella	7	20	1	2	0	0	0	0	.100
Ron Cey	6	9	0	2	1	0	0	0	.222
Gino Cimoli	1	1	0	0	0	0	0	0	.000
Pete Coscarat	1	1	0	0	0	0	0	0	.000
Tony Cuccinello	1	1	0	0	0	0	0	0	.000
Tommy Davis	3	8	1	1	0	0	0	0	.125
Willie Davis	2	3	1	3	0	0	1	2	1.000
Don Drysdale	8	3	0	0	0	0	0	0	.000
Leo Durocher	2	6	1	2	0	0	0	0	.333
Bruce Edwards	1	0	0	0	0	0	0	0	.000
Carl Erskine	1	0	0	0	0	0	0	0	.000
Augie Galan	2	5	1	1	0	0	0	0	.200
Steve Garvey	8	22	6	9	2	2	2	6	.409
Jim Gilliam	1	2	1	1	0	0	1	1	.500
Billy Grabarkewitz	1	3	0	1	0	0	0	0	.333
Pedro Guerrero	2	2	0	0	0	0	0	0	.000
Tom Haller	1	2	0	0	0	0	0	0	.000
Billy Herman	3	9	0	4	1	0	0	0	.444
Kirby Higbe	1	1	0	0	0	0	0	0	.000
Gil Hodges	6	12	3	4	0	0	1	2	.333
Burt Hooton	1	0	0	0	0	0	0	0	.000
Steve Howe	1	0	0	0	0	0	0	0	.000
Sandy Koufax	4	0	0	0	0	0	0	0	.000
Clem Labine	1	0	0	0	0	0	0	0	.000
Norm Larker	2	1	1	0	0	0	0	0	.000
Cookie Lavagetto	2	3	0	0	0	0	0	0	.000
Jim Lefebvre	1	2	0	0	0	0	0	0	.000
Davey Lopes	4	5	0	2	0	0	0	1	.400
Al Lopez	1	2	0	0	0	0	0	0	.000
Mike Marshall	1	1	0	0	0	0	0	0	.000
Joe Medwick	3	5	0	0	0	0	0	0	.000
Andy Messersmith	1	0	0	0	0	0	0	0	.000
Rick Monday	1	2	0	0	0	0	0	0	.000
Wally Moon	2	4	0	0	0	0	0	0	.000
Manny Mota	1	1	0	0	0	0	0	0	.000
Van Lingle Mungo	2	0	0	0	0	0	0	0	.000
Charlie Neal	3	2	0	0	0	0	0	0	.000
Don Newcombe	4	3	0	1	0	0	0	1	.333
Claude Osteen	2	0	0	0	0	0	0	0	.000
Mickey Owen	2	2	1	1	0	0	1	1	.500
Babe Phelps	2	1	0	0	0	0	0	0	.000
Johnny Podres	2	1	1	1	1	0	0	0	1.000
Pee Wee Reese	8	17	0	2	1	0	0	2	.118
Pete Reiser	2	7	0	1	0	0	0	0	.143

Dodgers All-Star Batting Averages (Continued)

Player	G	AB	R	H	2B	3B	HR	RBI	Avg.
Jerry Reuss	1	0	0	0	0	0	0	0	.000
Rick Rhoden	1	0	0	0	0	0	0	0	.000
Jackie Robinson	6	18	7	6	2	0	1	4	.333
Preacher Roe	1	0	0	0	0	0	0	0	.000
John Roseboro	2	6	1	1	0	0	1	1	.333
Bill Russell	3	5	0	0	0	0	0	0	.000
Steve Sax	2	4	1	2	0	0	0	1	.500
Bill Singer	1	0	0	0	0	0	0	0	.000
Reggie Smith	3	6	0	1	0	0	0	0	.167
Duke Snider	6	10	3	3	1	0	0	0	.300
Eddie Stanky	1	2	0	0	0	0	0	0	.000
Don Sutton	4	0	0	0	0	0	0	0	.000
Fernando Valenzuela	2	0	0	0	0	0	0	0	.000
Arky Vaughan	1	2	0	0	0	0	0	0	.000
Dixie Walker	3	6	0	0	0	0	0	1	.000
Bob Welch	1	1	0	0	0	0	0	0	.000
Stan Williams	1	0	0	0	0	0	0	0	.000
Maury Wills	6	14	2	5	0	0	0	1	.357
Whit Wyatt	2	1	0	0	0	0	0	0	.000
Jimmy Wynn	2	5	2	2	0	0	1	1	.400
Totals		291	33	58	9	2	9	24	.199

Dodgers All-Star Pitching Averages

Player	G	IP	H	R	BB	SO	W	L	ERA
Ralph Branca	1	3	1	2	3	3	0	0	6.00
Jim Brewer	1	1	0	0	1	2	0	0	0.00
Don Drysdale	8	19⅓	9	4	4	19	2	1	1.40
Carl Erskine	1	⅔	1	0	0	1	0	0	0.00
Kirby Higbe	1	1⅓	5	4	1	2	0	0	27.00
Burt Hooton	1	1⅔	5	3	0	1	0	0	16.20
Steve Howe	1	⅓	0	0	0	0	0	0	0.00
Sandy Koufax	4	6	4	1	2	3	1	0	1.50
Clem Labine	1	1	3	3	0	1	0	0	9.00
Mike Marshall	1	2	0	0	1	2	0	0	0.00
Andy Messersmith	1	3	2	2	3	4	0	0	6.00
Van Lingle Mungo	2	3	6	8	4	2	0	1	18.00
Don Newcombe	4	8⅔	9	4	2	5	0	1	4.15
Claude Osteen	2	5	5	0	2	1	1	0	0.00
Johnny Podres	2	4	3	0	3	3	0	0	0.00
Jerry Reuss	1	1	0	0	0	3	1	0	0.00
Rick Rhoden	1	1	1	0	0	0	0	0	0.00
Preacher Roe	1	1	0	0	0	0	0	0	0.00
Bill Singer	1	2	0	0	0	0	0	0	0.00
Don Sutton	4	8	5	0	1	7	1	0	0.00
Fernando Valenzuela	2	2	2	0	2	0	0	0	0.00
Bob Welch	1	3	5	2	1	4	0	0	6.00

Dodgers All-Star Pitching Averages (Continued)

Player	G	AB	R	H	2B	3B	HR	RBI	Avg.
Stan Williams	1	2	2	0	1	2	0	0	0.00
Whit Wyatt	2	4	1	0	1	1	0	0	0.00
Totals		84	69	33	32	66	6	3	3.54

AWARDS
(First Year of Award in Parenthesis)
MOST VALUABLE PLAYER (1911)

1913   Jake Daubert (Chalmers Award)
1924   Dazzy Vance (League Award)
1941   Dolph Camilli
1949   Jackie Robinson
1951   Roy Campanella
1953   Roy Campanella
1955   Roy Campanella
1956   Don Newcombe
1962   Maury Wills
1963   Sandy Koufax
1974   Steve Garvey

CY YOUNG (1956)

1956   Don Newcombe
1962   Don Drysdale
1963   Sandy Koufax
1965   Sandy Koufax
1966   Sandy Koufax
1974   Mike Marshall
1981   Fernando Valenzuela

ROOKIE OF THE YEAR (1947)

1947   Jackie Robinson
1949   Don Newcombe
1952   Joe Black
1953   Jim Gilliam
1960   Frank Howard
1965   Jim Lefebvre
1969   Ted Sizemore
1979   Rick Sutcliffe
1980   Steve Howe
1981   Fernando Valenzuela
1982   Steve Sax

FIREMAN OF THE YEAR (1960)

1966   Phil Regan
1974   Mike Marshall

AWARDS
(continued)

SPORTING NEWS PLAYER OF THE YEAR (1948)

1953 Roy Campanella
1955 Duke Snider
1962 Maury Wills

SPORTING NEWS PITCHER OF THE YEAR (1948)

1951 Preacher Roe
1956 Don Newcombe
1962 Don Drysdale
1963 Sandy Koufax
1964 Sandy Koufax
1965 Sandy Koufax
1966 Sandy Koufax
1974 Mike Marshall
1981 Fernando Valenzuela

COMEBACK PLAYER OF THE YEAR (1966)

1966 Phil Regan
1971 Al Downing
1974 Jimmy Wynn
1976 Tommy John
1980 Jerry Reuss

GOLD GLOVE WINNERS

1957 Gil Hodges, 1B
1958 Gil Hodges, 1B
1959 Gil Hodges, 1B
1960 Wally Moon, OF
1961 John Roseboro, C
      Maury Wills, SS
1962 Maury Wills, SS
1966 John Roseboro, C
1967 Wes Parker, 1B
1968 Wes Parker, 1B
1969 Wes Parker, 1B
1970 Wes Parker, 1B
1971 Wes Parker, 1B
1972 Willie Davis, OF
      Wes Parker, 1B
1973 Willie Davis, OF
1974 Steve Garvey, 1B
      Andy Messersmith, P
1975 Steve Garvey, 1B
      Andy Messersmith, P
1976 Steve Garvey, 1B
1977 Steve Garvey, 1B
1978 Davey Lopes, 2B
1981 Dusty Baker, OF

PLAYER OF THE DECADE (1960-1969)

Sandy Koufax

UNIFORM NUMBERS RETIRED

4	Duke Snider
19	Jim Gilliam
24	Walt Alston
32	Sandy Koufax
39	Roy Campanella
42	Jackie Robinson

Jackie Robinson's #42 has been retired.

NICKNAMES

How The Dodgers Got Their Name

Would a Bridegrooms vs. Yankees World Series seem quite the same? Or the fierce Grooms-Giants rivalry?

But "Bridegrooms," shortened to "Grooms," was one of the first nicknames pinned on the Brooklyn Baseball Club which in its 100-year history has had a lot of them: Trolley Dodgers, Wonders, Fillies, the Superbas, Robins, Bums, Flock, Daffiness Boys, and finally the Dodgers.

When the club was first organized in 1883 and played for a season in the minor league Interstate League they were called the "Brooklyns" or "Church City Nine," Brooklyn being a city with many churches.

Since Brooklyn also was a city noted for its many trolleys, several of which criss-crossed near the Washington Park ball yard, the nicknames of "Trolley Dodgers"—or "Dodgers"—gained acceptance.

By now the team played in the major league American Association and in 1889 won its first pennant. When a half-dozen of the players all about the same time got married writers began calling the Dodgers "Bridegrooms," shortened to "Grooms."

Always, though, "Dodgers" lurked in the background and would be used infrequently. When John Montgomery Ward became manager in 1891 the team became "Ward's Wonders," changed to "Foutz's Fillies" when Dave Foutz followed as manager.

During this time Charles Hercules Ebbets, a young man who'd worked in the club's offices at various jobs since 1883, began acquiring stock. By late 1897 he had gained a controlling interest, and then early in 1899 Ebbets and Baltimore Orioles owner Harry Von der Horst exchanged half-interests in each other's teams.

As a result, Von der Horst shipped some of his better players—including batting champ Wee Willie Keeler—plus his fine manager, Ned Hanlon, to Brooklyn and the newly stocked team walked off with National League pennants in both 1899 and 1900.

There was, at the time, a vaudeville troupe called "Hanlon's Superbas" and so writers started calling the erstwhile Dodgers "Superbas," a name that really didn't fade out until the 1920's—long after Hanlon himself was gone from the team.

Still, occasionally, there would be reference to the "Dodgers." But when Wilbert Robinson—the storied "Uncle Robbie"—became manager in 1914 both Dodgers and Superbas gradually faded and the Brooklyn club became most popularly the "Robins."

While Ebbets was still alive and in full control, the "Robins"—or "Superbas"—won National League championships in 1916 and 1920 and even came close in 1924, the year pitcher Dazzy Vance won league Most Valuable Player honors.

But with Ebbets' death in 1925 came a period of turmoil, the team lacking strong leadership, falling into financial hardship, and ultimately making poor player selections.

Still, under "Uncle Robbie's" rather casual managership the team had a special charisma that New York writers picked up on and one of them, Westbrook Pegler, called the club the "Daffiness Boys."

With outfielder Babe Herman, who played from 1926 to 1931, the special target—or favorite—the "Daffiness" became daffy as in "Daffy Dodgers." Herman could hit a ton—.393 one season, for example—but he also had a penchant for misjudging fly balls.

And he's the one who hit the ball where three Dodgers wound up all together on third base, thus being the only player ever to "triple into a double play"—or, more exactly to double into a double play.

By the time Robinson was fired, after the 1931 season, the nickname always in the background—"Dodger"—was ready to burst forth. And that it did during the 1930s, '40s, and especially since.

When the new general manager, Larry MacPhail, arrived in 1938 and the ex-daffy

Dodgers got serious again a cult of super fans emerged, though Brooklyn had long been known for its partisan, numerous, and often-raucous spectators.

They were the "Flock" (from Flatbush), just as was their team the Flock though the name was never more than a synonym for Dodgers. Most famous of these fans was Hilda (The Bell) Chester who always arrived carrying a sign "Hilda Is Here" and would sit in the stands and ring a loud bell.

Indeed, in chummy Ebbets Field the spectators were so close to the field they almost became part of the action. The team itself—always unpredictable—also became known by these fans as the "Bums," or "Our Bums," "Dem Bums," a term of affection.

One day newspaper cartoonist Willard Mullin caught a cab outside Ebbets and the driver asked, "How'd those Bums do today?" An idea clicked and Mullin drew his famous Flatbush Bum that became almost a symbol of the team although "Dodgers" still prevailed.

"Bums," too, would fit when newspaper headline space was tight. Play-by-play announcer Red Barber added to the acceptance with his "FOB"—the bases are "full of Bums."

Alas, when the team moved West the "Bum" became history. One Los Angeles newspaper even had an edict: that never in its pages would the Dodgers be referred to as "Bums."

And so today the Los Angeles Baseball Club is the "Dodgers" and probably will be for many years to come.

Nicknames Used by the Brooklyn (now Los Angeles) Baseball Club

Brooklyns, 1883-1888
Trolley Dodgers, mid-1880s and mid-1890s
Grooms (Bridegrooms), 1889-1891
Ward's Wonders, 1891-1893
Foutz's Fillies, 1893-1897
Dodgers, 1895 to date.
Superbas, 1899-1920s
Robins, 1915-1930
Bums, 1940-1957

Names Most Frequently Used

Grooms, 1889-1890s
Superbas, 1899-1920s
Robins, 1915-1930s
Dodgers, 1930s to date.

Dodgers' Nicknames

ACE
Emil Batch

AD
Addison Gumbert
William Yale

ADONIS
Bill Terry

AIRDALE
Don Drysdale

ANDY
David Anderson
John Messersmith

ARK
Gerald Hannahs

ARKY
Joseph Vaughan

BABE
Werner Birrer
Ellsworth Dahlgren
Floyd Herman
Ernest Phelps
George Ruth*

BABO
Robert Castillo

BAD BILL
Bill Dahlen

BALD BILLY
Bill Barnie**

BARNACLE BILL
Bill Posedel

BARNEY
Burt Shotton**

BARON
Elmer Knetzer
Andy Messersmith
Boots Poffenberger

BAYONNE
Doug Rau

BEAR TRACKS
Johnny Schmitz

BEAUTY
Dave Bancroft

BEETLE
Bob Bailey

BIG BILL
Bill Schardt
Bill Steele

BIG D
Don Drysdale

BIG DADDY
Stan Williams

BIG DAN
Dennis Brouthers

BIG DEE
Daryl Spencer

BIG ED
Ed Konetchy
Ed Reulback
Ed Stevens

BIG FOOT
Michael Marshall

BIG JIM
Jim Murray
Jim Roberts

BIG POISON
Paul Waner

BIG SERB
John Miljus

BILLY BUCK
Bill Buckner

BILLY G.
Bill Grabarkewitz

BINKY
John Jones

BIRD
Jerry Royster

BLACKIE
Gus Mancuso
Frank O'Rourke

BLACK JACK
Jack Burdock

BLADE
Mark Belanger
Jack Billingham
Don Demeter

BLIMP
Babe Phelps

BOBO
Bob Milliken
Norman Newsome

BONES
Fred Ely

Dodgers' Nicknames (Continued)

BONNIE
John Hollingsworth

BOOG
John Powell

BOOM-BOOM
Walter Beck

BOOMER
Steve Yeager

BOOTS
Al Hollingsworth
Cletus Poffenberger

BRAT
Eddie Stanky

BREW
Jim Brewer

BRICKYARD
William Kennedy

BROADWAY ALECK
Alexander Smith

BROWNIE
Mace Brown

BRYAN
Billy Herman

BUCK
Charles Marrow
Norman Newsome
Lee Rogers
Zach Wheat

BUCKSHOT
Tommy Brown
Glenn Wright

BUD
Bernie Hungling
Clarence Podbielan

BUDDY
John Hassett
Eddie Solomon

BULL
Louis Durham
Bruce Edwards
Al Ferrara
William Wagner

BUNNY
Albert Fabrique

BUS
Cal McLish

BUSH
Bob Borkowski

BUSTER
Frank Burrell
Colonel Mills

BUTCH
Walter Henline

BUTTS
Albert Wagner

BUZZ
Ralph Boyle
Doug McWeeney

BUZZIE
Emil Bavasi***

CADDY
Leon Cadore

CAMPY
Roy Campanella

CANDY
George LaChance
Candido Maldonado

CANNONBALL
Edward Crane

CAPTAIN
Pee Wee Reese

CAPTAIN MIDNIGHT
Lee Walls

CASEY
Charles Stengel****

CHAPPIE
Ben Chapman
Charles McFarland

CHEWING GUM
John O'Brien

CHICK
Tony Cuccinello
Wilson Fewster
William Outen

CHICO
Humberto Fernandez
Luis Olmo

CHIEF
Ernie Koy
John Meyers

CHIEF PONTIAC
Dick Gray

CHILDE HAROLD
Hal Janvrin

263

Dodgers' Nicknames (Continued)

CHINK
Earl Yingling
Al Zachary

CHUCK
Clarence Churn
Charles Dressen**
Kevin Connors
Charles Essegian
Charles Kress
Charles Ward

CLANCY
George Cutshaw
Clarence Smyres

CLIMAX
Clarence Blethen

CLARK KENT
Andy Kosco

COCONUTS
Rube Walker

COLBY JACK
Jack Coombs

COLUMBIA GEORGE
George Smith

COMET
Willie Davis
Clyde King

CON
Cornelius Daily

COOKIE
Harry Lavagetto

COONSKIN
Curt Davis

COTTON
Joe Beckwith
Jim Tierney

COWBOY
Jim Winford

COZY
Patrick Dolan

CRASH
Richie Allen

CURLEY
Manuel Onis

CY
Eros Barger
Cyril Buker
William Moore

DARBY
William O'Brien

DAZZY
Clarence Vance
Gene Vance

DEACON
James McGuire
Edward Van Buren

DEE
D.C. Moore

DEL
Adelphia Bissonette

DELSEY
Derrell Griffith

DIAMOND JIM
Jim Gentile

DIRTY JACK
Jack Doyle

DIXIE
Homer Howell
Fred Walker

DIXIE THRUSH
Sammy Strang

DIZ
Howie Reed

DOC
Al Bushong
James Casey
Harry Gessler
James McJames
William Marshall
Eustace Newton
Frank Reisling
Johnny Rutherford
William Scanlan

DODGER BLUE
Tommy Lasorda****

3-DOG
Willie Davis

DOLLY
Monroe Stark

DOLPH
Adolph Camilli

DOMINICAN DANDY
Juan Marichal

DOUBLE D
Don Drysdale

Dodgers' Nicknames (Continued)

DOUBLE NO NO
Alan Foster

DOUBLE O
Al McBean

DR. STRANGEGLOVE
Dick Stuart

DUCKY WUCKY
Joe Medwick

DUDE
Tom Esterbrook
Myron McCormick

DUKE
Charles Farrell
Duane Sims
Edwin Snider

DUKE OF FLATBUSH
Edwin Snider

DUMBO
Norm Larker

DUSTER
Walter Mails

DUSTY
Johnnie Baker

DUTCH
Erve Beck
Frank Henry
Adolph Jordan
Emil Leonard
Walter Ruether
Fred Schliebner
Charles Stengel
Sterling Stryker

EARACHE
Benny Meyer

Ee-Yah
Hughie Jennings

EGGIE
Ed Lennox

EL LATIGO
Rene Valdez

ELMER
Don Sutton

EL TORO
Fernando Valenzuela

FARMER
George Bell
Ray Moore
Morris Steelman

FAT FREDDIE
Fred Fitzsimmons

FATS
John Dantonio

FERGY
Joe Ferguson

FIDDLER
Eddie Basinski

FIREBALL
Jim Brewer

FLASH
George Fallon

FLEA
Bobby Lillis

FLIP FLAP
Oscar Jones

FOOTSIE
Wayne Belardi

FRENCHY
Stanley Bordagaray
Jim Lefebvre

FRITZ
Fred Ostermueller

GABBY
Doyle Alexander
John Roseboro

GABE
Len Gabrielson

GEE-GEE
Gus Getz

GENTLEMAN AL
Al Downing

GENTLEMAN FROM
INDIANA
Carl Erskine

GENTLEMAN GEORGE
George Haddock

GERMANY
Joe Schultz
George Smith

GERONIMO
Manny Mota

GIBBY
Gilbert Brack

GIGGI
Al Downing

Dodgers' Nicknames (Continued)

GILLY
Carden Gillenwater

GIMPY
Lloyd Brown

GINK
Harvey Hendrick

GLADIATOR
Pete Browning

GLASS ARM EDDIE
Eddie Brown

GOLDEN ARM
Sandy Koufax

GOLDEN VOICED TENOR
Al Mamaux

GOLDIE
Jim Golden

GOMER
Claude Osteen

GOOD TIME BILL
Bill Lamar

GOODY
Goodwin Rosen

GOO-GOO
Augie Galan

GRABBY
Bill Grabarkewitz

GREEK
Charles George

GULFPORT
Jack Ryan

GUMMY
Joe Wall

GUNNER
Guy Cantrell
Bill McGunnigle**

GUS
August Weyhing

HACK
Lawrence Miller
Lewis Wilson

HANDSOME HARRY
Harry Howell

HANDSOME RANSOM
Ransom Jackson

HANDY ANDY
Andy High
Andy Pafco

HANK
Henry Aguirre
Henry Behrman
John DeBerry
Henry Edwards
Henry Webb
Henry Winston

HAP
Henry Myers
Henry Smith

HAPPY
Burt Hooton

HARDIE
James Henderson

HATCH
Tom Haller

HAWK
Ralph Branca

HEINIE
Emil Batch
Henry Manush

HERKY JERKY
Elmer Horton

HICKIE
George Wilson

HIGHPOCKETS
George Kelly

HIPPITY
Johnny Hopp

HOD
Horace Ford

HOLIDAY
Charles H. Ebbets***

HONDO
Frank Howard

HONEST JOHN
John Anderson

HOPE DIAMOND
Charlie Hough

HORSE
Frank Howard
Bob Lee

Dodgers' Nicknames (Continued)

HOSS
Billy Cox
Terry Forster

HOT POTATO
Luke Hamlin

HOWZER
Steve Howe

HUB
George Collins
Oscar Knolls
Hubbard Northen

HUEVO
Vicente Romo

HUMAN FLEA
Frank Bonner

HUMPHREY
Steve Bilko

HUMPY
Pryor McElveen

HUNKEY
Henry Hines

HY
Henry Myers

IKE
Issac Boone
Danny Ozark*

IRISH
Emil Meusel

IRON MAN
Joe McGinnity
Joe Oeschger

IRON MIKE
Mike Marshall

IVY
Ivan Olson

JACQUES
Jack Fournier

JAKE
Jacob Daubert
D'Arcy Flowers
Herman Hehl
Merwin Jacobson

JAY
John Johnstone
James Partridge

JEFF
Edward Pfeffer

JERSEY JOE
Joe Stripp

JIBARO
Luis Olmo

JIGGER
Arnold Statz

JOSH
Von Joshua

JUDGE
Walter McCreedie
Frank Robinson

JUGHANDLE JOHNNY
John Morrison

JULIUS
George Cisar

JUMBO
Bob Barrett
Jim Elliott

JUNIOR
Lonny Frey
Jim Gilliam

KAISER
Irvin Wilhelm

KAMPY
Alex Kampouris

KELLY
Tommy Holmes

KEMER
Ken Brett

KEMO
Phil Ortega

KID
Wilfred Carsey
Mal Eason

KIKI
Hazen Cuyler
Al Ferrara

KING
John Karst
Eddie Solomon
Karl Spooner

KIPPER
Fred Kipp

Dodgers' Nicknames (Continued)

KIT
James McKenna

KLIP
Johnny Klippstein

KNUCKLES
Hoyt Wilhelm

KONEY
Ed Konetchy

LADY
Charles Baldwin

LANCE
Clarence Rautzhan

LAVE
Lafayette Cross
Lafayette Winham

LAWMAN
Rudy Law

LEE
Leondaus Lacy

LEFTY
Ralph Birkofer
Alfonzo Davis
George Dockins
Jim Faulkner
Nelson Greene
Leo Grissom
Fred Heimach
C.F. Hopper
Frank Lamanske
Bob Logan
Paul Minner
Frank O'Doul
Charles Perkins
Harold Phillips*
Joe Shaute
Dwain Sloat
Tom Sunkel
Hank Thormahlen

LINDY
Fred Lindstrom

LION
Leo Durocher****

LIP
Leo Durocher****

LITTLE COLONEL
Pee Wee Reese

LITTLE GLOBETROTTER
Billy Earle

LITTLE JOE
Joe Yeager

LITTLE POISON
Lloyd Waner

LITTLE POTATO
Camilo Pascual

LONG TOM
John Winsett

LORD
Jimmy Jordan

LUKE
Ray Lucas

MACK
McKinley Wheat

MAD HATTER
Glenn Burke

MAD MONK
Russ Meyer

MAHATMA
Branch Rickey***

MAX
Albert Butcher

MICK
Pete Mikkelsen

MICKEY
Dan Daub
Michael Doolan
Cornelius Finn
Michael Hughes
Thompson Livingston
Manny Mota
George O'Neil
Arnold Owen
Danny Walton

MIKE
Harry Mowrey

MOE
Morris Berg
Greg Mulleavy*

MONKEY
Pete Hotaling

MONTE
John Ward

Dodgers' Nicknames (Continued)

MONTY
Romanus Basgall*

MOON
Joe Harris

MOONIE
Otto Millier

MOON MAN
Jay Johnstone

MOOSE
John Clabaugh
George Earnshaw
Walt Moryn
Bill Skoron

MOUSY
Maury Wills

MR. CHIPS
Bob Chipman

MR. CLEAN
Steve Garvey

MR. CLUTCH
Ron Fairly

MR. MUSCLES
Gil Hodges

MR. RED, WHITE
AND BLUE
Rick Monday

MUDCAT
Jim Grant

MUGSY
Eddie Stanky

MURPH
Willie Crawford

MUSCLES
Joe Gallagher
Joe Medwick

MYSTERIOUS
Frederick Walker

NAP
George Rucker

NEEDLE
Watty Clark

NEMO
Les Munns

NEWK
Don Newcombe

NEWT
Newell Kimball

NICK
Otho Nitcholas
Jon Willhite

NIG
Bobby Bregan
Charles Fuller

NONCHALANTSKI
Ron Perranoski*****

NO NO
Bill Singer

OISK
Carl Erskine

OLD DOG
Lew Ritter

OLD FOLKS
Art Fowler

OLD PARD
Win Ballou

OLD STRONGHEART
Luke Hamlin

OL' HIGGLEBY
Kirby Higby

OL' STUBBLEBEARD
Burleigh Grimes

OPIE
Dave Patterson

OSKIE
Gordon Slade

OX
Oscar Eckhardt

OYSTER
Thomas Burns

PA
John Harkins

PACKY
Stanley Rogers

PARD
Al Epperly

PARISIEN BOB
Bob Caruthers

PAT
Ezra McGlothin
Don Ragan

Dodgers' Nicknames (Continued)

PATSY
Patrick Donovan****

PEACH
Chauncey Fisher

PEACHES
John Werhas

PEA RIDGE
Clyde Day

PEEPUL'S CHERCE
Dixie Walker

PEE WEE
Nate Oliver
Harold Reese

PEG O' MY HEART
Carl Furillo

PENGUIN
Ron Cey

PEPE
Jesus Frias

PEPPER
Eddie Morgan

PERRY
Ron Perranoski*****

PHENOMENAL
John Smith

PICKLES
Mike Garman

PIGGY
Joe Pignatano

PISTOL PETE
Harold Reiser

POLO
Stan Andrews

POODLES
Joe Hutcheson

POOSH 'EM UP
Tony Lazzeri

POP
John Corkhill
Frank Dillon
Paul Popovich
William Shriver
Harry Shriver

POSSUM
Larry Burright
George Whitted

POUND CAKE
Ken McMullen

PREACHER
Elwin Roe

PRIDE OF HAVANA
Dolf Luque

PROVIDENCE EXPRESS
Davey Lopes

PRUSCHKA
Andy Pafco

PUDGE
Sid Gatreaux

PUG
Horace Allen

QUAKER
Johnny Oates

QUIET MAN
Walt Alson**

RABBIT
Walter Maranville

RATTLESNAKE
Tom Baker

RAW MEAT
Steve Yeager

READING RIFLE
Carl Furillo

REBEL
Tommy McMillan

RED
Charles Adams*
Walter Barber*******
John Barkley
Bob Barrett
Lindsey Brown
Sam Crane
Alexander Downey
Fred Downs
Elmer Durrett
Russell Evans
Ray Hayworth
Thomas Owens
Don Padgett
Jim Russell
James C. Smith
Jim Smythe

REDSKIN
Raleigh Aitchison

Dodgers' Nicknames (Continued)

RED TOP
Fred Johnston

REINDEER
Rick Auerbach

RICK
Fred Auerbach
Robert Monday
Richard Rhoden
Richard Sutcliffe

RIP
Eldon Repulski

ROARING BILL
Brickyard Kennedy

ROCK
Ed Rakow

ROCKS
Harry McIntire

ROCKY
Everett Bridges
Rocco Colavito
Glenn Nelson

ROD
Raoul Dedeaux

ROLLS ROYCE
Jerry Reuss

ROPES
Bill Russell

ROSY
John Roseboro
Wilfred Ryan

ROWDY
Harold Elliott
Gene Moore

RUBE
Ed Albosta
Ray Bressler
Frank Dessau
Welton Ehrhardt
Richard Marquard
Reuben Melton
Harry Vickers
Al Walker
John A. Ward
Byron Yarrison

RUDY RUTGERS
Jeff Torborg

SADIE
John McMahon

SAL THE BARBER
Sal Maglie

SAMBO
Sam Leslie

SANDY
Edmundo Amoros
Charles Burk
Art Herring
Sanford Koufax
Gene Vance

SCAT
Otis Davis

SCHNOZZ
Ernie Lombardi

SCHOOLBOY
Alta Cohen
Waite Hoyt
Lynwood Rowe

SCISSORS
Dave Foutz****

SCOOPS
Max Carey****

SCOW
Fay Thomas

SCRAP IRON
Bob Stinson

SCRAPPY BILL
Bill Joyce

SENIOR STOPPER
Fernando Valenzuela

SHECK
Jimmy Sheckard

SHERIFF
John Gaddy
Hal Lee

SHERRY
Sherrod Smith

SHOOK
Elmer Brown

SHOTGUN
George Shuba

SHUFFLIN' PHIL
Phil Douglas

SILENT CAL
Ray Benge

Dodgers' Nicknames (Continued)

SILENT JOHN
John Hummel

SILVER
Tommy Hutton

SILVER FOX
Jesse Petty
Duke Snider

SIMMY
Simeon Murch

SINGER THROWING
MACHINE
Bill Singer

SIR THOMAS
Tommy Corcoran

SIZE
Ted Sizemore

SKEETER
Hal Gregg
Joe Moeller

SKIP
Gene Mauch

SKOONJ
Carl Furillo

SLATS
Bob Aspromonte

SLICK
Lou Johnson

SLOPPY
Hollis Thurston

SMILING AL
Al Maul

SMITTY
Reggie Smith

SMOKE
Dave Stewart

SMOKEY
Walt Alston**

SMUTTS
Morrie Aderholt

SNOOKS
Ray Dowd

SPARTANBURG JOHN
John McMakin

SPEEDY
Fred Miller

SPIDER
John Jorgensen
Mike Strahler

SPITTIN' BILL
Bill Doak

SQUIRE OF FLATBUSH
Charles Ebbets***

STAN THE MAN
UNUSUAL
Don Stanhouse

STEADY EDDIE
Ed Goodson

STEEPLE
Howie Schultz

STICK
Gene Michael

STILL BILL
Bill Hill

STORMY
Jack Doyle

STOUT STEVE
Steve Bilko

STRETCH
Howie Schultz

STUFFY
John Stewart

SUDS
Bill Sudakis

SUKEY
Clyde Sukefourt*****

SUT
Don Sutton

SWEETBREADS
Abraham Bailey

SWEET LOU
Lou Johnson

TABASCO KID
Norman Elberfeld

TACKS
Clifford Latimer

TAMI
Ralph Mauriello

TARZAN
Joe Ferguson

Dodgers Nicknames (Continued)

TEX
Jim Carlton
Ross Erwin
Gomer Wilson

THE DODGER
Roger Craig

THE GREAT
Walter Mails

THE POINT
Johnny Podres

THE VANISHER
Van Lingle Mungo

TIDO
Tom Daly

TIGER
Joe Becker*
Don Hoak
Wes Parker

TIM
Thomas Harkness
Charles Thompson

TINY
Claude Osborne

TITO
Pedro Guerrero

TJ
Tommy John

TOMATO FACE
Nick Cullop

TOMMY
Herman Davis
Fresco Thompson******

TOMMY THE CORK
Tommy Corcoran

TOP CAT
Fred Norman

TOPSY
George Magoon

TOT
Forest Pressnell

TOY CANNON
Jimmy Wynn

TRADER AL
Al Campanis******

TRIXIE
Dick Tracewski

TROLLEY LINE
John Butler

TUCK
George Stainback******

TURK
Dick Farrell

TWIG
Wayne Terwilliger

TY
Albert Tyson

UNCLE ROBBIE
Wilbert Robinson**

VANDY
Van Lingle Mungo

VIN
Vincent Scully*******

VITO
Vitautis Tamulis

VON
Paul Schreiber

VULTURE
Phil Regan

WATTY
William Clark

WEASEL
Don Bessent

WEE WILLIE
William Keeler

WELCHIE
Bob Welch

WHEEZER
Bill Dell

WHIT
John Wyatt

WHITEY
Charles Alperman
Ed Appleton
Harold Ock
Lawton Witt

WILD BILL
William Donovan
Bill Leard

WILLIE C.
Willie Crawford

WILLIE D.
Willie Davis

Dodgers' Nicknames (Continued)

WILLIE THE KNUCK
James Ramsdell

WIMPIE
Tom Paciorek

WIMPY
Claude Osteen

WINDY
Ike Benners

WOODY
Elwood English

ZACH
Zachariah Wheat

ZEKE
Ron Hunt
George Wrigley

ZIM
Don Zimmer

ZORRO
Zoilo Versalles

*Dodger coach
**Dodger manager
***Dodger executive
****Player and manager
*****Player and coach
******Player and executive
*******Broadcaster

BALLPARKS WHERE THE DODGERS HAVE PLAYED

(original) Washington Park, 1883-1890
Location: Between 4th and 5th Avenues and 3rd and 5th Streets, South Brooklyn.
First game (major league but pre-league): April 12, 1884—Cleveland 5, Brooklyn 1.
First game (American Association): May 5, 1884—Brooklyn 11, Washington 3.

Eastern Park, 1891-1897
Location: Vesta Avenue, Powell Street, Sutter Avenue, and Eastern Parkway, suburban East New York City.
First game: April 27, 1891—New York 6, Brooklyn 5

(second) Washington Park, 1898-1912
Location: Between 3rd and 4th Avenues and 1st and 3rd Streets, South Brooklyn, adjacent to original Washington Park.
First game: April 30, 1898—Philadelphia 6, Brooklyn 4

Ebbets Field, 1913-1957
Location: Sullivan Place and Cedar (later McKeever) Place bordered by Bedford Avenue, Brooklyn.
First game (Exhibition): April 5, 1913—Brooklyn 3, New York Yankees 2
First game (National League): April 9, 1913—Philadelphia 1, Brooklyn 0

Memorial Coliseum, 1958-1961
Location: Santa Barbara Avenue between Figueroa and Vermont in Exposition Park, just south of downtown Los Angeles.
First game: April 18, 1958—Los Angeles 6, San Francisco 5.

Dodger Stadium, 1962-
Location: 1000 Elysian Park Avenue off Sunset Boulevard in Elysian Park just west of downtown Los Angeles.
First game: April 10, 1962—Cincinnati 6, Los Angeles 3.

HALL OF FAME

Dodgers in the Hall of Fame

(Year elected in parenthesis)

Roy Campanella (1969)
Max Carey (1961)
Don Drysdale (1984)
Burleigh Grimes (1964)
Billy Herman (1975)
Willie Keeler (1939)
Joe Kelley (1971)
Sandy Koufax (1971)
Rube Marquard (1971)
Joe McGinnity (1946)
Joe Medwick (1968)
Jackie Robinson (1962)
Wilbert Robinson (1945)
Duke Snider (1980)
Casey Stengel (1974)
Dazzy Vance (1955)
Zach Wheat (1959)

Selected For Meritorious Services

Red Barber (Broadcaster)
Larry MacPhail
   (Executive)
Branch Rickey
   (Manager-Executive)
Vin Scully (Broadcaster)
Walter Alston (Manager)

Others Who Have Worn Dodger Uniforms That Are Enshrined

(Year elected in parenthesis)

Dave Bancroft (1971)
Dan Brouthers (1945)
Kiki Cuyler (1968)
Waite Hoyt (1969)
Hughie Jennings (1945)
George Kelly (1973)
Al Lopez (1977)
Heinie Manush (1964)
Rabbit Maranville (1954)
Tommy McCarthy (1946)
Frank Robinson (1982)
Lloyd Waner (1967)
Paul Waner (1952)
Monte Ward (1964)
Hack Wilson (1979)

7
ALL-TIME ROSTER INDEX (1884-1983)

A

Abbey, Bert	1895-96
Abrams, Calvin	1949-52
Aderholt, Morris	1944-45
Aguirre, Henry ("Hank")	1968
Ainsmith, Edward	1923
Aitchison, Raleigh	1911,1914-15
Albosta, Edward	1941
Alcarez, Angel ("Luis")	1967-68
Alexander, Doyle	1971
Allen, Frank	1912-14
Allen, Horace	1919
Allen, Johnny	1941-43
Allen, Richard ("Richie")	1971
Almada, Baldomere ("Mel")	1939
Alperman, Charles ("Whitey")	1906-09
Alvarez, Jesus ("Orlando")	1973-75
Amoros, Edmunds ("Sandy")	1952
	1954-57,1959-60,1967
Anderson, David	1983
Anderson, Ferrell	1946
Anderson, John	1894-99
Andrews, Stan	1944-45
Ankenman, Fred ("Pat")	1943-44
Antonello, Bill	1953
Appleton, Edward	1915-16
Archer, Jimmy	1918
Aspromonte, Robert	1956, 1960-61
Auerback, Frederick ("Rick")	1974-76

B

Babb, Charles	1904-05
Babich, Johnny	1934-35
Bailey, Abraham ("Sweetbreads")	1921
Bailey, Arthur ("Gene")	1923-24
Bailey, Bob	1967-68
Baird, Howard ("Doug")	1919-20

Baker, Johnnie ("Dusty")	1976-83
Baker, Tom	1935-37
Baldwin, Charles ("Lady")	1890
Ballou, Noble ("Win")	1929
Bancroft, Dave	1928-29
Bankhead, Dan	1947, 1950-51
Banta, John ("Jack")	1947-50
Barber, Tyrus ("Turner")	1923
Barbieri, Jim	1966
Barger, Eros ("Cy")	1910-12
Barkley, John ("Red")	1943
Barnes, Jesse	1926-27
Barney, Rex	1943,1946-50
Barr, Robert	1935
Barrett, Robert ("Red")	1925,1927
Bartley, Boyd	1943
Bashang, Albert	1918
Basinski, Edwin	1944-45
Batch, Emil ("Heinie")	1904-07
Baxes, Dimitrios ("Jim")	1959
Beck, Erwin ("Erve")	1899
Beck, Walter ("Boom-Boom")	1933-34
Beckwith, Joe	1979-83
Behrman, Henry ("Hank")	1946-48
Belanger, Mark	1982
Belardi, Carroll ("Wayne")	1950-51
	1953-54
Bell, Frank	1885
Bell, George	1907-11
Benge,Ray	1933-35
Benners, Isaac	1884
Berg, Morris ("Moe")	1923
Bergen, Bill	1904-11
Berres, Ray	1934, 1936
Bessent, Fred ("Don")	1955-58
Bilko, Steve	1958

277

Eayrs Edwin	1921
Eckhardt, Oscar ("Ox")	1936
Edwards, Charles ("Bruce")	1946-51
Edwards, Henry ("Hank")	1951
Egan, Richard J.	1914-15
Egan, Richard W.	1967
Ehrhardt, Welton ("Rube")	1924-28
Eisenstat, Harry	1935-37
Elberfeld, Norman ("Kid")	1914
Elliott, Harold ("Rowdy")	1920
Elliott, James ("Jumbo")	1925, 1927-30
Elston, Don	1957
Ely, Frederick ("Bones")	1891
English, Elwood ("Woody")	1937-38
English, Gilbert	1944
Enzmann, Johnny	1914
Epperly, Albert	1950
Erskine, Carl	1948-59
Erwin, Ross ("Tex")	1910-14
Espy, Cecil	1983
Essegian, Charles ("Chuck")	1959-60
Esterbrook, Tom ("Dude")	1891
Evans, LeRoy	1902-03
Evans, Russell ("Red")	1939

F

Fabrique, Albert ("Bunny")	1916-17
Fairey, Jim	1968, 1973
Fairly, Ron	1958-69
Fallon, George	1937
Farmer,Alex	1908
Farrell, Charles ("Duke")	1899-1902
Farrell, Dick	1961
Farrow, John	1884
Faulkner, Jim	1930
Felix, August ("Gus")	1926-27
Ferguson, James ("Alex")	1929
Ferguson, Joe	1970-76, 1978-81
Fernandez, Humberto ("Chico")	1956
Fernandez, Sidney	1983
Ferrara, Alfred	1963, 1965-68
Ferrell, Wesley	1940
Fette, Louis	1940
Fewster, Wilson ("Chick")	1926-27
Fimple, Jack	1983
Finlayson, Pembroke	1908-09
Finn, Cornelius ("Mickey")	1930-32
Fischer, Bill	1913-14
Fisher, Bob	1912-13
Fisher, Chauncey	1897
Fitzsimmons, Fred	1937-43
Fitzsimmons, Tom	1919
Fletcher, Sam	1909
Flood, Timothy	1902-03

Flowers, Charles ("Wes")	1940, 1944
Flowers, D'Arcy ("Jake")	1927-31,1933
Ford, Horace ("Hod")	1925
Forster, Terry	1978-82
Foster, Alan	1967-70
Fournier, John ("Jack")	1923-26
Foutz, Dave	1888-96
Fowler, John ("Art")	1959
Frankhouse, Frederick	1936-38
Franklin, James ("Jack")	1944
Franks, Herman	1940-41
Frederick, Johnny	1929-34
Freigau, Howard	1928
French, Lawrence ("Larry")	1941-42
French, Ray	1923
Frey, Linus ("Lonny")	1933-36
Frias, Jesus ("Pepe")	1980-81
Fuchs, Charles	1944
Fuller, Charles ("Nig")	1902
Furillo, Carl	1946-60

G

Gabrielson, Leonard ("Len")	1967-70
Gaddy, John	1938
Galan, August ("Augie")	1941-46
Gallagher, Joe	1940
Gallivan, Philip	1931
Garman, Mike	1977-78
Garvey, Steve	1969-82
Garvin, Virgil ("Ned")	1902-04
Gaston, Welcome	1898-99
Gastright, Henry ("Hank")	1894
Gatins, Frank	1901
Gautreaux, Sidney	1936-37
Geer, William ("Billy")	1884
Gentile, Jim	1957-58
George, Charles ("Greek")	1938
Geraghy, Ben	1936
Gessler, Harry ("Doc")	1903-06
Getz, Gustave ("Gus")	1914-16
Giallombardo, Robert	1958
Gilbert, Charles	1940
Gilbert, Pete	1894
Gilbert, Walter ("Wally")	1928-31
Gillenwater, Carden	1943
Gilliam, Jim	1953-66
Gionfriddo, Albert	1947
Giuliani, Angelo ("Tony")	1940-41
Gleason, Roy	1963
Glossop, Alban ("Al")	1943
Goschaur, John	1901
Golden, Jim	1960-61
Goltz, David	1980-82
Gooch, Johnny	1928-29
Goodson, James ("Ed")	1976-77

Howe, Steve 1980-83
Howell, Harry 1898, 1900
Howell, Homer ("Dixie") 1953, 1955-56
Hoyt, Waite 1932, 1937-38
Hubbell, Wilbert ("Bill") 1925
Hudson, Johnny 1936-40
Hudson, Rex 1974
Hug, Edward 1903
Hughes, James J. 1899, 1901-02
Hughes, James R. ("Jim") 1952-56
Hughes, Michael ("Mickey") 1888-90
Hummel, John 1905-15
Humphrey, Albert 1911
Hungling, Bernard ("Bernie") 1922-23
Hunt, Ronald 1967
Hunter, George 1909
Hunter, Willard 1962
Hurley, Patrick 1907
Hutcheson, Joe 1933
Hutchinson, Ira 1939
Hutson, Roy 1925
Hutton, Tommy 1966, 1969

I

Inks, Albert ("Bert") 1891-92
Irwin, Charles 1901-02

J

Jacklitcsh, Frederick 1903-04
Jackson, Ransom ("Randy") 1956-58
Jacobson, Merwin 1926-27
James, Cleo 1968
Janvrin, Harold ("Hal") 1921-22
Jarvis, LeRoy ("Roy") 1944
Jeffcoat, George 1936-37, 1939
Jenkins, Jack 1969
Jennings, Hugh 1899-1900, 1903
John, Tommy 1972-78
Johnson, Lou 1965-67
Johnston, James ("Jimmy") 1916-25
Johnston, Wilfred ("Fred") 1924
Johnstone, John ("Jay") 1980-82
Jones, Arthur 1932
Jones, Charles 1884
Jones, Fielder 1896-1900
Jones, John ("Binky") 1924
Jones, Oscar 1903-05
Jordan, Adolph ("Dutch") 1903-04
Jordan, James ("Jimmy") 1933-36
Jordan, Timothy 1906-10
Jorgenson, John ("Spider") 1947-50
Joshua, Von 1969-71, 1973-74, 1979
Joyce, Bill 1892
Judge, Joe 1933

K

Kampouris, Alex 1941-43
Karst, John 1915
Keeler, William ("Willie") 1893, 1899-1902
Kehn, Chester ("Chet") 1942
Kekich, Mike 1965, 1968
Kelleher, John 1916
Kellert, Frank 1955
Kelley, Joe 1899-1901
Kelly, George 1932
Kennedy, Bob 1957
Kennedy,, Edward 1886
Kennedy, John 1965-66
Kennedy, William ("Brickyard")
 1892-1901
Kent, Maurice ("Maury") 1912-13
Kilduff, Pete 1919-21
Kimball, Newell ("Newt") 1940-43
Kimber, Samuel 1884
King, Cldye 1944-45, 1947-48, 1951-52
Kinslow, Tom 1891-94
Kipp, Fred 1957-59
Kirkpatrick, Enos 1912-13
Kitson, Frank 1900-02
Klippstein, Johnny 1958-59
Klugman, Josie ("Joe") 1924
Klumpp, Elmer 1937
Knetzer, Elmer 1909-12
Knolls, Oscar ("Hub") 1906
Knowles, Jim 1884
Koch, Barnett ("Barney") 1944
Koenecke, Leonard ("Len") 1934-35
Konetchy, Edward 1919-21
Korwan, Jim 1894
Kosko, Andrew 1969-70
Koufax, Sanford ("Sandy") 1955-66
Koukalik, Joe 1904
Koupal, Louis 1928-29
Koy, Ernest 1938-40
Kress, Charles 1954
Krieg, Bill 1885
Krueger, Ernest 1917-21
Kruger, Abraham ("Abe") 1908
Kustus, Julius 1909

L

Labine, Clement ("Clem") 1950-60
LaChance, George ("Candy") 1893-98
Lacy, Leondaus ("Lee") 1972-78
LaGrow, Lerrin 1979
Lamanske, Frank 1935
Lamar, Bill 1920-21
LaMaster, Wayne 1938

Lamb, Raymond	1969-70	Mails, John ("Duster")	1915-16
Landestoy, Rafael	1977, 1983	Malay, Charles	1905
Landreaux, Kenneth	1981-83	Maldonado, Candido ("Candy")	1981-83
Landrum, Joe	1950, 1952	Malinosky, Anthony ("Tony")	1937
Larker, Norman	1958-61	Mallette, Malcolm ("Mal")	1950
Lary, Lynford ("Lyn")	1939	Malone, Lewis	1917, 1919
Lasorda, Tom	1954-55	Maloney, William ("Billy")	1906-08
Latimer, Clifford ("Tacks")	1902	Mamaux, Albert	1918-23
Lavagetto, Harry ("Cookie")	1937-41, 1946-47	Mancuso, August ("Gus")	1940
		Manuel, Charles	1974-75
Law, Rudolph ("Rudy")	1978, 1980	Manush, Henry ("Heinie")	1937-38
Lazzeri, Anthony ("Tony")	1939	Maranville, Walter ("Rabbit")	1926
Leard, Bill	1917	Marichal, Juan	1975
Lee, Bob	1967	Marquard, Richard ("Rube")	1915-20
Lee, Harold ("Hal")	1930	Marriott, Bill	1925-26
Lee, Leron	1975-76	Marrow, Charles ("Buck")	1937-38
Lefebvre, Jim	1965-72	Marshall, Michael A. ("Mike")	1981-83
Lehman, Kenneth	1952, 1956-57	Marshall, Michael G. ("Mike")	1974-76
LeJeune, Sheldon ("Larry")	1911	Marshall, William ("Doc")	1909
LeJohn, Donald	1965	Martin, Morris ("Morrie")	1949
Lembo, Stephen	1950, 1952	Martinez, Teodoro ("Teddy")	1977-79
Lennox, James ("Ed")	1909-10	Mattingly, Laurence ("Earl")	1931
Leonard, Emil ("Dutch")	1933-36	Mauch, Gene	1944
Leonard, Jeffery	1977	Maul, Albert	1899
Leslie, Samuel	1933-35	Mauriello, Ralph	1958
Lewallyn, Dennis	1975-79	Mauro, Carmen	1953
Lewis, Philip	1905-08	Mays, Albert	1888
Lillis, Bob	1958-61	McBean, Alvin	1969-70
Lindsey, Jim	1937	McCabe, Bill	1920
Lindstrom, Fred	1936	McCann, Henry ("Gene")	1901-02
Livingston, Thompson ("Mickey")	1951	McCarren, Bill	1923
Loes, William ("Billy")	1950, 1952-56	McCarthy, John A. ("Jack")	1906-07
Loftus, Dick	1924-25	McCarthy, John J. ("Johnny")	1934-35
Logan, Bob	1935	McCarthy, Tommy	1896
Lohrman, Bill	1943-44	McCarthy, George ("Lew")	1913-16
Lombardi, Ernesto ("Ernie")	1931	McCauley, Jim	1886
Lombardi, Victor ("Vic")	1945-47	McClellan, Bill	1885-88
Long, Tom	1924	McCormick, Michael J. ("Mike")	1904
Lopes, David ("Davey")	1972-81	McCormick, Myron ("Mike")	1949
Lopez, Alfonso ("Al")	1928, 1930-35	McCredie, Walter ("Judge")	1903
Loudenslager, Charles	1904	McCreery, Tom	1901-03
Lovett, Tom	1889-91, 1893	McDermott, Terrence ("Terry")	1972
Lucas, Ray	1933-34	Mc Devitt, Daniel ("Danny")	1957-60
Lucid, Cornelius ("Con")	1894-95	McDougal, John	1895
Lumley, Harry	1904-10	McElveen, Pryor	1909-11
Lund, Donald	1945, 1947-48	McFarland, Anderson ("Dan")	1899
Luque, Adolfo ("Dolf")	1930-31	McFarland, Charles ("Chappie")	1906
Lyttle, Jim	1976	McGamwell, Edward	1905
		McGann, Dennis ("Dan")	1899
M		McGinnity, Joe ("Iron Man")	1900
		McGlothin, Ezra ("Pat")	1949-50
Macon, Max	1940, 1942-43	McGraw, Bob	1925-27
Magee, Leo ("Lee")	1919	McGuire, James ("Deacon")	1899-1901
Maglie, Salvatore ("Sal")	1956-57		
Magoon, George	1898		

McIntire, John ("Harry")	1905-09
McJames, James ("Doc")	1899, 1901
McKenna, James ("Kit")	1898
McLane, Edward	1907
McLish, Calvin	1944,1946
McMahon, John ("Sadie")	1897
McMakin, John	1902
McManus, Francis ("Frank")	1903
McMillan, Tommy	1908-10
McMullen, Kenneth	1962-64, 1973-75
McTamany, Jim	1885-87
McVey, George	1885
McWeeny, Douglas	1926-29
Medwick, Joe	1940-43, 1946
Melton, Reuben ("Rube')	1943-44, 1946-47
Merkle, Frederick	1916-17
Messersmith, John ("Andy")	1973-75, 1979
Meusel, Emil ("Irish")	1927
Meyer, Bernhard ("Benny")	1913
Meyer, Lee	1909
Meyer, Russell	1953-55
Meyers, John ("Chief")	1916-17
Michael, Gene	1967
Mickens, Glenn	1953
Mikkelsen, Pete	1969-72
Miksis, Edward	1944, 1946-51
Miles, Donald	1958
Miljus, Johnny	1917, 1920-21
Miller, Bob	1963-67
Miller, Frederick	1910
Miller, John	1969
Miller, Larry	1964
Miller, Lawrence ("Hack")	1916
Miller, Lowell ("Otto")	1910-22
Miller, Ralph	1898
Miller, Rodney	1957
Miller, Walter	1911
Millies, Walter	1934
Milliken, Bob	1953-54
Mills, Colonel ("Buster")	1935
Minner, Paul	1946, 1948-49
Mitchell, Clarence	1918-22
Mitchell, Frederick	1904-05
Mitchell, Johnny	1924-25
Mitchell, Loren ("Dale")	1956
Mitchell, Robert ("Bobby")	1980-81
Moeller, Joe	1962, 1964, 1966-71
Mohart, George	1920-21
Monday, Robert ("Rick")	1977-83
Moon, Wallace ("Wally")	1959-65
Moore, D.C. ("Dee")	1943

Moore, Gary	1970
Moore, Gene	1939-40
Moore, Graham ("Eddie")	1929-30
Moore, Randolph ("Randy")	1936-37
Moore, Raymond	1952-53
Moore, William	1929-32
Morales, Jose	1982-83
Moran, Joseph ("Herbie")	1912-13
Morgan, Edwin ("Eddie")	1937
Morgan, Robert ("Bobby")	1950-53
Morrison, Johnny	1929-30
Moryn, Walter	1954-55
Moss, Raymond	1926-31
Mossor, Earl	1951
Mota, Manuel	1969-80
Moulder, Glen	1946
Mowe, Raymond	1913
Mowrey, Harry ("Mike")	1916-17
Mullen, William ("Billy")	1923
Mulvey, Joe	1895
Mungo, Van	1931-41
Munns, Leslie	1934-35
Murch, Simeon ("Simmy")	1908
Murray, Jim	1922
Myers, Henry ("Hy")	1909, 1911, 1914-22

N

Nahem, Samuel	1938
Naylor, Earl	1946
Neal, Charles	1956-61
Negray, Ronald	1952, 1958
Neis, Bernard	1920-24
Nelson, Glenn ("Rocky")	1952, 1956
Nen, Dick	1963
Newcombe, Donald	1949-51, 1954-58
Newsome, Norman ("Bobo")	1929-30, 1942-43
Newton, Eustace ("Doc")	1901-02
Niedenfuer, Tom	1981-83
Nitcholas, Otho	1945
Nixon, Albert	1915-16, 1918
Nops, Jeremiah ("Jerry")	1900
Noren, Irving	1960
Norman, Fredie ("Fred")	1970
North, Bill	1978
Northern, Hubbard ("Hub")	1911-12

O

Oates, Johnny	1977-79
O'Brien, Bob	1971
O'Brien, John J.	1891
O'Brien, John K. ("Jack")	1887
O'Brien, William ("Darby")	1888-92

Reulbach, Edward	1913-14
Reuss, Jerry	1979-83
Reyes, Gilberto	1983
Reynolds, Charles	1889
Reynolds, R.J.	1983
Rhiel, William ("Billy")	1929
Rhoden, Richard ("Rick")	1974-78
Richards, Paul	1932
Richardson, Daniel	*1893
Richert, Pete	1962-64, 1972-73
Riconda, Henry ("Harry")	1928
Riggert, Joe	1914
Riggs, Lewis	1941-42, 1946
Ripple, James ("Jimmy")	1939-40
Ritter, Louis ("Lew")	1902-08
Rivera, German	1983
Rizzo, Johnny	1942
Roberts, Jim	1924-25
Robertson, Dick	1918
Robinson, Charles	1885
Robinson, Earl	1958
Robinson, Frank	1972
Robinson, Jack ("Jackie")	1947-56
Robles, Sergio	1976
Rochelli, Louis	1944
Rodas, Richard	1983
Rodriquez, Eliseo ("Ellie")	1976
Roe, Elwin ("Preacher")	1948-54
Roebuck, Edward	1955-58, 1960-63
Roenicke, Ronald	1981-83
Roettger, Oscar	1927
Rogers, Lee	1938
Rogers, Stanley ("Packy")	1938
Rojek, Stanley	1942, 1946-47
Romano, Jim	1950
Romo, Vicente	1968, 1982
Roseboro, John	1957-67
Roseman, James ("Chief")	1887
Rosen, Goodwin ("Goody")	1937-39, 1944-46
Rosenfield, Max	1931-33
Ross, Donald	1940
Rowe, Kenneth	1963
Rowe, Lynwood ("Schoolboy")	1942
Roy, Jean Pierre	1946
Roy, Luther	1929
Royster, Jeron ("Jerry")	1973-75
Rucker, George ("Nap")	1907-16
Rudolph, Ernest	1945
Ruether, Walter ("Dutch")	1921-24
Rush, Jess ("Andy")	1925
Russell, Bill	1969-83
Russell, Jim	1950-51
Russell, John	1917-18

Rutherford, John	1952
Ryan, Jack	1911
Ryan, John	1898
Ryan, Wilfred ("Rosy")	1933

S

Sandlock, Michael	1945-46
Savage, Theodore ("Ted")	1968
Sax, David	1982-83
Sax, Stephen	1981-83
Sayles, Bill	1943
Scanlan, William ("Doc")	1904-07, 1909-11
Schardt, Wilburt ("Bill')	1911-12
Scheer, Allen	1913
Schenck, Bill	1885
Schliebner, Frederick ("Dutch")	1923
Schmandt, Raymond	1918-22
Schmidt, Henry	1903
Schmitz, Johnny	1951-52
Schmutz, Charles	1914-15
Schneiberg, Frank	1910
Schofield, John ("Dick")	1966-67
Schott, Arthur ("Gene")	1939
Schreiber, Paul	1922-23
Schriver, William ("Pop")	1886
Schultz, Howard ("Howie")	1943-47
Schultz, Joe	1915
Schupp, Ferdinand ("Ferdie")	1921
Scioscia, Michael	1980-83
Scott, Dick	1963
Seats, Tom	1945
Sebring, James	1909
Sells, David	1975
Sexauer, Elmer	1948
Shanahan, Paul ("Greg")	1973-74
Sharrott, George	1893-94
Shaute, Joe	1931-33
Shea, Mervin	1938
Sheckard, Samuel ("Jimmy")	1897-98, 1900-05
Sheehan, John ("Jack")	1920-21
Sheehan, Tom	1908
Sheridan, Eugene ("Red")	1918, 1920
Sherlock, Vincent	1935
Sherry, Lawrence ("Larry")	1958-63
Sherry, Norman	1959-62
Shindle, Bill	1894-98
Shirley, Barton ("Bart")	1964, 1966, 1968
Shirley, Steven	1982
Shoch, George	1893-97
Shriver, Harry	1922-23
Shuba, George ("Shotgun")	1948-50, 1952-55

U

Underwood, Fred	1894

V

Valdez, Rene	1957
Valentine, Bob	1969, 1971-72
Valenzuela, Fernando	1980-83
Valle, Hector	1965
Valo, Elmer	1957-58
Van Buren, Edward ("Deacon")	1904
Vance, Clarence ("Dazzy")	1922-32, 1935
Vance, Gene ("Sandy")	1970-71
Van Cuyk, Christian ("Chris")	1950-52
Van Cuyk, Johnny	1947-49
Vaughan, Floyd ("Arky")	1942-43, 1947-48
Versalles, Ziolo	1968
Vickers, Harry ("Rube")	1903
Visner, Joe	1889
Vosmick, Joe	1940-41

W

Wachtel, Paul	1917
Wade, Benjamin	1952-54
Wagner, Albert ("Butts")	1898
Wagner, William ("Bull")	1913-14
Walker, Albert ("Rube")	1951-58
Walker, Fred ('Dixie')	1939-47
Walker, Frederick ("Mysterious")	1913
Walker, Oscar	1884
Wall, Joe	1902
Wall, Stanley	1975-77
Walls, Ray ("Lee")	1962-64
Walton, Daniel ("Danny")	1976
Waner, Lloyd	1944
Waner, Paul	1941, 1943-44
Ward, Charles ("Chuck")	1918-22
Ward, John A. ("Rube")	1902
Ward, John M. ("Monte")	1891-92
Ward, Preston	1948
Warner, Frederick	1884
Warner, John ("Jack")	1929-31
Warren, Tommy	1944
Warwick, Carl	1961
Wasdell, James ("Jimmy")	1940-41
Washington, Ronald	1977
Watkins, George	1936
Weaver, William	1886
Webb, Henry ("Hank")	1977
Webber, Lester ("Les")	1942-46
Weiss, Gary	1980-81
Welch, Bob	1978-83
Wells, John	1944
Werhas, Johnny	1964-65, 1967

West, Walter ("Max")	1928-29
Weyhing, August ("Gus")	1900
Wheat, McKinley ("Mack")	1915-19
Wheat, Zachariah ("Zack")	1909-26
Wheeler, Edward	1902
White, Larry	1983
White, Myron	1978
Whiting, Jesse	1906-07
Whitman, Dick	1946-49
Whitted, George ("Possum")	1922
Wicker, Kemp	1941
Wilhelm, Irvin ("Kaiser")	1908-10
Wilhelm, James ("Hoyt")	1971-72
Willhite, Jon ("Nick")	1963-66
Williams, Dick	1951-54, 1956
Williams, Leon	1926
Williams, Stanley	1958-62
Williams, Woodrow ("Woody")	1938
Wills, Maurice ("Maury")	1959-66, 1969-72
Wilson, Bob	1958
Wilson, Edward ("Eddie")	1936-37
Wilson, George ("Hickie")	1884
Wilson, Gomer ("Tex")	1924
Wilson, Lewis ("Hack")	1932-34
Windhorn, Gordon	1961
Winford, Jim	1938
Winham, Lafayette ("Lave")	1902
Winsett, John ("Tom")	1936-38
Winston, Henry ("Hank")	1936
Witt, Lawton ("Whitey")	1926
Wojey, Pete	1954
Wright, Clarence	1901
Wright, Forrest ("Glenn")	1929-33
Wright, James ("Rick")	1982-83
Wrigley, George ("Zeke")	1899
Wurm, Frank	1944
Wyatt, John ("Whit")	1939-44
Wynn, James ("Jimmy")	1974-75

Y

Yale, Williams ("Ad")	1905
Yarrison, Byron ("Rube")	1924
Yeager, Joe	1898-1900
Yeager, Stephen ("Steve")	1972-83
Yingling, Earl	1912-13

Z

Zachary, Albert ("Chink")	1944
Zachary, Jonathan ("Tom")	1934-36
Zachry, Patrick	1983
Zahn, Geoffrey	1973-75
Zimmer, Donald	1954-59, 1963
Zimmerman, Bill	1915
Zimmerman, Edward ("Eddie")	1911

8

CHRONOLOGICAL INDEX

BARNEY, Rex 9/9/48
BARNIE, Bill 6/7/1898
BARRETT, Dick 9/30/45
BARUCH, Andre 4/13/54
Bases on balls
   17 issued (five to Mel Ott) in one game
      by Dodgers 4/30/44
   seven issued by Fernando Valenzuela vs.
      Yankees 10/23/81
   six consecutive issued by Brickyard
      Kennedy 8/31/1900
   13 collected by losing Dodgers
      in game 5/18/53
   148 collected by Eddie Stanky sets
      one-season major league record 9/30/45
   winning run scored on by Dodgers 6/2/25
   ninth complete game without pitched
      by Sandy Koufax 4/14/64
   Giants' Christy Mathewson goes 13—then
      47 consecutive—innings without 4/29/13
   otherwise perfect game by Carl Erskine
      ruined 6/19/52
      and by Sandy Koufax 5/11/63
Bat
   John Roseboro hit over the head by Juan
      Marichal with 8/22/65
   breaks, injures Steve Yeager waiting in
      on-deck circle 9/6/76
Batting slump, by Gil Hodges 5/23/53
Batting title, won by Zach Wheat 9/2/18
   Tommy Davis (second time) 9/28/63
Beanball(s)
   Pee Wee Reese hit by Cubs'
      Jake Mooty 6/1/40
   Joe Medwick hit by Cardinals'
      Bob Bowman 6/18/40
   Pete Reiser hits homer off pitcher who
      previously skulled him 5/24/41
   Hi Bithorn of Cubs throws at Leo Durocher
      in dugout 7/15/42
   Whit Wyatt, Braves' Manny Salvo have
      personal duel 8/8/42
   Dodgers-Giants "war" during
      double header 9/8/52
   Braves' Joe Adcock hit, Dodgers' Jackie
      Robinson decked 8/1/54
   Ron Cey hit by Yankees' Goose
      Gossage 10/25/81
BECKWITH, Joe 12/8/83
BEDELL, Howie 6/8/68
BEHRMAN, Hank 5/3/47
BELL, Gus 5/17/53
BENNETT, Dennis 6/2/62
BERRA, Yogi 10/4/55

```
26 . . . . . . . . . . . . . . . . . . . . . . . . .   6/21/01
25 . . . . . . . . . . . . . . . . . . . . . . . . .   6/21/22, 6/29/23
24 . . . . . . . . . . . . . . . . . . . . . . . . .   8/20/74
21 . . . . . . . . . . . . . . . . . . . . . . . . .   8/24/19, 8/31/50
20 . . . . . . . . . . . . . . . . . . . . . . . . .   4/26/59, 5/26/70
19 . . . . . . . . . . . . . . . . . . . . . . . . .   5/24/72
18 . . . . . . . . . . . . . . . . . . . . . . . . .   6/30/1893
17 . . . . . . . . . . . . . . . . . . . . . . . . .   8/1/25, 6/28/69
```
High scoring games (20 runs or more)
```
38 (Dodgers 22, Pittsburgh 16) . . . . . . . .   6/30/1893
36 (Dodgers 20, Philadelphia 16) . . . . . .   5/18/29
34 (Giants 26, Dodgers 8) . . . . . . . . . . .   4/30/44
31 (Dodgers 25, Pittsburgh 6) . . . . . . . . .   5/20/1896
   (Dodgers 25, Cincinnati 6) . . . . . . . . .   9/24/01
29 (St. Louis 22, Dodgers 7) . . . . . . . . . .   7/27/18
   (Dodgers 15, Pittsburgh 14) . . . . . . . .   6/21/22
   (Dodgers 23, Pittsburgh 6) . . . . . . . . .   7/10/43
28 (Dodgers 17, St. Louis 11) . . . . . . . . .   4/26/59
27 (Dodgers 22, Boston 5) . . . . . . . . . . .   9/21/1897
   (Dodgers 18, Giants 9) . . . . . . . . . . . .   8/13/32
   (Dodgers 15, Chicago 12) . . . . . . . . . .   5/18/45
   (Dodgers 20, Cincinnati 7) . . . . . . . . .   8/8/54
26 (Dodgers 22, Philadelphia 4) . . . . . . .   9/23/39
   (Dodgers 18, Chicago 8) . . . . . . . . . .   8/20/74
   (Dodgers 14, Chicago 12) . . . . . . . . .   5/5/76
25 (St. Louis 13, Dodgers 12) . . . . . . . . .   5/19/1897
   (Dodgers 19, Pittsburgh 6) . . . . . . . . .   6/23/30
   (Cincinnati 23, Dodgers 2) . . . . . . . . .   6/8/40
   (Giants 16, Dodgers 9) . . . . . . . . . . .   5/13/58
24 (St. Louis 18, Dodgers 6) . . . . . . . . .   6/17/1885
   (Dodgers 21, Cincinnati 3) . . . . . . . . .   6/21/01
23 (Giants 17, Dodgers 6) . . . . . . . . . . .   5/28/54
   (Dodgers 17, Cincinnati 6) . . . . . . . . .   5/25/79
   (Dodgers 16, Astros 7) . . . . . . . . . . .   4/5/83
22 (Dodgers 12, Giants 10) . . . . . . . . . .   10/18/1889
   (Dodgers 15, Boston 7) . . . . . . . . . . .   8/11/41
   (Pittsburgh 17, Dodgers 5) . . . . . . . . .   9/6/45
   (Dodgers 19, Boston 3) . . . . . . . . . . .   8/31/50
   (Milwaukee 15, Dodgers 7) . . . . . . . .   7/31/54
   (Dodgers 19, Giants 3) . . . . . . . . . . . .   5/26/70
   (Dodgers 18, San Diego 4) . . . . . . . .   9/13/77
21 (Dodgers 20, Pittsburgh 1) . . . . . . . . .   8/1/1890
   (Philadelphia 11, Dodgers 10) . . . . . .   6/5/34
   (Dodgers 13, New York Yankees 8) . .   10/5/56
20 (Dodgers 13, Giants 7) . . . . . . . . . . . .   7/17/1900
   (St. Louis 17, Dodgers 3) . . . . . . . . . .   9/15/24
   (Dodgers 19, Cincinnati 1) . . . . . . . . .   5/21/52
   (Milwaukee 13, Dodgers 7) . . . . . . . .   8/24/57
```
HILL, Marc 8/18/77
Hit batsman, four by pitcher Carl Doyle 6/8/40
Hits pitcher in head with line drive 5/25/22
Hit(s), for the cycle (single, double, triple and home run)
    Oyster Burns 8/1/1890

double header in Pittsburgh played
   despite field that resembles a "lake"
   because of backed up sewers 7/4/02
Dodgers batter the 10th southpaw pitcher
   in 11 games that faces them 8/1/25
every total in game's box score
   the same 8/3/10
Dodgers and Cubs each win by a score of
   9-2 in double header 8/22/25
Cincinnati concedes game after four
   innings 9/24/01
runner scores from third when Dodger
   pitcher Jack Coombs drops ball while
   winding up 6/15/18
same number of assists as putouts against
   Pittsburgh 6/14/06
Bill Sharman only player kicked out of a
   game though he never played in
   one. 9/27/51
St. Louis protests umpire's continuance of
   game by lighting candles 9/7/1889
three runners wind up on third base after
   Babe Herman's extra-base hit 8/15/26
an injured Jake Daubert lays down six
   sacrifice bunts during double
   header 8/15/14
George Cutshaw's long drive hits at base of
   Ebbets Field fence, then "climbs" over
   for a homer 6/6/18
Cincinnati has 10-run 13th inning to break
   open scoreless tie and win, 10-0 . . . . . 5/5/19
Pitcher Sloppy Thurston gives up six
   homers to Giants, but he also gets
   four hits. 8/13/32
pitchers Harley Payne (Dodgers) and Joe
   Corbett (Baltimore) hurl two 3-3 ties
   against each other same season 8/10/1897
Giant manager John McGraw retires to
   clubhouse in fifth inning, claiming his
   players aren't trying to beat Dodgers . . 10/3/16
Dodger minor league pitcher, in Navy,
   takes leave for a day, is shelled by Cards
   in first inning, quickly returns to
   Navy. 7/27/18
Dodgers' Jack Sheehan only player ever to
   get as many hits during season as he
   does in World Series 5/31/21
18 runners stranded against Cincinnati . . 5/18/53
pitcher Ben Wade gives up four homers in
   one inning 5/28/54
Larry Cheney tosses up five wild
   pitches 7/9/18

Sunday game(s), Brooklyn
    first between Dodgers-Giants 7/18/1898
    first at Washington Park, no charge 4/17/04
    arrest by police for test case 6/17/05
    first with admission charge 7/1/17
    first following legislative approval
      by New York 5/4/19
SUTCLIFFE, Rick 5/3/79, 5/25/79
SUTTON, Don
    throws shutout in first Championship
      Series game of Dodgers 10/5/74
    20-game winner first time 9/24/76
    named Most Valuable in All-Star
      Game 7/19/77
    twirls record fifth one-hitter 8/18/77
    starts his seventh straight opener 4/7/78
    ejected for "defacing baseball" 7/14/78
    fights Steve Garvey in locker room 8/20/78
    surpasses Don Drysdale as all-time
      Dodger winner 5/20/79
    pitches Dodger-record 52nd shutout 7/4/80
    other subjects 4/15/72, 4/6/73, 5/9/74, 8/24/74,
      10/1/74, 10/5/74, 10/9/74, 5/31/75,
      4/7/77, 8/28/77, 4/7/78, 9/15/78,
      8/10/79, 5/12/80, 10/4/81

T

TAFT, William Howard 4/7/10
TAYLOR, Jack 8/9/06
TAYLOR, Tony 6/8/68
TAYLOR, Zach 10/4/36
Television, first-ever major
    league game 8/26/39
TEMPLE, Johnny 8/4/63
TERRY, Adonis
    starting pitcher for first Dodger major
      league game 4/12/1884
    pitches clincher for first American
      Association championship 10/14/1889
    twirls first "official" Dodger-Giant
      game 10/18/1889
    other subjects 4/18/1884, 7/24/1886, 5/27/1888,
      10/29/1889, 9/1/1890
TERRY, Bill 1/24,34, 5/28/34, 9/30/34
THOMAS, Derrell 5/25/79, 4/16/80
THOMASSON, Gary 5/25/79
THOMPSON, Fresco 11/24/53, 10/21/68
THOMPSON, Hank 7/8/49
THOMSON, Bobby 10/3/51, 10/20/51, 4/23/58, 7/14/62
Three men on third base 8/15/26
THURSTON, Sloppy 8/13/32
Tie Games
    0-0 for 3 innings, vs. Giants 9/27/31

Winning streak, major league record, set by
    Rube Marquard against Dodgers 7/3/12
Win(s)
    two in one day, Bill Scanlan 10/3/05
    two in one day, against the Dodgers
        Amos Russie 9/26/1891
        Iron Man McGinnity.............. 8/8/03
        Ed Reulbach (both shutouts) 9/26/08
        Bill Doak (and Grover Alexander) 9/18/17
    20th (as youngest-ever Dodger pitcher) of
        season, Ralph Branca............ 9/11/47
    50th in National League, Sandy Koufax .. 8/24/61
    100th by Don Newcombe 7/29/56
    191st by Don Drysdale, then
        Dodger record 4/13/68
    210 by Don Sutton 5/20/79
Wins, 2,000th by Walt Alston as manager .. 7/17/76
Wins, Dodger team
    first-ever in Brooklyn 5/12/1883
    first in American Association 5/1/1884
    first in National League 4/19/1890
    1,000th since joining National League... 8/3/03
    first-ever in World Series 10/10/16
    first World Series championship 10/4/55
    first as Los Angeles franchise 4/16/58
    first Los Angeles World Series title 10/8/59
Wins, consecutive, by Dodgers
    5 in World Series at Ebbets Field 10/5/56
    7 over New York Giants.............. 8/20/53
    8 games........................ 8/2/61, 8/10/82
    9 games, start of season 4/30/40
    10 games, start of season 4/22/55
    10 at Candlestick Park 5/31/72
    13 games....................... 8/20/53, 6/2/62, 9/30/65
    15 games....................... 9/6/24
    22 at home, reference to 5/22/1899
Wins, consecutive, Giants extend streak
    to 16.......................... 7/3/12
    Giants launch 26-game major-league
        record skein 9/6/16
"World Championship" games
    Dodgers vs. Giants 10/18/1889, 10/19/1889, 10/29/1889
    Dodgers vs. Louisville 10/27/1890
World Series, Dodgers
    vs. Baltimore..................... 10/6/66, 10/9/66
    vs. Boston....................... 10/7/16, 10/9/16, 10/10/16, 10/12/16
    vs. Chicago 10/1/59, 10/2/59, 10/4/59, 10/6/59,
                                 10/8/59
    vs. Cleveland 10/6/20, 10/10/20, 10/11/20, 10/12/20
    vs. Minnesota 10/9/65, 10/14/65

THE AUTHOR

Cliff Gewecke is a freelance writer and former newspaperman who has worked in the Los Angeles area for 25 years. While sports editor of the *Daily Signal,* he also was correspondent for the *Christian Science Monitor,* covering for both publications a wide variety of subjects–including the Dodgers.

A graduate of USC, where he played baseball under coach Rod Dedeaux (Dodgers, 1935), he has a master of arts degree and has authored two other books—on tennis and jogging—plus an assortment of magazine articles.

He is a cousin of professional singer Sue Raney, whom he first met at a Dodger Oldtimers Day luncheon where she sang "Dodger Blue," the flip side of her recording of "Van Lingle Mungo."